COMING OUT, COMING HOME

Coming Out, Coming Home

Helping Families Adjust to a Gay or Lesbian Child

Michael C. LaSala, Ph.D.

COLUMBIA UNIVERSITY PRESS   NEW YORK

COLUMBIA UNIVERSITY PRESS

Publishers Since 1893

New York Chichester, West Sussex

Library of Congress Cataloging-in-Publication Data

LaSala, Michael C.

Coming out, coming home: helping families adjust to a gay or lesbian child /

Michael C. LaSala, Ph.D.

p. cm.

Includes bibliographical references and index.

ISBN 978-0-231-14382-0 (cloth: alk. paper) — ISBN 978-0-231-14383-7 (pbk.: alk. paper) —

ISBN 978-0-231-51299-2 (e-book)

1. Parents of gays. 2. Gays—Family relationships. 3. Parent and child. I. Title.

HQ76.25.L36   2010

306.874—dc22   2009045335

THIS BOOK IS DEDICATED TO

my parents, Michael LaSala and Carole Guardino LaSala,

my brother, Jaime LaSala,

my partner, Timothy Murphy,

the families in this study,

and all other sources of unconditional love.

CONTENTS

Monica McGoldrick

M ICHAEL LASALA HAS WRITTEN A LANDMARK STUDY OF the experiences and relationships of parents and their children in the coming-out process. It is a moving exploration of families working through the disruption of finding out their children are homosexual. Parents, as LaSala describes, "agonize that their children will be unsafe as they launch them into a world where gay and lesbian youth are discriminated against, assaulted, even murdered." The important news is that parents can buffer the effects of these harsh realities, so LaSala's book is essential reading for all clinicians working to facilitate family development and connectedness.

LaSala's narrative challenges many of the myths about family relationships before, during, and after the coming-out process, such as the myth that families cannot be close before they are open about their child's homosexuality. He conveys with touching descriptions that even though there is avoidance about the homosexuality, parents and children may be very caring and connected on many levels. What impressed and humbled him in doing the study, he says, is the way the parents and children held on to each other and even grew closer despite their fears and shattered expectations. Children must try to figure out their own identities while working to stay connected to parents on whom they are still reliant for emotional and financial support, while parents go through a "maelstrom of feelings" during this phase. LaSala was awestruck by the depth and persistence of family connections, which led him to reflect on the mysterious ties that bind families together. Reading his book, I was similarly awestruck by the power, mystery, and persistence of families to stay connected in spite of everything. It also made me feel the tragedy and loss of those families not included in this study, those who could not appreciate the importance of family relationships and do not manage to stay connected. I wish they would read this book and realize what they are missing.

LaSala's writing is refreshing, with humor and tenderness for the parents and children in these sixty-five families. He found these families' stories went beyond the stereotypical narrative that children are victims of parents' negative attitudes toward homosexuality and that once the parents are educated they relate better and relationships improve. LaSala achieved a broader understanding of the experiences of children and parents in the coming-out process.

The larger context for these families is, of course, facing the fear, shame, ostracism, and rejection from societal groups: religious, cultural, and social. The courageous effort of so many parents in this book to hold on to their own values and relationships in spite of such pernicious societal pressures is inspiring. LaSala discusses what has been called homosexual stigma—"society's shared belief system through which homosexuality is denigrated, discredited, and constructed as invalid relative to heterosexuality" (Herek, Chop, and Strohl 2007:171). We have to remember it is only a few decades ago that the *Diagnostic Manual* ceased to call homosexuality a mental illness. Families live in the shadow of such societal negativity. The devastating impact of peer abuse, religious and societal intimidation and condemnation is hard to overcome. So every family here has a courage that must be appreciated.

LaSala has a deep understanding of family process. He explores with rich understanding the relationships of the parents and children in his study. As he describes the love of mothers he says, "It is hard to imagine anything quite as soothing for a distressed child as a mother's love, particularly for children in this study who were being harassed by peers and felt like potential outcasts." Most had strong relationships with their mothers, characterized by closeness, consistency, and warmth. On the other hand, as appears generally true between parents and children, mothers tend to have closer relationships with their children than do fathers, although there were examples where fathers were the ones with whom sons or daughters had an easier time dealing with the issues of coming out and, in general, staying connected.

LaSala says: "Fathers tend to live on the outside edge of the emotional lives of their families." Only seventeen fathers agreed to talk with him compared to sixty-two mothers; thirteen of the children had little or no relationship with their fathers. Sometimes, as has been shown in other research, fathers remembered their relationships with their children more positively than children did. Many families found themselves in the common triangle where the father's only communication with the children is through what the mother relays to him or is left out of the loop altogether. Many of the children in LaSala's study reported that their fathers knew of their sexuality, but only twenty-six had told them directly; in the other families, mothers informed fathers. LaSala also discusses the socialization of fathers, which teaches all men that homosexuality is incompatible with real masculinity or full manhood. Fathers have been raised not only to look down upon homosexuality but generally to fear it in themselves. LaSala wonders whether fathers choose to be peripheral in the lives of their children and then families organize around them or whether families keep fathers distant. This is an important clinical dilemma, because, as family therapists, we need to work hard to change this pattern.

Generally lesbian and gay youth do not disclose their sexual orientation until they have become somewhat comfortable with themselves. LaSala recommends having great respect for the distance that parents and children seem to need for a period of time, until the youth are comfortable discussing their identity. LaSala's careful descriptions of parent-child relationships conveys the important point that parents and children sometimes feel close and connected even though the child has not discussed his or her sexual orientation. For one thing, because in our culture parents and children are expected to avoid discussing their sexuality with each other, families can share many other things though they keep silence about that one thing. It is important not to undermine the connections between parents and children even as they are in a phase of development where they are not yet ready to deal with all the issues between them. Indeed, this is probably true for most families at certain points of development. LaSala's respect for the complexity of family relationships, and the timing of opening up extremely difficult issues that challenge what family members mean to each other, is a critical insight in many situations. LaSala conveys that in this developmental phase parent-child closeness may require more nuanced understanding. Mothers and sons may be close when discussing fashion or feelings but not regarding peers, school problems, or cross-gendered behavior. He believes the avoidance of talking about homosexuality until they are ready, while staying connected in other ways, may be important for maintaining nurturing connections until the time is right for the youth to come out.

LaSala conveys the importance of education in helping parents over-come the blame they tend to put on themselves, given the societal messages, despite all evidence to the contrary, that bad parenting makes a child lesbian or gay. He discusses the importance of intervening not only with families, to help them wend their way through the issues of coming out, but also within stigmatizing institutions and other environments. This is a strong mandate for us as clinicians. We must take the time to understand when and how to intervene with different family members, when to encourage them to talk together and when to coach them separately. The importance too of siblings, extended family members, friends, and other members of the family's social network cannot be minimized. Clearly, the wider the net we spread, as a container for young adults coming out to their parents, the better. The issues are not only personal or even familial but also social and societal, and this awareness is a critical part of our clinical mandate. LaSala's study shows this extremely well through the voices of parents and children who have a deep attachment, but are driven apart by societal stigma and prejudice.

All clinicians should keep LaSala's insights in mind as they work to create a therapeutic context to help families hold on to their connections in the face of painful social realities of ostracism, shame, and rejection, which, given our society's closed-mindeness, can too often break loving families apart.

The family—that dear octopus from whose tentacles we never quite escape nor, in our inmost hearts, ever quite wish to.
—DOROTHY GLADYS SMITH

THROUGH MY EXPERIENCES AS A THERAPIST, A SCHOLAR, and, not least important, a family member, I continue to be in awe and humbled by the power and influence of the family. A family can be a safe haven from a difficult world, a loving place to raise children, a destructive source of emotional and physical violence, or some combination of all these. It seems, no matter what our families were like when we were growing up, they always remain a part of us, for better or worse. Whatever our experiences, invisible cords reach through time and space to forever connect us to our mothers, fathers, siblings, and children—and no matter how hard we try, if we try at all, we can never completely free ourselves from their influence.

However, the discovery that a son or daughter is gay or lesbian is like an earthquake whose tremors threaten to permanently weaken even the strongest family. A father fears his lesbian daughter will face discrimination in the workplace, preventing her from having a successful career. A mother panics that she did something wrong to make her son gay. Both mothers and fathers find themselves reeling as their long-held ideas about sexuality and relationships are upended. Furthermore, they agonize that their children will be unsafe as they launch them into a world where lesbian and gay youth are discriminated against, assaulted, even murdered. Gay children worry they will lose the love of the most important people in their lives, their parents.

Parents matter. Ann Muller, a mother of a gay child who wrote a book with this title reminded us of this simple truth in 1987, but she didn't need to, especially those of us who were gay or lesbian and thinking of coming out to our fathers and mothers. Not long ago it was believed that lesbians and gays distanced from their families to avoid facing their disapproval and rejection, creating families of their own out of friendship networks (Kurdek and Schmitt 1987; Weston 1991). However, currently, more and more are coming out during adolescence and young adulthood—before they are old enough to find the community necessary to form these networks.

The good news is that accepting parents can buffer the effects of a harsh, stigmatizing world on a gay or lesbian young person (D'Augelli 2002). The not so good news is that despite recent signs of (slowly) growing societal acceptance, parents still struggle with their children's gay sexual orientation, and too many lesbian and gay youth are still ejected from their homes by parents who will not or cannot accept them (Wilber, Ryan, and Marksamer 2006). Thus it is no wonder that the biggest fear of many children who have yet to come out is that they will be rejected by their parents and lose the one resource that has the potential to offer safety in a harsh world—their families.

In addition to Muller (1987), several others have given us important, insightful glimpses into the family lives and relationships of lesbian and gay children. Everyone who is in the business of helping lesbian and gay young people and their families, or who lives in such a family, owes these researchers, clinicians, and parents an enormous debt of gratitude. However, these descriptions, studies, and models of coming out tend to be individually focused and rely almost exclusively on either the perception of the youth (Cass 1979; Savin-Williams 2001a; Troiden 1989) or parents (Borhek 1993; Griffin, Wirth, and Wirth 1997; Herdt and Koff 2000; Robinson, Walters, and Skeen 1989). What would parents and children from the same family say about the coming out experience? What do parents think helps their adjustment? What do children think is beneficial? How are parent and child impressions similar and different and why?

The traditional thinking about parental adjustment goes something like this: 1. parents get upset or angry when they learn their kid is gay, 2. their frightened, helpless children who are seeking love and acceptance are victims of their parents' disapproval, 3. parents get educated about homosexuality, 4. they feel better and their attitudes toward their children improve, 5. the end. As a gay man and a family therapist, I have long suspected that this story was way too simple and far from complete. So I undertook this study of sixty-five gay and lesbian youth and their parents to see if I could get a fuller picture, one that included the perspectives of parents and children in the same family.

However, as I interviewed the young people and their parents, I found what I had long suspected in my clinical work, that there was a *family* adjustment process. Parental reaction and adjustment to the news that a child is gay or lesbian did not occur in isolation. The children's personal characteristics and the relationships they maintained with their families played a significant role in parental recovery. Furthermore, the interviews seemed to suggest that family adjustment occurred in stages or phases—revealing a process not fully encompassed by grief-recovery models suggested in the earlier literature (Mattison and McWhirter 1995; Robinson et al. 1982). These stages were not necessarily temporal but were instead typified by reciprocal parent-child interaction patterns unique to each phase of the family adjustment trajectory. These interaction patterns provided insight into family struggles and suggest guidelines that can assist therapists in working with these clients.

In addition, previous models of gay self-acceptance and coming out describe a mostly *individual* process during which a lesbian or gay male traverses a path from confusion and distress to eventual self-acceptance (Cass 1979; Coleman 1982; Troiden 1989). However, what the interviews in this book uncover is the potentially powerful role of the family in gay and lesbian self-acceptance, which further underscores the importance of considering the family in working with lesbian and gay youth.

This book is not meant to contradict or replace the findings of the excellent research, clinical guides, and articles already available, some already mentioned and others cited in the body of this book. Instead, I hope readers integrate the information herein with that of my fellow colleagues, adding their own clinical wisdom to the mix so as to provide the most sensitive and effective treatment possible.

In the spirit of grounded theory, this work was inductive in nature. The themes and patterns that emerged from the interviews were compared, contrasted, and, when relevant, integrated with existing literature. However, in putting together my ideas, if the findings could be considered bricks, clinical wisdom was the mortar. No one study answers all the questions in a particular area and most raise additional questions. Thus I drew from my twenty-five years of practice experience to make cohesive sense of the results, fill holes in the data with tentative explanations as well as develop practice suggestions. My theory and clinical implications are not evidence-based where they have not been empirically tested with this population. I hope the reader keeps in mind that my findings are best considered hypotheses, no matter how strongly asserted. Nevertheless, the clinical recommendations in this book are based on research findings and, if combined with the practitioner's clinical wisdom and common sense, should prove useful.

Furthermore, it is important to understand that most of the parents in these families were at least somewhat adjusted by the time I interviewed them. This does not mean they did not go through difficult times—as you will see, many did. But, for the most part, these tough times were behind them. With few exceptions, I did not attract families with parents who did not recover, at least somewhat, from the news that a daughter or son was gay or who persistently rejected their children. My general experience as a researcher and clinician has taught me that it is difficult to get people who are unhappy or in the middle of a crisis to talk to a research interviewer about their experiences—those are the folks who come to see us as therapists. So these findings are not necessarily representative of the entire population of gay and lesbian families (whatever that is), but more likely indicative of the adjustment that is possible—and what therapists can help families strive for.

"Life isn't about waiting for the storm to pass; it's about learning to dance in the rain" (anonymous). The simple yet profound wisdom reflected in this quote is made evident in the stories of these families. I was moved and humbled by the way parents and children held onto one another, growing closer despite their fears and shattered expectations. Once again, as in my previous work, I was awestruck by the depth and persistence of family connections, which led me to reflect on the mysterious ties that bind families together, including those that bind me to my own.

I learned a lot from these families—I hope you will as well.

ACKNOWLEDGMENTS

I T TAKES A VILLAGE TO RAISE A CHILD, AND IN SOME WAYS, the same can be said about writing a book, and I owe a debt of gratitude to the many people who helped make this one possible.

First and foremost, I must thank the National Institute of Mental Health at the National Institute of Health, which funded this project (1 R03 MH068272–01) and therefore made it possible. A special thanks goes to my program officer, Emeline Otey, who believed in this project from the start and played a big role in making it happen.

Of course, this study would never have happened if it were not for the sixty-five families who were gracious and generous enough to share their stories with me. They taught me the importance of unconditional love and the persistence of family bonds and for this I am eternally grateful. Their stories will stay with me forever.

Additionally, I also thank Lauren Dockett at Columbia University Press, not only for her patience and her assistance with this book but also for her continued commitment to knowledge building for the human services. Furthermore, I am grateful to my pioneering and prolific colleague, Gerald (Gary) Mallon, from the School of Social Work at Hunter College, for his encouragement and for introducing me to CUP. I also wish to thank the external reviewers whose feedback helped me enrich this work.

I was lucky to find two really smart, really sensitive research assistants in Bethann Albert and Rita Velez Carreras. Their assistance with interviewing and analysis was invaluable. I also wish to thank my transcribers, Linda D. Phillips and Astrid Hufnagel, whose accuracy and countless hours of hard work greatly contributed to the success of this project.

I owe an enormous debt of thanks to my home institution, the School of Social Work at Rutgers, the State University of New Jersey, and especially Dean Emeritus Mary Edna Davidson. Her support and belief in my abilities during the early years of my academic career helped give me the confidence to write a successful grant proposal. My current dean, the talented and masterful Richard Edwards, along with my colleagues at Rutgers, supported me with their words of encouragement and their willingness to put up with my absences when I was busy writing. A special thanks to you all.

I was initially introduced to family therapy by Professor Max Siporin when I was a Master of Social Work student at the State University of New York at Albany. I distinctly recall being inspired by a videotape he presented in class showing Virgina Satir's sensitive work, which, as a student, I suspected was magic. (Now, as a seasoned clinician, I am certain of it.) My formal family therapist training really began at Project Strive, Inc., a home-based foster care prevention program where David Bosworth, the executive director, had the wisdom to hire Anne Itzkowitz from the Philadelphia Child Guidance Center to train us in structural family therapy. From that point on, I was fortunate to have received training and inspiration, either through formal programs, workshops, or consultations, from Salvador Minuchin, Carl Whitaker, Michael Kerr, Monica McGoldrick, Insoo Kim Berg, Steve DeShazer, and Maurizio Andolfi. I am grateful to have known and learned from these gifted individuals, and each has left an imprint on my thinking and my clinical work.

A very special thank you must go to my dear friend and mentor Michael P. Nichols. Good teachers model and demonstrate skills for their students to copy. The really great ones help their students find these abilities within themselves. In his ongoing support of my work, including his sensitive review of previous drafts of this book, Mike pushed me to find the heart and smarts inside of me and gave me the courage to infuse them throughout the text. Having him in my life has been a gift for which I am eternally grateful.

My mother and father taught me many valuable things. One is to always aim high. From an early age they taught me the sweet pleasure of achieving lofty goals. They also demonstrated the importance of staying connected to loved ones, no matter what. If anyone is wondering, my parents had a very difficult time when they learned in 1979 that I was gay, and it took them several years to adjust. But we never let go of each other, and, eventually, like the parents in this study, they came around. When you have a family such as mine, whose members are passionate people with strong opinions, bruising arguments are inevitable. However, I always know that, no matter what happens, we will still love one another, and, in each other, we can always find a home to return to.

Finally, I must thank my partner of twenty-seven years, Timothy Murphy. Anyone who lives with someone who is writing a book knows how difficult and lonely it can be. Tim deserves a lot of credit for this book, as he did all the things that made it possible for me to have the necessary blocks of time to write it, including, but not limited to, maintaining the house, caring for our garden, and putting up with my alternating periods of crippling self-doubt and towering grandiosity punctuated by long emotional absences. One of the great mysteries of my life is how I managed to be lucky enough to have this smart, strong, devoted, and sensitive man as my partner. What I do know is I will never be able to thank him enough—and that I will love him forever.

COMING OUT, COMING HOME

CHAPTER I

Family Sensitization

If the family were a fruit, it would be an orange, a circle of sections,
held together but separable—each segment distinct.
—LETTY COTTIN POGREBIN

FOR SOME GIRLS, IT MIGHT BEGIN WITH A CRUSH ON AN
older sister's best friend or a strange physical sensation that occurs
while watching Xena, the Warrior Princess on television. For a boy,
it might be a fantasy to take a bath with a buddy or a strong urge to run his
hand across his gym teacher's bearded cheek. At first, these children might not
pay much attention to these early stirrings—when they first appear boys and
girls are usually too young to know what they mean. However, at some point as
they get older they come to realize to their horror that there is something wrong
with these feelings—horribly wrong. These urges threatened to pull them away
from everything and everyone they know, leaving them as lost and alone as an
unmoored boat, bobbing and drifting on a cold, dark, dangerous sea.

Children with these feelings often want nothing more than to be like
everyone else, to be accepted and well-liked by their peers. However, they
soon realize that if they were found out they would be ridiculed as outcasts.
They could lose everything: their friends, the respect of the teachers and classmates at school—and—perhaps the most frightening prospect of all, they
could lose the love of their parents.

Now imagine you are a parent of one of these children. You noticed that
your tomboy daughter does not seem to be developing interests in boys like her

older sister did at her age and also seems to have a particularly intense friendship with the girl next door. Your sensitive son prefers to help his mom around the house rather than play ball outside with the other boys. Like a gentle summer breeze, the thought occurs to you. "Does this mean . . . could it mean . . . ?" but, before you could finish it, the notion, like that breeze, is gone. You push away any nagging worry the thought leaves behind and try to forget it.

During adolescence, a particularly difficult time for many families, children are testing their wings, sometimes pushing against ideas and values with which they were raised in an effort to develop their own identities. However, it is a mistake to view child development in isolation. Sociologists and family therapists have recognized *family* stages of development, which are evolving, reciprocal relationship patterns during each phase of the child's growing maturity (Carter and McGoldrick 1999; Hill and Rodgers 1964). In families with teenagers, parent-child relationships must become more flexible than ever before in order to accommodate the adolescent's growing needs for independence and exploration outside the family (Garcia-Preto 1999).

A major challenge for families at this time is for parents and children to establish and maintain relationships that allow children the freedom to develop their own identities but also keep them safe—no easy task. Children must figure out who they are while remaining connected to parents on whom they still must rely for physical and emotional support. Parents cope with a maelstrom of feelings during this phase. Certainly, they are anxious, knowing that their children will be spending more time away from the family, exposed to dangers such as drugs and alcohol, out of reach of supervising adults. Parents may project their fears onto their children who in turn react by either internalizing these anxieties or fighting their parents to avoid doing so. No wonder this is a difficult time for many families—and we haven't even talked about sex yet.

The first stirrings of sexual feelings bring a confusing mix of awkwardness, anxiety, and pleasure. For most adolescents, when hormones begin to surge, the opposite sex once regarded neutrally, or even with scorn, becomes a fascinating source of fantasy, mystery, angst, and frustration as teenagers recognize their emerging sexual attractions and attempt to relate to each other. Observing parents may react with a combination of bemused pleasure, as they reminisce about their own puppy loves and pangs of regret that their "babies" are growing up too fast. As parents witness their children's sexual maturation, they may dream of the day when their sons and daughters will marry and have children of their own continuing the family into the next generation. However, the emergence of their children's sexuality may also inspire fears of teen pregnancy or HIV infection, leading parents to become excessively restrictive. In response, children may become fearful and avoidant or angry and combative, arguing "You worry too much!" "You never give me enough freedom!" "You treat me like a baby!"

Nevertheless, today's families face the difficult task of coping with their children's sexuality in a world that sanctions and celebrates these attractions. Whatever their romantic or sexual problems, heterosexual men and women and their families can find available guidance and potential solutions in art, the media, psychology, etc. Because they live in a society that endorses heterosexuality, parents and children can easily find resources to help them understand, adjust, and even celebrate these growing urges and attractions. There are opportunities within families, schools, and communities to openly discuss with young people the risks of heterosexual sex, such as pregnancy and sexually transmitted diseases, and how they can be avoided. Furthermore, heterosexual youth can look forward to love and legally and socially sanctioned marriage— ways to satisfy their longing for sexual fulfillment without risk or taboo.

However, about one in ten children do not have the luxury of living in a world that embraces their burgeoning sexual maturity. As recalled by Joelle,[1] a young African American college student who felt a strong sense of alienation when she began to realize she was attracted to other girls: "I'd say like third grade, it would be like, I don't feel like the rest of these kids. And for long periods of time, I'd just be sitting in class not doing work and just be like, 'God, I feel so different.'" And this young student teacher, Mike, who, once he realized he was gay, attempted to commit suicide: "When I was twelve, I used to watch porn and I focused more on the penis and not the female . . . it was just something that I just thought about and no one knew but me. . . . [I realized this] very young, I guess, about ten or eleven. I know it felt fine to me on the inside, but I was very, very scared of anyone finding out."

Many of the prevailing models of lesbian and gay identity development describe coming out as primarily an individual experience starting with a troubling emerging awareness that one is somehow different from her peers (Cass 1979; Coleman 1982; Troiden 1989). Troiden uses the term *sensitization* to describe this first stage of gay and lesbian identity development, and, as the sixty-five adolescents and young adults in this study recalled their early

---

1. Respondent names and identifying information has been changed to protect their confidentiality.

lives, this term resonated. However, as I interviewed the gay and lesbian young people and their parents, I found there was a *family* stage process that was related but also different from the family development stages identified by Carter and McGoldrick and others. To borrow from Troiden, the first of these stages is what I am calling the *family sensitization* phase. Like Troiden's sensitization phase, the period for family sensitization occurs anywhere from the time when children realize something is different, often without knowing why—to the three months or so before they come out to their parents. However, what makes this a *family* phase is the interaction between the children's awareness of stigma, their emotional distancing from their mothers and fathers, and their parents' suspicions.

As these previous quotes suggest, facing the fear of shame, ostracism, and rejection is a central theme in the lives of the adolescents and young adults who were interviewed for this book. Once parents eventually knew that their children were lesbian or gay, they also feared the harsh judgment of those who would blame them for their children's homosexuality. However shame and stigma are not the whole story. The recollections of these families also demonstrate the persistence and potential healing power of family connections that endure despite personal guilt, anxiety, and societal condemnation.

Stigma and Isolation

All stories have a beginning. For the families discussed in this book, their stories of coping and adjustment began long before children understood what their attractions meant and certainly well before parents knew about them. Most of the young respondents in this sample described the realization that they had same-sex attractions as a slow dawning coupled with a nagging realization that something was wrong—very wrong, with the way they felt. They understood that if their peers or their parents discovered their sexual feelings, they risked becoming objects of rejection and abuse.

Stigma has been defined as a personal quality or condition that is considered deviant and diminishes the bearer's worth and status (Dovidio, Major, and Crocker 2000; Goffman 1963; Link and Phelan 2001). Goffman described stigma not as a personal attribute but as a function of relationships; a stigma exists because the individual with the deviant characteristic is considered tainted by others and is therefore marginalized and discredited. Despite slowly growing improvement in the public's attitudes toward homosexuality (Avery et al.

2007; Brown and Henriquez 2008), in a Gallup poll close to half of the sample believed that homosexuality should not be "considered an acceptable alternative lifestyle" and 40 percent thought homosexual relations between two consenting adults should be illegal (Gallup Organization 2006). Thus, there still very much exists what Herek, Chopp, and Strohl (2007) call a *homosexual stigma*, defined as "society's shared belief system through which homosexuality is denigrated, discredited, and constructed as invalid relative to heterosexuality" (171).

Children are taught that love and marriage between a man and a woman is the romantic ideal to which everyone is expected to aspire. Those growing up with same-sex attractions learn what is considered normal long before they discover, to their horror, that they themselves are abnormal. Shame, stigma's evil handmaiden, is defined by Nichols (1995b) as the feeling of being looked down upon by others: of feeling worthless, weak, and dirty. As gays and lesbians begin to recognize their same-sex attractions, they are already aware that such feelings are shameful and must be denied, hidden, and repressed — at great cost to their own self-esteem.

Schulze and Angermeyer (2003) have identified interpersonal interaction as one of the primary domains where stigma manifests, and many of the young people in this study first learned that their homosexuality was wrong at the hands of their peers. Their classmates saw their cross-gendered or otherwise atypical behavior as justification for cruelty. Both of the following respondents recalled being physically assaulted by peers who believed them to be gay or lesbian long before they recognized their own same-sex attractions.

> Once I hit middle school I think really other kids figured out before I did. I used to get picked on for being gay all the time and I didn't know what it meant. . . . I wasn't the most masculine kid (twenty-one-year-old gay man).

> I got beat up a lot. I didn't have many friends, they were kind of put off. A lot of the guys would pick on me. . . . They would call me dyke and beat me up (twenty-year-old lesbian).

Schulze and Angermeyer (2003) also identify a structural dimension of stigma, namely, how discrimination is embedded in institutional policies and practices. Youth who were verbally and physically harassed by peers recalled how school employees who witnessed their abuse did nothing to stop it. The confusion and shame experienced by these youth was compounded by the indifference of adults who could have protected them but didn't. One eighteen-year-old gay man, recalling abuse he experienced in high school, remembered feeling helpless and abandoned: "Yeah, no one else saw it. Which is pretty ironic considering there is a teacher at every doorway—every five feet—but no one ever heard it. No one ever saw it. So then I didn't know what to do. I was completely clueless. I had no idea what to do." Jay, a twenty-five-year-old gay male, recalled:

> Well see the thing of it was I got colitis the summer after my sixth-grade year, which was my worst year in school ever. The kids beat me up with no mercy and my teacher did nothing about it, absolutely nothing. And he is the vice principal now! I am convinced, because of the stress of that year I developed colitis the summer following sixth grade and I was very sick. By the fall the doctors figured out what it was, gave me medicine and I was fine . . . but halfway through eighth grade the bullies started up again and this time it was girls, two white trash girls that were just angry and just hated me. . . . But it [also] seemed like every boy was just trying to get me—kick me in the hallway, push me over, push my books on the floor—crap like that. And I developed colitis again in the spring of that year.

The devastating emotional impact of peer abuse was compounded by the respondents' helplessness and isolation. One way oppressed people protect themselves from the shame that can result from stigma is to form groups with others like themselves so they can learn effective coping methods such as externalization, which is when people place the blame for their stigma on its source where it belongs. (e.g., "It's not us who are sick, it's them!") (Corrigan and Watson 2002; Frable, Wortmen, and Joseph 1997). However, for the most part, a resource such as a supportive group of gay peers was not available to the young men and women in this study. As stated by a sixteen-year-old young man: "As far as I knew I was the only person [who was gay]." And recalled by this twenty-three-year-old lesbian: "When I started thinking that I was gay, it was just really odd. There were no out gay people where I live, no out gay people on either side of my family. I know because I am the only one. But I didn't know anybody."

Such isolation and mistreatment (or fear of mistreatment) takes a toll on a gay or lesbian person's physical and mental health, as reported by Jay who developed colitis and who also became school phobic as a result of the abuse he experienced. As lesbian and gay adolescents and young adults attempt to reconcile their sexual orientation with their status as stigmatized persons, they may develop a denigrated self-image that bodes poorly for their mental health and ability to maintain long-term intimate relationships (Corrigan and Watson 2002; Gallo 1994; Greenan and Tunnell 2003; Meyer 2003; Meyer and Dean 1998). Among samples of gay males and lesbians, reported incidents of discrimination and violence have been associated with psychiatric problems including suicidal thoughts and attempts (D'Augelli 2002; D'Augelli, Pilkington, and Hershberger 2002; Huebner 2002; Meyer 2003; Vives 2002), and the destructive effects of being stigmatized were found among the young respondents interviewed for this study, whereby most recalled experiencing symptoms of depression and anxiety before coming out.

Experts in the area of stigma describe the way in which people develop self-protective behavior once they become aware of their potential to be stigmatized (Herek, Chopp, and Strohl 2007; Scambler 1989). The young people in this sample learned painfully and powerfully that their burgeoning homosexuality was shameful and punishable by social exclusion and violence, so they attempted to hide their attractions in an effort to protect themselves from ostracism and rejection.

Peer Harassment and Parents

For those who haven't experienced it, it is difficult to imagine how humiliating, lonely, and horrible it is to be terrorized on a daily basis and be afraid to tell anyone. Parents of children who were harassed by peers during family sensitization were sometimes (but not always) aware that their children were having problems with other kids in school. However, they were never aware that their sons and daughters attracted the ire of their peers because they appeared gay or lesbian.

Jay's mother Adele knew that he was experiencing peer problems but was unaware that he was victimized because he was perceived to be gay. Another gay male recalled being the target of frequent verbal and physical assaults in junior high school for what his peers perceived were his effeminate behaviors. However, his father and mother only knew that he was experiencing trouble with other kids in school—they did not know why. Two young lesbians had similar stories. What all four youth had in common was that they were so afraid that their parents would think they were gay that they could not bring themselves to tell their mothers and fathers why they were being hassled. As recalled by one of the lesbians who had been harassed in school before she even realized she might be lesbian: "I would never, never have told my parents the kids were calling me a lesbian, because it was so embarrassing and also then they would begin to suspect that I was [lesbian]."

The family is the usual place children turn to when they need help and a safe haven from the turmoil of the outside world. Nevertheless, in this study, all by themselves, these children had to face frightening feelings of confusion and shame about their sexual orientations—and some had to do so while enduring their schoolmates' cruel treatment. For most children, parents are a source of comfort, support, and protection during tough times. However, this much-needed safe haven was unavailable to these children during the family sensitization phase because they felt they needed to hide themselves— or else risk parental rejection.

Family Sensitization: The Initial Phase of Family Discovery and Adjustment

Even though they feel isolated, young lesbians and gays do not realize their emerging sexual orientation in isolation. The reports of both the parent and child respondents suggest a *family process* in which there are distinctive changes in the family interactions and relationships as the child slowly realizes and eventually discloses his sexual orientation. Family sensitization, the first stage of this process, accounts for what occurs in families at the time children begin to recognize feeling different and attracted to members of the same sex.

Parents and children reported that maternal relationships, especially between mothers and sons, were particularly close up to and sometimes beyond the time the children began to realize they were gay or lesbian. However, in some families there existed what Ponse (1976) has called a *counterfeit secrecy* in which both parents and children suspected the children might be gay or lesbian but implicitly agreed not to acknowledge it. For some families, the children's burgeoning realization that they were gay and needed to hide it, along with the parent's growing suspicions, rendered parent-child relationships distant and, in some instances, conflicted.

Mothers and Closeness

Though it seems like a cloying cliché to say so, it is hard to imagine anything quite as soothing for a distressed child as a mother's love, particularly for many of the children in this study who were being harassed by peers or who felt like potential outcasts. Among the sixty-five youth respondents, fifty-one described having historically strong relationships with their mothers characterized by closeness, consistency, and warmth. For example, this young woman, who while being interviewed was preparing to dress as a man for a drag performance at her college, talked about what it was like for her growing up: "I never really felt like I fit in. I always felt something was wrong. I never had boyfriends." However, in speaking about her relationship with her mother, she related: "My mom and I have a very close relationship. We've always been really close. And . . . she was always there when I needed her, even before I came out." Her mother recalled: "She is my kid. . . . I think we've been very close forever. . . . She has always talked to me, told me what is going on in her life. She always told me what she and her friends were doing . . . if they smoked pot or whatever. She was open."

M. C. was a scapegoat in high school and college because of his effeminate behavior. He talked of the closeness he shared with his mother growing up:

My mother and I can best be described as [having] a friendship as well as a family relationship. We got along very well. We shared a lot of the same interests. We would play Scrabble together and we would talk politics together. We would watch political shows together, like *Hardball*, and we still do. We liked going on vacations. We shared some of the same tastes in food—some disagreements here and there, but we joked around. She was very caring and still is a very caring . . . mother. I would say it was almost like a friendship between us. I know we are not equals and could never be as a mother and son. But, as much as possible, we were able to talk to each other as almost equals.

His mother, Charlotte, a legal secretary, recalled, "[M. C.] and I have been especially close . . . an extremely close bond."

Chauncey, a twenty-year-old gay male, and his mother Marie were born in Haiti and have lived in New York City for the past fifteen years. Chauncey had significant problems with neighborhood bullies, which are described in chapter 4. However, he also recalled his close relationship with his mother: "I wasn't interested in football or going out and playing, that's true. I was more interested in being with my mother and just being secluded in the home. I was definitely never interested in sports, and I just basically was staying with my mother, you know, just being secluded in the house." This young man's mother agreed with her son's recollections, remembering that she and Chauncey were very close when he was growing up—much closer than she and her older son.

Like Marie, mothers tended to agree that they enjoyed a special closeness with their sons before they came out, although, unlike their sons, they did not look back and attribute this closeness to their boys' emerging homosexuality. This was in contrast to the reports of the young men who believed that their burgeoning homosexuality made them more empathic and sensitive and thus better able to communicate with their mothers. The following twenty-four-year-old African American college student described why he felt closer to his mother as he grew up:

I think personally it [being gay] made me a more emotional person, more sensitive, more in touch with both the male and female sides of myself, but allowing me to even acknowledge that other side made me closer to my mother. I was OK with braiding her hair, OK with sewing, OK with cooking—not trying to be very macho. Yes, definitely, it made me closer to her.

Unfortunately, this respondent's mother was deceased at the time of the interview, so her opinions could not be captured. However, this next mother from a white working-class family recalled: "Jack is definitely my closest [of three sons]. You know, we just always had a special bond. I could just relate to him better than the other two." Like the other boys, when Jack, a senior in high school, was asked how his emerging sexual orientation played a role in his relationship with his parents, he replied:

Well, my relationship with my mother has always been the strongest and the best relationship probably with anyone in my family, so it was always wonderful. I could tell her anything and felt comfortable doing that. I always felt like, from a very young age, she respected me very much for who I was and that there was something a little different between me and my brothers and she loved me for that. And so, in turn, I think I gave her a certain amount of respect that my brothers may not have been able to. I felt as though my brothers treated her in a way similar to the way my father treated her, and sometimes I think they forget that she's not just a mother but a human being with feelings and stuff like that. And I think that the way that my mother handled experiences that I had growing up . . . I was able to realize that and appreciate it and in turn treat her with a certain amount of the same empathy and compassion that she had with me.

Perhaps it is not surprising that mothers and children described their relationships as close. Mothers typically have an advantage whereby they usually interact more with their children than do fathers (Kimmel 2004). However, being gay might be a factor that makes mothers and sons even closer. In his study of gay and lesbian youth, Savin-Williams (2001a) found that most of his respondents reported feeling close to their mothers before coming out, and some of the boys entertained the idea that this closeness caused their homosexuality. This idea corresponds to prevailing stereotypical notions that male homosexuality is caused by family dynamics in which "sissy" boys and their mothers cling to each other—a myth that had implications for the respondent mothers' later reactions once they suspected and then knew for sure their sons were gay.

However, the young gay males in this study believed the causal relationship worked in the opposite direction: that their burgeoning sexual orientation made them closer to their mothers. These boys recalled sharing interests in common with their mothers, such as fashion and cooking, and were also sensitive to their feelings. Perhaps these mother-son connections were fueled by the boys' need for extra security because they felt like pariahs outside their homes. Whatever its cause, this feeling of commonality and connection to mothers could potentially be considered a unique aspect of the parent-child relationship in some gay families.

However, even though respondents who reported that their sexuality made them closer to their mothers were mostly gay males, Joelle, the African American young woman who was previously quoted as feeling alienated from her peers, reported recollections that indicate it is possible for a lesbian to believe her sexuality contributed to a special closeness with her mother: "At the moment it didn't seem like it did. It just seemed like normal. But, looking back, I think it did because of wanting a sense of security in terms of having a female relationship in my life—emotional security, which she offered me."

Nevertheless, despite this history of warm closeness, some of these sons (and daughters) recalled a change in their maternal relationships as they got older. Kenneth, a twenty-three-year-old aspiring actor recalled: "We had a great relationship. We were always friends when I was growing up. And in high school I got a little bit distant, I was going through your typical teenage stuff. I was really busy in school and always doing my own thing, but we had a really good relationship." His mother, Cynthia remembered the changes:

> It changed when, I can't remember the exact time, I think he was around fifteen, tenth grade. It was right after we moved to Colorado and he changed schools. Things started changing. He started becoming more quiet—stayed in his room more. He became extremely aware of his weight . . . So he just became more to himself. I would go up to his room and ask if there was something wrong. He didn't want to talk to me. And my husband told me that boys are like that when they become teenagers—he is probably going through puberty so you need to just leave him alone. Boys don't hang out with their moms when they get to be a certain age.

Like Cynthia's husband, most parents in this study generally assumed that this growing distance was caused by the children's burgeoning independence and need to separate themselves from their mothers to find their own identity. However, almost invariably, the children in this study saw this distance as attributable to their growing realization that they were gay. This dynamic will be further explored in later sections of this chapter.

Fathers

It's a sad fact that men's relationships with their children tend to be more distant than those with their mothers (Kimmel 2004), and in this sample there were few exceptions to this phenomenon. Fathers tend to live on the outside edge of the emotional lives of their families and, as a result, family members, family therapists, and family researchers often find them difficult to engage. In this sample only seventeen fathers agreed to be interviewed compared to sixty-two of the mothers.

Fathers in these families were preoccupied and tired from work, distant and a bit intimidating, or simply not present in the lives of their children. Of the sixty-five sons and daughters in this sample, eighteen had no contact with their fathers. Five of these young respondents reported that their fathers were dead, yet the other thirteen never experienced a relationship with their fathers—or they had one when they were very young but now no longer had contact with them. For the forty-seven young respondents who reported relationships with their fathers, the majority (forty) described them as distant particularly in comparison to their maternal relationships. The small number of fathers who agreed to be interviewed could be attributed to this remoteness.

Distant father-child relationships are not unique to families of gay and lesbian children. Despite changing sex roles, as evidenced by the number of mothers working outside of the home and the increasing willingness of men to take on household and child rearing duties, children are still closer to their mothers than their fathers. Mothers still spend more time with their children than fathers (Craig 2006) and continue to bear the responsibility of communicating with their children, particularly when the topic is sex (Kirkman, Rosenthal, and Feldman 2002).

One reason for this might be that men's family roles tend to be more instrumental (discipline, providing income, moral/ethical development, assisting with career development) compared to the more expressive functions that are the domain of the mother (caregiving, companionship, facilitating emotional, social and spiritual development; Finley and Schwartz 2006). Despite a cultural shift in which these functions are expected to be shared, traditionally distinct, complementary parental roles are still socially scripted and reinforced, inevitably leading to family relationships in which fathers and their children expect less interaction and more emotional distance (Rosen 1999).

Paternal distance was definitely found in the families in this study. As this father described:

> I like to give the kids a lot of space. They don't need to be around me all the time; I don't need to be around them all the time. I have kind of like a "don't ask, don't tell" attitude. I tell my wife; "You don't have to tell me every little detail of everything that they're involved in. I want to know big, important stuff, but I don't need to know every little thing that's going on."

And this next father:

> Well to a certain extent I kind of feel I have abdicated a lot of responsibility to my wife . . . it was partly an issue of not wanting to conflict with her, but having a real sense along the way of [how] I wouldn't be doing it her way more or less. And at the same time, in a retrospective look, I think her sensibilities were much more on target than mine.

In discussing his relationship with his father, this son recalled:

Well, we were never that close, but there were never really big things that went wrong between us. I always loved him and I felt we could relate on certain things. . . . And I don't know, it was probably your typical father-son relationship. He wasn't very warm, wasn't much for emotions or hugging or stuff like that.

Even though the parent-child relationships in this study seemed to match what we would expect in most American families, the gay sons believed that their homosexuality was the reason they had a lack of shared interests with their fathers and, in their minds that was the cause for this distance. As recalled by this young man:

INTERVIEWER: Were you close when you were younger?
RESPONDENT: Not really, just a father and son. We know we love each other and that kind of thing, but, it's not like we have to tell each other everything.
INTERVIEWER: Did you do things together, you and Dad?
RESPONDENT: No not really because my dad was always into stuff that I really wasn't into, like he could tell that I really never was into fixing the car. . . . We never really did anything since I was little, like baseball and stuff like that.

M.C., who was quoted previously as playing Scrabble and watching political shows with his mother, recalled the distance between him and his father:

Things were more distant with my dad. I would say we just didn't share the same interests, whereas my mother nurtured me with my piano music, which is something I did get to enjoy. I guess he was the one who got me into soccer, which I stunk at, and that kind of stuff. He likes to fish, and I never enjoyed it. We never did much together in that regard. He didn't have that same desire to go out and experience new things, and we just didn't really share many things of interest. I wouldn't say it's been hostile, just more distant. We had a different perspective politically as well.

For the most part, fathers and children agreed that the father-child relationship was not as close as the mother-child counterpart. This young lesbian, remembered: "We never really talked about anything important ever, so anything that went on was never between my father and I. It was always between my mother and my father, and then my mother would tell me what my father said." And her father agreed: "She's definitely closer to her mother."

Sometimes, as in the following case, fathers remembered their relationships with their children more positively than their sons and daughters did. Bob, a corporate attorney, recalled a better relationship than his daughter Ellie did, at least when she was younger, even though he remembered it deteriorating as she grew into adolescence:

> It was what I perceived at the time as being a normal relationship. I found her as a youth to be very lovable and cuddle-able and sweet as she went through the usual growth stages. I found as she reached her young teenage years we started to grow apart and there was more rebelliousness and unwillingness to conform to parental norms.

However, Ellie, a psychology graduate student, recalled:

> My mom was a stay-at-home mom, so I had a lot of access to her . . . a lot of time with her. And she was an extremely attentive person so she was also sort of fulfilling my needs. I forgot my lunch at school and she would come with a picnic basket full of stuff. She was very attentive in that way. My dad has always, until two years ago, worked twelve-hour days. He is a very hard worker so he would come home, he would eat, and fall asleep. So having an intense conversation with my dad had to be scheduled, which was difficult as a child but as an adolescent it made it easy for me to disengage from him. I never had to deal with a confrontation with him because he never had time. I am sure he would have made time if I would have asked for it but it just wasn't on his mind.

Although, based on these interviews it is difficult to know with any certainty the causes of these discrepancies, it is possible that fathers who perceive their relationships with their children as less distant than their children do might be reluctant to admit to an outsider that these relationships were less than optimal. A second factor might also be at play whereby the children and the fathers may have different standards as to what makes a good paternal relationship. As stated previously, divergent parental roles are believed to be socially scripted and reinforced, inevitably leading to family relationships in which fathers and children expect less interaction and more distance (Rosen 1999).

Just like some of the boys and their mothers, some of the girls in this sample remembered good relationships with their fathers based on common "masculine" interests they shared, at least until adolescence. Tara, whose father was a chemist, was a college student majoring in chemistry at the time of her interview. She recalled:

> When I was really younger, I was a lot closer with my father. . . . When I was little, I guess I was like daddy's little girl and I would always go to my father. Like I really like to fix things and stuff, so if he was fixing something around the house, I would always go help him. Or something outside like I'm always the one who does yard work. I like mowing the lawn for some reason. But I would always do that, so we would bond over that.

Her father, Luke, recalled sharing common interests, even though there were changes in their relationship as she approached adolescence:

> She was always athletic, and we participated in her athletic activities. She's always been a good student, so we've stayed abreast of her academics, encouraged her, interacted with her in that degree. She's always been a little combative, so that's always put some strain, and she became a little more combative as she got older. So that would maybe be the biggest difference as she grew into adolescence.

Thus common interests seem to support closeness between daughters and fathers and, in particular, mothers and sons. As would perhaps be expected in any American family, these relationships became somewhat strained during adolescence. Fathers, like mothers, viewed these changes from a developmental perspective: the family relationships were changing because the kids were becoming adolescents. However, as we will see, the youth recalled putting distance between themselves and their mothers and fathers not necessarily as a way to develop autonomy but rather to hide their homosexual feelings.

Further, the relative closeness in the mother-child relationship accounts for the common family dynamic of children communicating mostly with their mothers and then for mothers to either relay information to fathers or leave them out of the loop completely. This dynamic has implications for later in the coming out process.

Suspicion During Family Sensitization

It is safe to say that all therapists have encountered the unmentioned "elephant in the room" when working with families. As a matter of fact, when our clients come to us, it is our job to point it out—often to the consternation of family members. Beginning therapists might be surprised that there is something important happening in the family and no one is discussing it. However, as we get more seasoned, we come to realize that families become accustomed to living with certain secrets—if they live with them long enough, they forget they exist.

In forty-five of the sixty-five families, parents recalled that they suspected their children were gay or lesbian before finding out for sure, and, with rare exception, the children in these families knew that their parents suspected. Nevertheless, in the great majority of these families, the children's sexual orientation was not directly acknowledged or openly discussed during family sensitization. Without any direct discussion, parents and children appeared to have made a silent pact to keep this issue a secret.

REASONS FOR PARENTAL SUSPICION. During the family sensitization phase, one of the primary reasons parents suspected their daughters were lesbian was that they did not show the usual early adolescent interest in boys. One forty-year-old divorced mother recalled: "The fact that she didn't date and didn't talk about boys made me suspicious. . . . Boys didn't call." When asked if she thought her parents suspected, this mother's twenty-four-year-old daughter knew her lack of interest in boys during adolescence gave a meaningful indicator. "I think they both did. I never dated men. I never showed the least bit of interest."

Parents noticed that, instead of showing an interest in boys, their daughters developed particularly close relationships with other females—closer than what they considered to be normal—and this made them suspicious. Nancy, the African American school administrator who was the mother of Joelle, was suspicious: not only was her daughter not dating boys, she seemed to have an intense relationship with another girl.

> Junior year of high school she had a friend, because I talked to my husband about this, and I knew that her intensity of feeling and reaction to this person was beyond the scope of a normal high school girlfriend type of situation. So my clue was the intensity and the obsession and the passion.

All the drama surrounding the relationship with this person said to me that something else was going on here.

Looking back, Joelle knew that her close friendship was sending out signals that led her mother to suspect. When asked if she thought her mother suspected before she came out, she replied: "Definitely. Because of the whole incidence of how I discovered it through realizing my attractions towards a friend and the way that I would talk about that friend. It just became so obvious over time that I was [gay]—to everyone."

For many parents of lesbians, their daughters' tendency not to groom themselves to attract male attention was an additional factor that led them to suspect. The expectation that teenage girls, even previous tomboys, are going to dress and act in ways to inspire the romantic and sexual interest of boys is perhaps so engrained in our culture that a girl who fails to do so calls attention to herself and raises the suspicion of parents. This father, a successful building contractor, recalled that his daughter did not seem to be trying to attract boys:

> Over the last four years . . . it started subtly, when she wasn't getting dates with boys and things like this, coming to the new school, getting a little success in the track team, but still never really wanting to look nice or dress nice. I am sensitive to these things, because nobody likes to look better than me. I could see she wasn't even trying. . . . She wasn't grooming herself to be attractive to anybody, frankly. But she had a little success with the track thing, and I kind of forgot about it a little bit. But, like I said, the last four years, it became pretty obvious to me. She doesn't date boys.

His daughter was clear:

> My father definitely suspected. After I came out to them, it was actually really funny. My mother cried and did the typical thing. My father was like, well, "So what? Like I didn't know." Later he said he had suspected for a while, but he wasn't going to bring it up. And when I was a sophomore in high school, he asked me if one of my friends were a lesbian. He has actually picked out a couple of my friends and asked me if they are, which was interesting.

Mac, a retired fireman who was gay himself, suspected his young daughter Jillian was a lesbian because of her seemingly careless grooming as well as her intense relationship with another girl:

> I guess maybe a lot of kids do it today, but this is one thing we do fight about a lot; she's in sweat suits all the time. She hung out with this girl. . . . Before I knew for sure I thought that this girl was a girlfriend. There was also what turned out to be a $1,000 phone bill, because this girl was in Florida.

This next mother, a widowed legal secretary, suspected her daughter Janie might be gay because of her preference for masculine clothes:

> She never wanted to wear dresses . . . from infancy. From infancy we couldn't put a dress on her, we had to fight with her to get a dress on. And then her brother gave her a leather jacket. . . . She would rather wear that. She wanted to wear my husband's shoes all the time . . . anything that had to do with boys.

Despite this last example, for the most part, such masculine behavior was not a primary reason for the parents of this study to suspect that their daughters were lesbians. This might be because a girl's tomboy behavior or interest in masculine clothing before puberty is socially acceptable and is usually transitory—not necessarily an indication of future lesbianism (Carr 2007).

However, for boys, cross-gendered mannerisms or "sissy" behavior is considered a more serious aberration, presumably because masculine gender roles are more rigid, and girlish behavior in boys is seen as a rejection of normal masculinity (Kimmel 2004). Furthermore, boys' sissy behavior is not seen as temporary but as an engrained, permanent (and undesirable) personality characteristic. This may explain why cross-gendered behavior was the primary sign that led parents to suspect their sons were gay during the family sensitization phase.

As remembered by Eula, an African American social service worker and widowed mother who lived with her eighteen-year-old son, Andrew, in a neighborhood known for its high crime rate:

> He had somewhat effeminate moves . . . and a lack of interest in the "manly" type things. Andrew loved to sing and dance and perform. And in watching

him . . . he had some effeminate tendencies when he would move around and so forth. And that was pretty much it. My husband and I started watching from then on. And it's like, "OK, we see where this is going," and it started to worry me. And I am like, OK, now I am going to have to go through this with him of not wanting to be an overprotective mother, but to a degree having to watch a little more who he is around and so forth to protect him from gay bashing and things like that. Because, even though it is open more and accepted more than when I was kid, you have got some crazy people out there, which is why I took him out of the local public high school. I told him that I did not feel it was conducive to his physical or emotional health . . . I was thinking: "Uh oh, I am going to really have to protect this kid."

Andrew, a pharmacy assistant, recalled: "My mother always knew. She was just waiting for me to tell her. She tells me that all the time. . . . She was just waiting for me . . . for the right time when I felt comfortable to tell her."

Like Eula, many parents who suspected their sons were gay understood how their cross-gendered behaviors, interests, and mannerisms might make them objects of discrimination and even violence, as stated by the following African American mother. "I was upset at first. Because I was like, 'Not my child! Why my child? How my child?' and then I sat down and I prayed about it. I talked about it. It was something like, 'Oh my God, is Jarrell gay?' But I didn't feel disgusted. I just felt like, 'Wow, this is a hard life.' That is really it." Fears for their children's well-being, which emerged as a concern for parents once they suspected their sons or daughters were gay, later surfaces as an ongoing worry once they knew for sure.

SUSPICION NOT DISCUSSED. Like virtually all the youth of suspecting parents, the son of this previously quoted mother knew his parents suspected he was gay before he came out. However, what is also apparent is that, almost without exception, the youth's burgeoning sexual orientation was never discussed. There was one family in which the daughter recalled her mother asking her several times if she was gay: "Yes. She asked me a couple of times. I was sixteen—she kept asking me. I would just deny it."

Almost all models of individual lesbian/gay identity development describe how lesbians and gay men will not disclose their sexual orientation to others until they are at least somewhat comfortable with it themselves (Cass 1979; Troiden 1989). What the findings herein suggest is that there is a period when parents and children *both* suspect but are not ready or able to discuss it. If parents confront their sons and daughters and try to make this subject a topic of family discussion before their children have come to terms with their homosexuality themselves, they will simply deny it. Trying to push this issue during family sensitization is like taking a cake out of the oven before it is fully baked — it's just not ready.

PARENTAL GUILT.   Nancy, the African American mother whose daughter Joelle was first quoted in this chapter, talked about how she and her husband wondered if they were at fault when they first suspected their daughter was a lesbian. It is worth noting that Joelle suffered from learning and emotional problems during her adolescence.

> I just kind of felt—like she doesn't have enough problems. Now she is going to choose an even harder path in life. My husband and I have had conversations where we go, "OK, is it something that we did?" And not in a belligerent way . . . We will even joke with each other about it, and he will go, "If you haven't been so whatever . . . " And I will go, "No, it's your fault." And we will go, "OK, nature, nurture. Nobody else in the family is gay." But it is weird because my husband is an adopted child, so who knows anything about his family's background?

This mother of an eighteen-year-old gay youth recalled:

> You know what? Bud has always had like a little bit of . . . feminine tendencies. He used to wear long T-shirts and pretend they were dresses and put makeup on and walk around the house like that. And, you know, he would—even earlier on, maybe when he was thirteen, he would see guys on TV and say, "Oh, he's cute." I felt like "What did I do wrong?"

Generally, it is not uncommon for parents to blame themselves when something goes wrong with their kids (Ferriter and Huband 2003). Mothers in particular often feel guilty about their parenting—even when there is nothing wrong with their children (Jackson and Mannix 2004). No doubt, the tendency for parents to feel guilty when they suspect a child is gay is aggravated by the general idea that parents are to blame for their children's homosexuality. So it must be particularly distressing for parents to see their children develop into people whose behavior attracts ridicule, discrimination, and violence—and think it's their fault!

Goffman (1963) defines *courtesy stigma* as the negative impact felt by those who are connected or related to the stigmatized individual, and in this sample, some parents began to experience this type of stigma when they initially suspected their children were gay. Based on their research of parents of the mentally ill, Corrigan and Miller (2004) distinguished two types of courtesy stigma; *vicarious stigma,* or the suffering parents feel empathically because their loved one is suffering, and *public stigma,* which is the stigma family members experience directly—they are tainted because they are thought to be to blame for their child's illness.

Although homosexuality is not a mental illness, it is similarly stigmatized and, like families of the mentally ill, parents of lesbians and gays share in their stigma. Courtesy stigma is found throughout the stories of these families and begins to rear its head during the family sensitization phase. Parents who suspect their child is gay and worry about his safety and well-being are experiencing an anticipatory vicarious stigma. Furthermore, when they feel to blame for their child's homosexuality, they fear public stigma in the form of the harsh judgment of others.

Although most of the parents who mentioned self-blame were mothers, some fathers also experienced guilt when they suspected their children were gay. This father, the previously quoted building contractor, felt shame when he suspected his daughter was a lesbian:

RESPONDENT: I was suspecting, but, I thought no, maybe I'm wrong. That type of thing . . . Yeah. I'm reading the signs wrong. Because of how I was raised . . . what a man was supposed to be. Not *my* daughter, I'm a virile Italian man, supposedly, and my offspring is not supposed to be a lesbian.
INTERVIEWER: So, that's a reflection on your manhood?
RESPONDENT: Maybe. Yeah. Again, I never went that deep into it. But, I'm sure that has a lot to do with it.

Joe, a recovering alcoholic, talked about how when he suspected, he felt guilty because he initially hoped for a daughter when his son Tony was born. Although that wish faded soon after his son's birth, when he suspected his son was gay it seemed as if the fates were meting out a cruel punishment for his old wish:

[I suspected] when he was a little boy. And I talked to my cousin afterwards. She is a psychiatric social worker. And she told me the same thing;

she said; "I wondered about that myself." Apparently he talked to her about wishing he was a girl. And you know, I felt very badly about that at the time, because when he was born, I think I said to someone; " I just wish in a way Tony had been a girl." because I thought I might have gotten along better with a little girl than a little boy, just because of my own relationship with my own father. . . . My first wife really got on my case about that. She said, "You really shouldn't talk about that around him." I said; "You are right, I shouldn't." So, I stopped. I was a little concerned. I don't know whether that clearly ever had any impression on him or not. So I sort of began to wonder if I had implanted that in his mind. . . . Who knows, but I don't think it did. The point is he did tell my first cousin he wished he was a girl.

The idea in our society that parents are to blame if their children are gay has been fueled by the influence of the helping professions, particularly psychiatry. Up until the 1970s psychiatrists asserted that homosexuality, which they considered a form of mental illness, was caused by pathological parenting, namely an overly close mother-child relationship and a distant father. Some studies biased by this premise implicated dysfunctional family relationships in its etiology (Bieber et al. 1962; Loney 1973; Thompson et al. 1973; West 1959). Despite ample findings disproving such notions (Hooker 1957; Shavelson et al. 1980; Siegelman 1974, 1981a, b), this idea persists and painfully surfaces for parents when they suspect their child is gay or lesbian.

INKLINGS AND DENIAL. Some parents, rather than fully suspecting, experienced fleeting notions that their children might be gay, which they tried to ignore. Similar to the young respondents quoted earlier in this chapter who denied or pushed aside their premonitions, parents in five families recalled hunches that their children might be gay before they knew for sure, but found ways to quickly vanquish such notions. Ann, a fifty-year-old homemaker and mother of Mike, the previously quoted student teacher, recalled: "I didn't suspect. But . . . one day I was out for a walk and, I don't know why, but I was thinking about the kids in general and it was kind of like the thought that he might be gay was almost like a bird coming and landing on a branch and then flying away. And, as fast as the bird came, I thought, no, that can't be it."

Mike's father, Fred, denied suspecting that his son was gay. However, Mike, like many of the youth whose parents repressed their suspicions, thought his parents *must* have suspected, largely due his obvious fascination with men and their anatomy: "Well, let's see. There were the penis-puppets-in-the-nursery-school thing. We were making puppets, a little arts and crafts thing, and I made mine with a big old dong, just because I felt like it. And then they kicked me out." A fifty-three-year-old mother of a nineteen-year-old gay son denied suspecting her son was gay, even though she recalled some indications:

> I did not really suspect. . . . If I look back, you know in retrospect I see signs, but I always tell this at PFLAG [support group for parents of lesbian and gay children]. I say that I hate stereotypes, so when people will say, "Oh the kid is into theater or he doesn't like sports, he must be gay" I get annoyed. It was annoying when people would say that, not about him, but about anybody in general, because I know a lot of people who have those characteristics who aren't gay. So I think my husband had more of a suspicion than I did. But only when it was close to the time, like within the year that he told us, did I start to suspect a little bit, but kind of on a very subconscious level.

Nevertheless, like Mike, this woman's son was sure his mother as well as his father knew well before he came out to them.

Looking back, this next mother, Janet, who was a psychiatrist, could remember overlooking signs of her son Robert's homosexuality, but denied she ever suspected before he came out to her:

> I absolutely should have, but I did not. He *is* kind of effeminate. I think he was maybe less so younger, but he got more so over the years. But he had interests that were gay like theater . . . musical theater. He never liked sports. His friends were girls. And I also had a gay stepson. I suspected Robert was gay, but really only because as a teenager he would go out with girls who sort of liked him, but he never liked any of them. So I sort of figured something was up. But I really did not suspect that Robert was gay.

Robert agreed that his mother did not suspect. Coincidentally, the subject did come up between them when he was younger, but not in a way that facilitated honest exchange:

> She and I were always close . . . and she never thought I was going to turn out gay, I don't think. She didn't suspect. . . . The reason it has been hard

for her is because she was very close to two gay men when she was younger and they both died of AIDS . . . and I remember when I was maybe ten or something her friend had just died of AIDS and she said, "Please don't be gay," which probably wasn't the best thing to say. And I said, "I am not gay, Mom. I am not gay." But that was really the only time sexual orientation ever came up before [coming out].

As stated by this mother of a twenty-one-year-old son who did not suspect:

No [I did not suspect]. But, you know, the funny part is—this is years ago—I was with my friend. We both had boys born the same year. And they both played with dolls, and we used to tease each other and say, "Can you imagine, they like dolls, what if they grow up to be gay?" I tell you the truth, we joked about it then, because he used to take the dolls and hide them. He would take his baby sister's dolls. We would find them, and I would say, "What are you doing with this doll?" I jested about it at the time. But, you know, years later I knew he was home a lot, he didn't go out. He would be on the phone . . . he would be like a busybody—like a girl would be more than a guy. But I never suspected.

Her son recalled:

I think they were in denial. I think when she looks back, she suspected. She makes jokes all the time about how she suspected. At the time when I was twelve, do I think my mom thought I was gay? No. But when I now discuss it, she will always say: "There were so many signs. I was just in such denial." My first album I ever bought was Cindy Lauper, *Girls Just Want to Have Fun*. And I used to play it on my record player all the time and dance around. That was my favorite song. So she always jokes that she should have known. No, I don't think she knew when I was twelve that I was gay. But now, looking back, I think she is very aware that there were signs the whole time—that she was in denial.

What these interviews suggest is that like their children who try to push aside same-sex attractions, parents also try to ignore the signs that their sons or daughters are gay. During family sensitization, suspecting parents might not want to confront their children, or even acknowledge the signs, because they are unwilling or unable to face that their child is gay. They understandably want to avoid the fear, worry, loss, and self-blame this reality would bring. So they might suspect but are hoping it's not true. Both parents and children are involved in a mutual dance of denial, which helps them avoid facing a difficult reality before either is ready.

Despite this unspoken agreement not to recognize or discuss the child's burgeoning sexual orientation—as earlier described, some parents and children, particularly mothers and sons, recalled their relationships as historically close, and some (though not all as will be described later) reported parent-child closeness right up until the time the children came out. On the surface, it seems contradictory that parents and children can believe that they are close when such an important issue is not recognized or discussed. However, a closer look suggests why this might indeed be possible. First of all, in our culture children and parents are expected to avoid directly discussing each others' sexual feelings, even in families that are considered close. Thus, the sexual orientation of a child can remain hidden behind this wall of silence, even if family members share themselves freely in other areas of their lives.

Secondly, it should be remembered that gay and lesbian people, particularly those who are in the closet, have learned to hide their sexuality in response to hostility such as that faced by some the respondents. Gays and lesbians seal their sexuality and related feelings in a metaphorical locked drawer, keeping this component of their lives separate from other parts of their identity.

Parents may be doing the same thing. When children enter the world, parents project their fondest hopes and wishes onto them. They fantasize about a future which they happily assume will include weddings (to someone of the opposite sex) and grandchildren. Parents, afraid to face the idea that their child might be gay or lesbian are perhaps, like their children, denying or suppressing their own suspicions to avoid experiencing distressing feelings that will damage their relationships with their children.

Family therapists might assume that this mutual avoidance creates disengagement in the family, in which people feel isolated and unsupported. Family relationships in which children hide parts of themselves are thought to be tenuous and unhealthy (Tharinger and Wells 2000). Shernoff asserts that "when people grow up in a family system where they cannot be or acknowledge who they truly are, they are placed in a system of dysfunction" (2008:178).

However, parent-child closeness might be a more complicated phenomenon than these ideas reflect, and the findings from this study suggest a more nuanced view might be in order. Perhaps it is a mistake to dichotomize parent-child relationships as close or distant, good or bad, while ignoring the likelihood that family closeness may be situation specific—mothers and sons might feel close when they discuss fashion or feelings but feel more distant when the topic is sexuality or related issues such as homosexuality, cross-gendered behavior, or peer problems at school.

Franklin, a twenty-one-year-old man of Guyanese descent talked about how hard he worked to get along with both his mother and father but how his attempts to hide his homosexuality led to distancing from his dad, Norman. However, contrary to what one would suspect, in some ways he felt his paternal relationship got stronger once he realized he was gay:

> As I said, I think being somewhat aware of my own sexual orientation made me aware of myself gender-wise, both male and female. I was able to identify with both sides. So with my dad, I was a boy, a guy. With my mom, I was a guy that was sensitive. But with my dad, I think maybe it did strengthen our bond, but at the same time in some way I think that was the only place where I had a sort of wall towards him. Because when I was younger I heard my father, my brothers and his friends make a lot of comments about gay people and what it means to be a man. So I assumed automatically that if they saw me doing things that weren't manly that they would make fun of me. So I would kind of shy away from them in those ways. With everything else there were no boundaries, but with that, anything that bordered on not being typical of a male, I would avoid.

If we are to believe the families in this study, it is possible for parents and children to feel a sense of closeness even though this important part of the child is not discussed. The avoidance of this difficult topic before the family is ready to deal with it could help parents and children maintain helpful, nurturing connections until the time is right for the child to come out. As a matter of fact, some of the closeness these youth described during the family sensitization period proved to be beneficial to the coming out process.

PARENTS WHO DIDN'T SUSPECT. Although most of the parents in this study suspected their children were gay or lesbian, and some had passing inklings that they ignored or pushed aside, twenty-five parents claimed they had no idea before their children came out to them. Nevertheless, seven of the children of these twenty-five parents found this simply impossible to believe.

According to them, their parents *must* have known, suggesting a tendency for some of the youth to either overestimate their parent's early awareness or underestimate their tendency for denial. This twenty-five-year-old biracial girl was sure her mother suspected: "She would just watch me and watch who I liked and see the posters I would put up. She would say, 'Don't you like this guy such and such?' and I would be like, 'No, not really. I really like this girl.' So I think she knew." However, her mother reported that she was taken completely by surprise when she learned her daughter was a lesbian.

Sometimes children of unsuspecting parents assumed their parents always knew based on what they perceived to be their own cross-gendered mannerisms. One twenty-two-year-old girl stated, "Yes. I was always a tomboy, so everybody thought that I was gay." Despite this, the girl's parents both denied ever suspecting their daughter was a lesbian before she came out, perhaps because, as stated earlier, tomboy behavior is not considered abnormal or a harbinger of future lesbianism. Mitch, a college freshman, whose parents discovered his sexual orientation one year prior to the interview, was previously quoted as enjoying a close relationship with his mother while growing up. He believed his parents must have known because of what he thought were obvious signs: "To be completely honest, I definitely fall under the stereotype of a homosexual male. So, yes, if she read anything or knew anything about homosexuality, I think she could piece it together." However, his mother claimed she had no idea.

These young people had difficulty believing their parents did not suspect. Some were quite certain that parents had an intuitive sense, which they chose to ignore: "Parents always know whether or not they want to admit it. I think they always know" (twenty-four-year-old lesbian).

Parents of both these last two quoted children denied knowing or even suspecting before they found out for sure. In two additional families the youth insisted their parents told them they suspected they were gay before they came out, but the parents stated they were completely surprised. Although this is a small minority of parents, it does lend further credence to the notion that parents and youth can have very different impressions of a parent's suspicion as well as what communication on this topic has actually occurred.

Sometimes, cultural taboos played a role in parents not wanting to recognize their children's sexual orientation. Norman, the previously quoted father of Franklin, who was from Guyana, talked about the tendency to push any suspicions away based on his culture's disapproval of homosexuality.

INTERVIEWER: Did you suspect your son was gay before you knew for sure?

NORMAN: No, I did not. That came as a complete surprise and I must say I come out of a homophobic culture in the Caribbean, homosexuals have no protected rights in the Caribbean, and it is a whole cultural put down. So when that sprung up on me that he was gay, I guess maybe I had my head in the sand and didn't want to see it, so I didn't accept it consciously. I didn't see that at all. Even though talking to other folks in the extended family later on, they said: "We knew that." I mean even his brothers were talking about it, but I didn't [suspect before he told me].

Still, Franklin believed his father must have suspected:

He's pretty smart. I think he knew a lot more about me than I knew about me. Meaning I think he could tell, I think he knows so many things about me, because I just tell him. And he is able to read between the lines. So I think he probably did suspect before I said anything, but he didn't necessarily come to a concrete conclusion.

Chauncey and his mother Marie, both from Haiti, were quoted earlier in this chapter as enjoying a close relationship. Chauncey explains why his mother might not have been able to acknowledge something was "different" about her son.

Every mother knows. She [my mother] was very religious and very traditional. She had the sort of attitude that if something didn't make sense, religiously or according to her own thinking, then she would just reject it—it didn't exist. So when I did tell her, she was like, "I don't believe you." She knew—she had to know. But she pushed it out of her mind.

Besides these cultural factors, there are other possible reasons youth might believe their parents suspected (or recalled their parents telling them they suspected) when their parents denied this. First of all, in this study parents might have been embarrassed to admit they were overlooking the signs or repressing the idea that their daughter or son might be lesbian or gay. Good parents are supposed to know what is going on with their children, particularly if they are struggling with something of such great magnitude. It might be embarrassing for these parents to admit to a stranger, and especially to the interviewers, that they were ignoring this important piece of information about their children. It should be noted that the interviewers were a gay man, a lesbian, and a mother of a lesbian, and parents might have feared the judgment of such clearly gay-positive people.

Second, as stated earlier, parents might be trying to deny or repress this information, much as their children do when they are in the early stages of coming to terms with their sexuality. Fear for their children's well-being, cultural taboos, and a wish to avoid thinking about a child's sexual feelings might be some of the reasons many parents do not recognize their children's homosexuality or try to push aside any suspicions. Perhaps parents who either suspected, reported fleeting inklings, or who had denied suspecting were hoping against hope it wasn't true—and that, if they didn't think about it, it would go away.

Third, it is also possible that parents did not even recognize their child being gay or lesbian within the realm of possibility—it was just not on the radar. So they did not look for or recognize any indicators. As stated succinctly by Frank, a butcher who was the father of a lesbian: "I don't think a father would want to look for it. You want me to be honest, right?"

This next parent's response suggests that a father's focus on protecting his daughter from aggressive males, which is an expected role for the father of a daughter, can get in the way of recognizing that his daughter might be lesbian. When asked if he ever suspected his daughter was gay before she came out to him, Bob, the previously quoted overworked stockbroker replied: "No . . . I think fathers try to avoid focusing [on] sex for their daughters except to pound the shit out of any guy who shows up at the door with his tongue hanging out."

Finally, children might be overestimating either their parents' powers of perception or the clarity of the signals they are sending out. Youth might have been comforting themselves with the notion that their parents were at least somewhat aware of their sexual orientation, so that when they told them their parents wouldn't be surprised. The prospect of coming out to parents is terrifying, and if sons and daughters can convince themselves their parents already suspect, they can also persuade themselves that telling their parents is only a small step—they are only confirming what their parents already know. The reality is that even parents who admitted to suspecting their children were gay were shocked and devastated when they eventually found out for sure. Nevertheless, the frightening prospect of having to someday come out to their parents might have led the youth to wishfully overestimate their parents' awareness. Unfortunately, this tendency could leave children unprepared for the shocked reaction they might receive when they come out to them.

Distance and Conflict During Family Sensitization

If someone is hiding a shameful secret, one that if exposed could result in ostracism and rejection, he feels at least somewhat safe as long as nobody knows. Toward the end of the family sensitization stage, once they realized they were gay, the frightened and ashamed young respondents drew the shades around themselves to carefully hide their homosexuality. This put additional emotional space between their parents and themselves, which strained family relationships, including some of the historically close mother-child relationships. When asked if her relationship with her mother changed when she first started to wonder if she was a lesbian, one twenty-year-old African American college student and psychology major responded, "For a while—it was like we've always been very open and I felt that I had to put on this charade with her . . . this act for her." This distancing did not go unnoticed by parents. As the mother of this young woman recalled: "When she got [to be] about eleven, twelve; she was standoffish, to herself. You know, she didn't talk a whole lot. I think I was closer to her than she was to me. . . . She started getting rebellious I guess at about thirteen, and started to have fits and tantrums."

However, like many of the parents in the study, though she was far from pleased by these changes, she did not believe they indicated something was wrong or abnormal. Instead, this mother attributed her daughter's withdrawal and irritability to her entry into adolescence. She recalled:

> She got very quiet. She didn't want to share with me. . . . She didn't want
> to tell me what was going on. She didn't want to be with the family or be
> involved with family activities. I thought, "This is the beginning of the end,
> the beginning of adolescence." I am sorry it happened, but I know this sort
> of thing is supposed to happen, so I am not going to sweat it. I will just
> let it ride, because life is supposed to be like that. Partings have to happen
> and growing up has to happen.

Certainly in the absence of any additional information, it is reasonable that parents would consider adolescent withdrawal to be normal and expected.

However, almost without exception, the young respondents attributed their own changes in relating behavior not to normal development but rather to their feelings about their sexual orientation. Their sexual and romantic attractions combined with their fears or actual experiences of being harassed by peers made them feel as if something was wrong with them, and they worried that parents and peers would ostracize and reject them if they knew they were gay. As this twenty-four-year-old woman, whose parents were divorced, recalled: "I would say it [feelings about being lesbian] influenced my relationship with everybody. I felt completely isolated, like no one had any idea. I felt that she [my mother] would understand me if I could bring myself to talk to her about it. But, because I didn't talk to her about what was really going on, it was really hard for me to do that." As for her relationship with her father: "I knew he wouldn't approve. So I don't know if it changed our relationship, but it made me feel that much farther away from him emotionally. Because it was a big deal to me and I didn't think he would understand."

As stated earlier, compared to their relationships with their mothers, the young respondents' paternal relationships felt more distant even before they came out. However, the realization that they were gay or lesbian seemed to pull them even further away from their fathers. As revealed by this nineteen-year-old African American woman: "I withdrew from him when I went through puberty. . . . I withdrew from him even more because I wasn't sure how his reaction would be because our relationship was already rocky and I didn't know what would happen. So I didn't share anything with him." This fifteen-year-old lesbian's parents divorced when she was six. She continued her relationship with her father through weekly visits; however, she always maintained a certain distance from him—even more so once she realized she was a lesbian: "I've always held back more information about myself from my dad than from my mom. So it was probably a more clamped feeling; as I was figuring it out, I had to watch more and more what I was saying."

Some young respondents attempted to throw their parents off-track by doing or saying something that confirmed that they were straight. Sometimes this worked—sometimes not. The previously quoted psychology major recalled her high school years

Like if we see a video or something, I'd go; "Oh yeah, he's cute. And the, "Oh yeah, he's really cute." But I'm really not feeling him. And it's just like the whole time I'm thinking, she can see right through me, she's seeing it, she's seeing it. And so secretly I was like "I hope she does and then—no, no, no, you're not ready for that!" So, for that year it was, it was really weird.

As she later discovered, her mother did not "see right through her" and did not suspect until her senior year, when she started spending time with gay friends.

Parent-Child Conflict

For some besieged youth, not only was there no shelter from the storm at home, but the weather there was also quite stormy. Sometimes the growing tension felt by youth as they started to realize their sexual orientation led not only to distancing, but to overt conflict with parents, adding to the enormous strain they were under. Tara, the previously quoted chemistry major who was eighteen at the time of her interview, described how distressed she felt when she started to suspect in middle school that she was gay: "I definitely think that the confusion in my own head over, like, what was going on and me not understanding it . . . made my relationships really, really hard with my parents. Like they even told me they didn't even want to be around me because I was just so bad." Her mother, Dora, recalled how belligerent her daughter became during this time and how, unlike most of the parents in this study, she suspected their mother-daughter problems went beyond those typical for adolescence:

> I would say up until she was about ten or eleven, we were close. She was really a sweet kid and very easy going and very nice. But she was like always with her friends too. She would disappear. Really, it was like the wind, we'd be eating dinner and then she would be done and be out the door. She had a lot of friends in the neighborhood, a lot of boys and girls. And then, when she got to be about eleven or twelve, she got to be a very, very difficult child, very hard to deal with. As a matter of fact, when she was in sixth or seventh grade—I forget which grade it was—I finally took her to a counselor. People were saying, "Well, you know, it's just typical kid's stuff." I said "No, I've got two other daughters and I never went through difficult kid stuff." But she would yell at us. She would just fight with us a lot. I want to say she was a decent student, but I guess sometimes she didn't want to do well, so we used to fight about academics—I mean so bad that I would go in the room and say you have to do this and she'd start screaming at me and I'd walk out. And then my husband would have to go in. It was like we had to play tag team because she was just so awful. She really was—she was awful to deal with.

Her father Luke, quoted earlier as remembering his daughter becoming "more combative" during adolescence, would agree.

In some families, conflict erupted because the young respondents felt their parents were pushing them to be "straight" or to act in ways congruent with expectations for heterosexual men and women. "I was a big tomboy. She tried to get me to dress differently, and we would argue . . . And I actually asked her the other day. I looked at my [old] pictures. I said, 'Did I pick out my own clothes?' She said I would pick out my own clothes out of the closet, but she would buy my clothes for me" (twenty-four-year-old woman). In speaking of her father, she recalled, with bitterness, "If I had friends who were guys, he would say: 'Oh, you should have him over for dinner' or 'Why don't you go out?'" Perhaps because she was struggling to come to terms with her sexual feelings and was particularly sensitive, she saw this pushing as his attempts to make her straight, which made her resentful.

In these families the children's and parents' anxiety seemed to generate a reciprocal pattern of parental pressure and youth resistance. Children might have been projecting feelings about societal disapproval onto their parents, while parents were projecting their hopes and dreams onto their children along with the fear that these dreams would go unfulfilled. Many of the young respondents felt distressed, even angry that they would not be able to meet their parents' (or society's) expectations of heterosexuality and, as a result, became combative. In response, parents understandably reacted in anger or withdrawal themselves.

When asked if her growing realization that she was a lesbian affected her relationship with her parents, this nineteen year old recalled how she perceived that her mother expected her to date and pursue more feminine interests: "I think it kind of hurt our relationship because I think in a way I started to resent her—her always wanting certain things from me and having these expectations and telling me the way I should act. But that wasn't her fault. She just didn't really get that wasn't what I wanted. It never occurred to her." Her mother, who did not suspect her daughter was a lesbian until right before she came out, recalled this period as a time when her previously happy, good-natured daughter abruptly became sullen and irritable. However, this mother attributed these changes to the growing pains of adolescence:

> I have thought about this a lot. When she was little, a small child, right up until, I would say, adolescence, she was the most cheerful, fun little girl. I mean she took dancing lessons, she laughed all the time. She was just

beloved by everybody from an infant on. And in adolescence [things got] very hard. She just was not happy.

The husband of this last respondent was quoted previously as suspecting his daughter was a lesbian four years before she came out to him. He recalled the ongoing discord between his daughter and her mother and how it led to arguments between him and his wife:

> Her mother would constantly ask, "Are you dating boys?" and it would almost, like, hurt me. Later we would have a fight. I would say, "How could you ask her if she is dating boys? You know she is not. Why make her uncomfortable?" But I couldn't talk to her about it. Her mother never really even suspected anything. I kind of, over these last four years, really came to accept that it was probably something—I never really said the word *gay*, I never thought of her as gay. . . . But I knew something wasn't right.

Like the mother previously quoted, the parents of children who felt pressured were mostly silent on the topic of whether they did things to push their sons and daughters to "be straight." For the most part, only the child respondents reported that their parents pressured them to act differently. This mother, Charlotte who along with her son M.C. discussed how close they were, was the only one who recalled thinking she *should* say something to her son. However, she denied doing so. "Quite honestly, I think I probably felt like, 'M.C., Stand up straight! Don't you know you look girlish the way you're standing?' I'm sure I didn't say anything to him. I'm absolutely certain I didn't say anything to him. But, in my mind, I'm sure I was correcting him." M.C., who later reported feeling pressure from his father to "act straight," did not feel the same push from his mother.

As we have seen earlier in this chapter, suspicious parents are struggling with feelings of guilt, loss, and worry. They care deeply for their children, but see them potentially taking a path that will put them in harm's way. Thus it is no wonder they would want to do anything they could to put their children on "the right track."

However, for the most part, parents in these disengaged or conflicted families did not believe their suspicions and guilt that their child might be gay or lesbian affected their relationships with them during the family sensitization stage. This contrast with their children's impressions suggests a couple of possible explanations. Parents might be disinclined to discuss or even admit that their own fears would impact their relationship with their children, particularly in the presence of strangers who are gay or who are clearly sympathetic to gay people and their causes. They might have thought that the interviewers would think poorly of them if they admitted to letting their negative feelings about their children's suspected sexual orientations influence their relationships and so therefore did not report such behaviors.

Another potential explanation for the children feeling pressured has more to do with their own perceptions. There is simply no safe haven for these kids. As described previously, youth are becoming painfully aware of their sexual feelings and, at the same time, they are learning that these feelings are considered wrong and even shameful. They might even be projecting their feelings of alienation, social pressure, anger, and disappointment for not being "normal" onto those convenient and closest to them—their parents. Thus, the young people in this study might have been particularly sensitive and reactive to any signs that their parents want them to be different. It's hard enough dealing with potential rejection from the outside world—dealing with it at home is just intolerable.

According to the children's reports, parents' suspicions and desires for their children to be different were clearly communicated, while, at other times, a simple statement from an unsuspecting parent might have been taken out of context. Sadly, during family sensitization gay issues were not open to the type of family discussion in which members could clear up any misunderstandings. Someday we will live in a world where children can talk with their parents about their same-sex attractions as soon as they recognize them, but that day has yet to arrive.

Boys and Fathers

Fathers in many families are mysterious, distant, intimidating figures—even more so for boys with homosexual attractions. They are the family torchbearers of manliness, and, as males young and old know, homosexuality is considered the dreaded opposite of masculinity. According to Kimmel (2004), men demonstrate their masculinity by repudiating all that is feminine and demonstrating an ever-ready willingness to engage in sexual intercourse with women whenever the opportunity arises—in a nutshell, to prove they are not gay. To be gay is to be powerless, weak, unable to break free from Mommy, and these characteristics are incompatible with real manliness.

Kimmel asserts that homophobia plays a central role in men's masculine self-concept and his contention initially seems rather extreme. However, go to places where men and boys congregate, like schoolyards, sports fields, fraternity houses, and locker rooms in this country and you will hear taunts such as "You're a sissy!" "That's so gay." "Cocksucker!" or "Wow, you really got fucked in the ass on that one!" Sex between males is seen as an act of violence and domination rather than an expression of love, affection, or mutual pleasure, and this mocking, whether it is done playfully or with hostile intent, is meant to degrade a man by deriding his manliness. A boy growing into a gay man will get the message loud and clear that he is weak, dirty, and, perhaps worst of all, less than a man.

Thus it is no wonder that the boys were so reactive to and at times fearful of the responses of their fathers — the people in their lives who were expecting them to receive and carry the torch of masculinity. As this eighteen-year-old young man described:

My father has always been very physical. He liked competitive sports and he played football. He was always pushing me to be on the football team or to do this or that. The kind of things I had absolutely no interest in doing at all, and I don't know how tied up that is in sexuality, but I certainly felt like I had something I needed to keep hidden from him.

M.C. reported feeling close to his mother, but, in contrast, he clearly resented what he perceived as his father's pressuring efforts to push him toward heterosexuality:

I guess I reacted more hostilely inwardly towards him (my father). I began treating him more or less as an enemy, as one who I had to hide everything from. And [I was] quite resentful too, because I figured he would want me to find a girl. And there were occasions when he would say, "when you get married . . . " and that just blew my mind. It was, like, "Bastard, you are assuming I am going to get with a girl." And on occasions when he would say, "I have this pornography, Marilyn Monroe, up in the attic if you need me to get it down . . . " That came up, and I thought, OK, this is getting sickening here, and I resented it and I became very distant.

Rico, a twenty-two-year-old Latino man who worked in a bookstore, described how his father's derision, which was possibly fueled by suspicion, made him fearful:

My father used to fear me into ever owning up to it, by calling them [gay people] names and stuff. Just saying that he didn't agree with it and thought it was wrong and all that stuff. . . . Yes, and he didn't want me to become that . . . one time I had just dyed my hair. I was eighteen, nineteen. I dyed it red. And he said: "Don't be a girl, you fag!" or something like that.

Rico, whose parents were long-divorced, perceived these admonitions as a threat, which is why, at the time of his interview, he had yet to come out to his father.

Jay was asked if his emerging sexual orientation played any role in his relationship with his father:

Yes. I think I was taking out my frustrations with all of the straight jocks at school . . . that he was this mister normal guy that had the normal family, the normal house and the normal job and normal, normal, normal. And I don't know . . . he was an easy target, too, because he wasn't always here and when he was here I could attack him.

For sons, paternal disapproval is a particularly bitter pill to swallow. Perhaps, deep down, they fear disappointing their fathers by not being the man they expected them to be. They realize if they are being chided in the outside world for not being real men that this will reflect poorly on their dads, who will be angry and disappointed once they come out.

Unfortunately, none of the fathers of the boys who reported feeling taunted or pressured by them consented to an interview, so we could not get their perspectives. However, like Jay, it is perhaps too tempting to make fathers an easy target, particularly in the absence of their voices. We must remember that fathers and sons live in the same world—one that teaches boys that homosexuality is incompatible with real masculinity and, by association, full male adulthood. Fathers too were raised to not only look down upon homosexuality, but to fear it in themselves. The fathers of these male respondents may have perceived that they failed at one of their most important tasks, passing masculinity onto their sons. Thus having a gay son might feel particularly shameful for a father, as he may believe it is an indictment of his own masculinity.

Moreover, it is perhaps humiliating for a father to have a son who engages in sex acts that are considered by many to be so disgusting and degrading that their very mention is used by men to insult each other. When a father in this study initially found out his son was gay, he repeated, over and over, "Do you know what two men do together? Is that what you want to do?" Add to this shame and disappointment men's tendency to be stoic about problems to avoid appearing incompetent or weak (Cochran and Rabinowitz 2003; Mahalik, Good, and Englar-Carlson 2003) and one gets a sense why many fathers, like those of the boys previously quoted, did not want to discuss such a topic with a stranger—a gay stranger, no less.

Isay (1989) believes that gay males undergo a reverse Oedipal complex whereby, as young boys, they become subconsciously sexually attracted to their fathers (rather than their mothers). When the boy is a toddler, the father anxiously senses the subliminal sexual charge in their relationship and, because he is socialized to be repelled and afraid of homosexuality, he consequently disengages from the son. Oedipal issues aside, a developing gay boy may demonstrate some traditionally feminine gestures or interests that foreshadow an adult homosexual orientation, which may in turn make his father uncomfortable and want to distance.

Sadly, father-son disengagement or strain may have particularly destructive consequences for gay men. Because a boy's relationship with his father is his first, most important relationship with a man, it is the primary arena where he learns not only how to interact in close contact with other men but also whether he is attractive and lovable in their eyes. If this primary relationship is rife with fear, distance, and hostility during childhood, as it is for many gay men, this will no doubt interfere with his ability to form and maintain intimate, committed relationships with male partners in his future adulthood.

Summary of Family Issues During Sensitization: Fear, Isolation . . . and That Elephant

During family sensitization, young women and men begin to recognize their sexual orientations in environments that are hostile, rejecting—even dangerous. In this study, many youth experienced antigay violence and rejection at the hands of peers before they themselves realized they were lesbian or gay. However, they had to handle their disturbing sexual feelings and victimization by themselves because they were so afraid that, if their families knew the source of their unhappiness or mistreatment, they would be rejected. These findings suggest the ways in which young people receive the message from their schools and families that their homosexuality is unacceptable and thus needs to be hidden. However, the pressure to hide their turmoil and victimization leaves children in frightening and painful isolation.

Most parents suspected their child was gay or lesbian before knowing for sure. However, in families in which parents reported they did not suspect, their children were certain that they did. This suggests that during family sensitization there might be a tendency among some youth to overestimate their parents' awareness. Professionals need to keep this in mind as they assist young gays and lesbians who are trying to decide whether or not to come out to their parents.

Parent-Child Interaction During Family Sensitization

As daughters and sons begin to fully realize their sexual orientation, they may pull away from their parents in an effort to hide themselves. Furthermore, youth might be projecting their resentment about societal disapproval onto their parents and therefore may be particularly sensitive or reactive in the face of real or perceived pressure from parents' to "act straight."

All parents have their own aspirations for their children, and suspecting their children might be lesbian or gay threatens their dreams. Parental fear during family sensitization may be communicated in subtle and not so subtle directives to the children to "act more heterosexual." Children, already scared and reactive, may be particularly sensitive to any parental negativity, and in turn may become distant and resentful. Parents are, of course, unhappy with these changes in the family, and may respond by becoming irritated, but, without knowing how alienated and distressed their children are, they might attribute such changes in family relationships to the normal growing pains of adolescence. Thus family sensitization can be a confusing period—there can be distance and strain in the family, but parents are in the dark as to its exact cause and, therefore, cannot fully understand or resolve it.

The sociologist Reubin Hill (1971) proposed a model that defines a family crisis as an interaction between the distressing event, the family's coping resources, and the interpretation the family makes of the event. Hill's work was based on the experiences of soldiers leaving their families as they were called to service during World War II. In the families he studied, he identified a stage of family crisis during which families anticipated the departure of the husband/father before he was actually deployed. This period was marked by what Hill called *anticipatory disturbance,* which strained family relationships. Families in the sensitization stage are experiencing similar anticipatory anxiety, particularly in light of the distance and conflict that can emerge once children recognize they are gay. The simmering anxieties and tensions of this period eventually come to a boil, leading to the child's coming out, as we shall see in the following chapter.

Implications for Treatment

During family sensitization, families might seek therapy for their children's behavioral or mental health difficulties without knowing that their sons and daughters are trying to come to terms with their same-sex attractions. However, because the children might not fully understand their sexual feelings, or because they fear other people's reactions, it is unlikely they will discuss this topic with a therapist.

Working with the Child

Before they came out, five young respondents were enrolled in individual treatment by their parents, who were concerned about sudden and unexpected deterioration in their children's moods and behaviors at some point during their adolescence or preadolescence. These parents recognized that these changes were beyond what was developmentally expected, but did not know their children were struggling with same-same attractions—and, sadly, neither did their therapists. As an illustrative example, one young woman discussed how she was sent to therapy at age twelve because her parents and teachers noticed that she had been depressed.

INTERVIEWER: Let me ask you. Why do you think you didn't tell the therapist you were feeling attracted to other girls and were worried you might be a lesbian?
RESPONDENT: Well, like in middle school I didn't even know that I was a lesbian.
INTERVIEWER: But you knew you were attracted to girls.

RESPONDENT: Yeah, I knew something was different. But at that point in time I figured everyone was like that . . . I figured, because socially, culturally, in this society it's OK for a girl to say, "Oh, that girl is pretty" or "She looks nice today." You know? So I figured it was more along the lines of that. But one time I had asked my friend Nancy, I was like, "Hey Nancy—are you ever, like, actually attracted to girls?" And she's like, "No." And I'm like, "OK." And I just stopped it. And I thought, "OK, so this is different." And, yes, I was just going through all the turmoil with my parents, so I didn't talk about it. And I just never felt comfortable. I wasn't even comfortable with it myself.

INTERVIEWER: Even though a lot of your upset had to do with that, you're telling me?

RESPONDENT: Yeah. Now, in retrospect, understanding it.

INTERVIEWER: So at that time you didn't know that was connected to your problems?

RESPONDENT: Yeah. I didn't even know it.

INTERVIEWER: What if your therapist asked you, at the time, "Do you find yourself attracted to girls?" Would you have told her?

RESPONDENT: Yeah. I think if she brought things up like that, then I'd be more inclined to talk about them. But I would never bring it up. Because she could judge me—she still has the opportunity to say, "Ooh, I'll never talk to you again." I definitely had a fear of rejection.

Another young lesbian recalled how she did not tell her therapist she was worried about her attractions to girls for fear that the therapist would then disclose this information to her parents. It is tragically sad that these children coped with their feelings by hiding them, leaving the source of their troubles out of their therapists' reach and precluding them from getting the support they so desperately needed.

Stone Fish and Harvey (2005) have written about the tightrope therapists must walk when they suspect a young client is wrestling with her sexual orientation but is unwilling to talk about it. On the one hand, it would be threatening to confront an adolescent or young adult who has same-sex attractions before she is ready to acknowledge them. On the other hand, if youth are struggling with their homosexual feelings and coming to terms with a gay identity, the therapist does not want to miss the opportunity to help them find safety and acceptance, which could go a long way in diminishing their distress.

The young woman quoted in this section described how she might have talked about her sexual attractions if the therapist raised this topic; however, she was deeply ashamed of her feelings at the time. Stone Fish and Harvey (2005) offer a list of sensitive, indirect questions for therapists who suspect that their young clients are questioning their sexual orientation but are ambivalent about discussing it. The beauty of these questions is that they leave the young gay clients in control of how much they acknowledge to the therapist, thus ensuring they can continue to hide their feelings if they are not ready to talk about them. For example:

What would you recommend a teenager do when she has a secret about herself and she wants people to get to know her but is afraid if she tells the secret, they won't like her?

What do you do when you know that you are different, you want to talk to someone about it, and yet you also think that if you talk about it, you will be really hurt—that somebody won't like you or accept you or something even worse?

Is it OK if a boy is attracted to other boys?

What do you think your parents would do if they found out someone was a lesbian? (Stone Fish and Harvey 2005:120–121).

It should be noted that it is never a good idea to push children to come out or even acknowledge same-sex attractions before they are ready. If clients fail to respond to these questions in a meaningful way, shutting down or becoming obviously anxious, angry, or defensive, therapists must retreat and understand that they are either mistaken or their client simply isn't ready. Considering the effects of stigma, if youth are attracted to others of the same sex, it is no doubt a wise choice to keep such feelings hidden from others and even oneself in order to survive both physically and psychologically. Thus clinicians need to honor and respect such defenses by backing off when their young clients are not yet ready to discuss their attractions. In these circumstances therapists might have to simply "let go" and remind themselves that the great majority of gay people reconcile their feelings about their sexual orientation without the assistance of mental health professionals. Like some of the parents and children in this study, therapists and their young clients can still have helpful therapeutic relationships without directly addressing the gay issue.

"I AM IN LOVE WITH MY BEST FRIEND! WHAT SHOULD I DO?" It is also possible that school counselors or therapists might be approached by young clients who are willing, at least somewhat, to discuss their attractions but are frightened by them. Therapists, human service and educational professionals, of course, care deeply for the children in their charge and want to be helpful. It might be tempting for well-meaning professionals, to declare, "Yep, you're gay" and then to push them forward in some way before they are ready. For example, professionals with good intentions might encourage their gay clients to tell others, to confess their love to their best friend in the name of honesty, and/or to connect them with support groups and services.

However, this type of premature encouragement might terrify young people who are not ready—who, despite their verbalized attractions, still fear that what their classmates are joking about or saying about them is true. Thus it is important to go slow. *Start where the client is,* the sage advice learned in graduate school, is perhaps no more relevant than when working with these young people. It is advised that the counselor explore the client's fears and worries in as neutral manner as possible. Client's need to know that it is not sick or strange to have same-sex attractions, but they also need their fears understood and validated. When children are first recognizing their same-sex attractions, the thought of acting on them in any way can be scary, and it is likely that doing so will result in peer harassment and rejection—especially during adolescence and early adulthood when peer pressure is so strong and peer acceptance so important.

Having same-sex attractions does not mean one is ready to identify as gay. In fact, one may never have to. For example, some progressive-thinking youth are eschewing labels and are unapologetically acting on their sexual and romantic feelings without adopting specific sexual identities (Savin-Williams 2005). Thus there is no rush, nor perhaps any need, for the young person who is coping with same-sex attractions to feel like he has to quickly (or ever) adopt a gay identity and all that entails.

Conversely, for a therapist worried that a child who declares she is lesbian is going to commit to a difficult, unalterable path, it might be just as tempting to push these client's feelings aside with comments such as "It's just a phase" or all "adolescents have these feelings," which, by the way, they don't. Again, the motto is to go slowly. It might be useful to help the young person identify the potential positive and negative outcomes of approaching a friend upon whom she has a crush, joining a lesbian/gay student group, telling parents, or taking any one step out of the closet.

For example, the therapist or counselor might say something like, "OK, I understand you want to tell Sarah you are in love with her. Let's take our time and look at all of the pros and cons of doing this. What do you hope will be the outcome if you tell her? Knowing her, what would be her most likely reaction? What is the worst that can happen? Could you handle it?" It is of utmost importance that these young clients carefully consider all possibilities so they can make decisions in an informed manner.

Working with the Environment

Bullies and harassing peers are not the devil's spawn, as tempting as it might be for those who witness their misdeeds to think so. Like parents, they are born and raised in a homophobic, heterosexist world and are thus products of their environment. Therefore, another way to assist youth who are struggling to come to terms with their sexual orientation is to intervene in their schools to address what was referred to previously as the structural dimension of stigma (Schulze and Angermeyer 2003). So doing, human service and education professionals can help make these places more conducive to their gay clients' healthy development.

As a first step, an environmental assessment would be in order (Netting, Kettner, and McMurty 2004). Is the school a place that welcomes and accepts gay and lesbian students? Are there any openly lesbian or gay faculty? Does the school sponsor a lesbian, gay, bisexual, transgender (LGBT) support group? Is material on LGBT people incorporated into programs that educate students about diversity? During this research I noticed that kids who attended schools that had such resources reported considerably less harassment than youth who went to schools that did not. How is antigay bullying and harassment between peers addressed at the institutional level? Do school professionals intervene or simply ignore it?

Elsewhere I have written about the importance of intervening not only with the gay person but also within the stigmatizing environment (LaSala 2006). Mental health and education professionals who care about youth should advocate for this vulnerable group by appealing to school administrators for services such as support groups as well as tolerance and antiviolence education for the entire student body (Kosciw 2001).

Granted, in schools with politically and religiously conservative parents, teachers, and school boards, establishing such programming would be difficult. However, there are resources available developed by those who have previously blazed these paths. Human service professionals or anyone wanting to assist LGBT youth can contact national organizations such as the Gay, Lesbian, and Straight Education Network (GLSEN, www.glsen. org, 212–727–0315) and Parents, Families, and Friends of Lesbians and Gays (PFLAG, www.pflag.org, 202–467–8180) for information and technical support on how to establish such groups as well as how to advocate for LGBT students in even the most hostile school settings.

Working with the Family

In this study there was one family in which particularly tolerant parents suspected that their child was gay before he told them. These parents found ways to indirectly communicate positive messages about gay people in their child's presence and indicated they would be accepting if and when he was ready to come out. When the child was ready, he was certain his parents would be accepting, which made for a smooth, low-stress coming out process. In my clinical work I have been approached by a small number of parents who suspected that their children were lesbian or gay, worried for their psychological well-being, and therefore wanted to know how best to be supportive.

Again, the therapist and the parents in these circumstances must be careful not to push the child to come out before she is ready. However, the practitioner can help parents find ways to communicate positive messages about gay people, which can help ease a child's anxiety. For example, in a positive manner, parents can discuss topical gay and lesbian issues, such as same-sex marriage and adoption rights, in the child's presence. If possible, parents can cultivate friendships with gay and lesbian neighbors, acquaintances, and relatives. Such relationships would have the twofold benefit of demonstrating parental acceptance and helping family members get more information about gay and lesbian people.

Furthermore, therapists, whether they are gay or straight, can model for their client families the importance of tolerance and acceptance by making sure their offices are welcoming places. To this aim, therapists can place LGBT-affirming reading materials in their offices, such as the *Advocate* (http://www.advocate.com) and *Out* (http://www.out.com) as well as *Curve* (http://www.curvemag.com)—national magazines catering to LGBT persons. Rainbow stickers and flags, which are the official signs of LGBT tolerance, can be prominently displayed in therapists' offices. The existence of such material could go a long way in communicating the therapist's tolerance and acceptance, that her office is a safe place to discuss issues related to sexual orientation. Clients struggling with their sexual orientation will sit in the waiting room and understand that it is not only OK to be LGBT but that it is also OK to talk about it.

Therapists Working on Themselves

It is impossible for therapists to know everything about all groups different from their own. However, it is the responsibility of human service professionals to be proactive, lifelong students of the cultures of their clients. While many human service undergraduate and graduate curricula cover the special needs of racial and ethnic minorities, such programs are often woefully inadequate when it comes to addressing LGBT issues. Therefore, clinicians will need to seek out this information on their own. In addition to this book, there are excellent sources therapists will find helpful (Griffin, Wirth, and Wirth 1997, Herdt and Koff 2000; Savin-Williams 2001a; Stone Fish and Harvey 2005). Full citations of these works can be found at the end of this volume.

However, books or articles alone are not going to help a therapist who is having trouble understanding and coping with his own feelings of disapproval toward lesbians and gays. Let's not forget that therapists, like the families they work with, are products of society, and, like their clients, it might be difficult for them to avoid being influenced by the oppressive messages heard about lesbians and gays in places of worship, in the media, and from public figures and politicians. For many years I taught a course called Diversity and Oppression. During one of my classes on LGBT people, I asked my mostly straight social work students how, if at all, they learned how two men or two women have sex. I was shocked to find that most of them discovered this information either by witnessing taunts in the schoolyard or reading graffiti in public bathrooms. Learning that such behavior is shameful, dirty, and depraved no doubt leads people to think the same about those who engage in it.

Nobody, including therapists, can be blamed for having initially negative reactions to homosexuality, however therapists who work with these clients are indeed responsible for recognizing and mitigating these feelings. When therapists are preparing to work with gay clients and their families, they must first look inward and examine how they really feel about LGBT people. They should be on the lookout for feelings of anxiety, pity, disgust, or rescue fantasies—even unexpected arousal. It is advisable that they take an inventory of their negative stereotypical thoughts, such as "all gay men are promiscuous" and "lesbians hate men." They need to be mindful that positive stereotypes (lesbians are relationship oriented, gay men are artistic) could also obscure their ability to understand their individual clients and hear their concerns. When it comes to their feelings about LGBT people, or anyone who is stigmatized, human service and educational professionals need to be sure their own houses are in order before stepping outside to help others.

For therapists who discover feelings or biases that threaten to interfere with their ability to assist lesbian and gay clients, I have a recommendation that goes beyond reading books. If the clinician does not know any openly lesbian or gay people, it would be a good idea to get to know some—and as soon as possible. It is pretty clear that contact with gay people can reduce one's antihomosexual bias (Brown and Henriquez 2008). Thus, mental health professionals would be advised to seek out openly gay and lesbian people socially as well as professionally to not only learn more about them but to get to know them as real human beings, both different and similar to themselves. Not all gays and lesbians want to educate naive heterosexuals. However, there are plenty of us willing to do so. Please find us. We can help you become as informed as possible to be maximally helpful to this vulnerable population.

CHAPTER 2

Family Discovery

The Youth Come Out

L IKE A RUNAWAY TRAIN, ONCE THE YOUNG MEN AND WOMEN in this study realized they were gay, something was set in motion that they felt they could not stop. Sooner or later they knew they would have to let others know, and this prospect was terrifying. Many of the youth already got a taste of what can happen when peers suspect someone is "different." What would the world do to them once it was known for sure?

Most important, what would their parents do? The young gay and lesbian respondents were more than familiar with stories of sons and daughters who were thrown out of their homes, and fear of this possibility loomed large. But, in their minds, fully realizing they were gay or lesbian meant they would eventually have to tell their parents, and as that time grew closer the youth became increasingly distraught.

The Precoming-Out Subphase: Anxious Youth, Mystified Parents

The precoming-out subphase of the family trajectory occurred in the one to three months before the child came out to her parents. During this pre-dawn period, the young respondents felt intensely burdened by the stress of hiding, the isolation, actual and anticipated peer harassment, difficulties in relationships with romantic or sexual partners, and worries for the future. For many, it felt as if the pressure was building and their lives were ready to explode.

Of the sixty-five youth interviewed, forty recalled feeling highly anxious and depressed during this period, fourteen to the point where they considered suicide. For these young gays and lesbians, hiding was no longer working as a coping mechanism. When asked what things were like the month before she came out, this twenty-five-year-old biracial woman, who worked in retail and lived in a tough urban neighborhood, confessed:

> I was sad because I was lonely, I didn't have anybody and I wanted to hang out with someone, be affectionate and all that stuff. Sometimes, I felt worthless because I was scared that if anybody found out that they would hurt me or make fun of me. Yes, I didn't want anybody to find out. I was pretty sure how they would react.

Toshi, a sixteen-year-old Japanese American gay boy, described the enormous strain of hiding himself right before he came out:

> Well, because when you are in the closet . . . you have to watch every single thing you do . . . every single word you say. Like you have to watch everything to make sure you don't give anything away. And that can be very stressful. There are people [whose] parents break down and cry, but they still tell them because that's how much you feel that you have to tell them. Because it really hurts . . . I mean like . . . you are talking to your parents, you are thinking, "They don't even know me."

Mitch, the nineteen-year-old young man quoted in the previous chapter, enjoyed a particularly close relationship with his mother Susan. He recalled what it felt like during the month before his parents found out he was gay. "I didn't know how to deal with everything. I was dealing with that, and also there was a guy I had gotten hooked up with through my friend. And he was spreading rumors about me, which upset me, and then the fact that I had to deal with coming out and realizing it myself and accepting it—it was just really hard." Janie's mother was quoted previously in chapter 1 describing how her daughter wouldn't wear a dress, even as a very small child. Two months before she told her mother she was a lesbian, Janie, who was a junior in high school at the time, was grieving the breakup of a romantic relationship, which worsened her sense of isolation: "The whole end of the relationship with my girlfriend . . . I don't know . . . it really hurt. I was kind of lost . . . I didn't know where to go from there. I was feeling like I would have to keep lying for the rest of my life because even though I am going out with girls, people don't know this and I just didn't want to cover it up anymore."

So what was happening in the families of these respondents during the precoming-out subphase? Some parents, like those of the previously quoted respondents, were largely unaware of their children's struggles immediately before they came out. They did not notice the acute distress that their children were experiencing. A reason for this might have been that their sons and daughters, long accustomed to keeping their feelings hidden, continued to do so up until the time they came out. It is worth noting that most parents who did not notice their child's distress also did not suspect their child was lesbian or gay before they knew for sure. As previously stated, in many families there was a growing distance between children and their parents, and this may have acted as a filter through which parents could not see their children's distress.

However, this was not the case for all families. As recalled by Kenneth, a twenty-three-year-old aspiring actor:

I think it just had been bottling up for so long that I definitely had real extreme spells of depression and sadness and I had a lot of emotional roller-coaster episodes during the month before [coming out to parents]. I mean, you know, it was tough . . . for the reason that there was this guy that I really had some feelings for, and he wasn't gay—and I couldn't share that, so I guess I was lonely.

Kenneth's mother Cynthia knew her son was upset during the month immediately before he came out to her, but she had no idea his distress was related to his homosexuality. Interestingly, Cynthia claimed she strongly suspected her son was gay ever since he was a toddler so that, when she eventually learned for sure, she was not surprised. She recalled that he had begun psychotherapy at this time, but she believed the reason for his distress was that his father, a man who fought depression and alcoholism his entire adult life, had committed suicide the previous year.

The following twenty-year-old lesbian recalled how lonely and desperate she felt having to handle her peers' persecution all by herself:

I thought I was all alone. And then I had to hide it. It was sad having to hide it and keep it in. . . . I remember walking through the halls at school and feeling like I wish I could just fall into the ground so that people couldn't see me. I remember every time I heard people whisper I would assume it was about me and I hated walking into classrooms because I would have to walk in front of everyone and then I just thought that every time they would see me certain things would just pop into their heads. I just wanted them to know me for Jennifer. I didn't want them to know me as "Jennifer, she's gay."

Under that pressure, Jennifer fantasized about suicide during the month before her mother found out she was gay: "I constantly thought about it, but never made a plan to do it. No plan but constantly thought it would be so much better if I did. I didn't want to feel it anymore. I didn't want to feel sick anymore. And I used to cut myself. I used to cut my arms and stuff."

Her mother, Martha, who worked in a Laundromat, remembered the months prior to when she learned her daughter was gay as a particularly frustrating time. She knew Jennifer was disturbed by something, but she didn't know what, and she felt understandably helpless. Martha had suspected her daughter might be a lesbian for quite a while before she learned for sure, but had no idea that this was what was causing her distress. She recalled: "In her fights she was having with herself . . . she would lash out. She lashed out more at me than anything. It seemed like my husband would always come to the rescue. It was me that she treated rotten."

Mike, the student teacher who was quoted in the last chapter, was eighteen and a college freshman when he came out to his parents. After years of struggling with his sexual orientation, culminating with the rupture of a friendship with a male crush, he was in so much pain that he attempted to take his own life. He recalled the pain he felt in the weeks before he came out, which was fueled by his unrequited infatuation:

I had to work through my senior year [in high school] because I really needed some money, so I worked at ShopRite. And I met some sixteen year old who was kind of everything that I wasn't at the time. He was very confident, like borderline cocky. Ahh, fiercely attractive and just flat-out cool. And I thought I was in love with him, but I think it was more that he was everything I would have liked to be at the time . . . everything that I valued at the time. But it felt like love, and so that hurt . . . it never came to anything. He ended up quitting around Thanksgiving that year, and I was really devastated about it. And to me that was kind of the final straw.

His parents, Fred and Ann, were aware that something was very wrong during the months before he came out, but did not know what. His mother was previously quoted as having a fleeting notion her son might be gay when he was younger, which she described in the last chapter as a bird briefly landing on a tree branch before flying away. However, she in no way attributed his distress to this possibility. She recalled her strong sense that her son was withdrawing from the family:

> We kind of had an idea that something was going on with him, for, I don't know how long, maybe a few months. . . . He was so active in high school and so social and then when he went to college he cut himself off from everybody he had gone to high school with and it seemed like he totally lost touch with them. He didn't want to deal with them anymore. He started saying things like, "Saturday night, it sucks, there's nothing to do. This is such a dull town, roll up the sidewalks." And I said, "Go to college, go down to the school and do something." We are eight miles away from the school. So, I couldn't quite figure out what was wrong. And he seemed to be withdrawing into his room a lot . . . I also noticed that emotionally he seemed to be pulling away from us. We are a huggy, kissy family. I saw him hug his grandmother one day, and he put his arms around her and kind of touched her back, but his arms never touched her. And I remember looking at it and saying, "It looks like he is afraid to touch his grandmother . . . " And we asked him several times if everything was OK, and he said, "Yeah, it is just the adjustment, you know, in high school it was a small school and we knew everybody. It is a big adjustment in college."

Fred, his father, also noticed his son's sudden unhappiness: "He wasn't happy. So, ah, there he is, he starts college, and he seems to be struggling, he is not happy and it is obvious to us that there is a problem and every time we try to confront him about it he doesn't want to talk about it. He is thinking about dropping out. We are trying to talk him out of it."

There is something extremely sad about the disconnection in these families during the precoming-out subphase. Many parents knew something was upsetting their children, but did not know what, which left them feeling frustrated and helpless. Young people struggled with loneliness, shame, crushes, and feeling different—some, like Jennifer and Mike, to the extent that they felt suicidal. However, without knowing the source of their pain, nobody, not even their parents, could help them

Precoming Out and Suicide Ideation

Although there is consistent evidence that youth with same sex attractions are more likely to think about or attempt suicide (D'Augelli et al. 2005; Russell and Joyner 2001), questions have been raised as to whether gay and lesbian youth who attempt suicide do so because of their sexual orientation (Savin-Williams 2001b, 2005). Savin-Williams (2001a) warns against what he calls the "clinicalization of sexual minority youth" (237), which is the tendency for gay rights activists and mental health and school professionals to promote the idea that all or most young gays and lesbians experience the kind of profound angst that leads to feelings of suicide. He recalls the story of a young gay respondent who wondered if he was really gay because he had *not* been suicidal. Savin-Williams wisely cautions mental health workers to be mindful of their expectations. Most LGBT youth in research samples have never been suicidal, despite the stigma and loneliness they face, which underscores the considerable strengths and resiliency of many of these young people.

However, findings in this study along with those of others suggest that the relative suicide risk among gay and lesbian youth might be higher, and education and mental health professionals should be on the lookout for the signs and symptoms. Fifteen of the young respondents discussed feeling suicidal at various times in their lives and twelve of them reported feeling suicidal the month before they came out to their parents. Three of the young respondents had made serious suicidal attempts, and two did so immediately before they came out.

Those who felt suicidal spoke of loneliness, isolation, anxiety, depression, and anger, which, in turn, left them wishing they were dead. Most of the young gays and lesbians who felt suicidal attributed their feelings to their sexual orientation, however there were two who believed that their feelings were part of a larger sense of alienation.

Ellie, the daughter of Bob the stockbroker quoted in the last chapter, recalled being addicted to drugs and wanting to end her own life before she came out:

I think there was a combination of feeling like I didn't fit into the environment I was existing within. Not just for being queer but just who I am. I went to a stuck-up private school and I was the kid who wanted to be outside with my skateboard smoking cigarettes. It didn't fit. But the drugs were a symptom of the problem, not the problem, although, they certainly made more problems.

The other respondent was a young woman who was having difficulty understanding and accepting her own sexual feelings, but right before she came out she felt suicidal because her parents were in the throes of a difficult divorce.

This study does not conclusively establish a causal link between being lesbian or gay and suicidal risk. However, these findings suggest that clinicians need to carefully assess their young lesbian and gay clients and be especially watchful for suicide ideation, particularly if their clients are feeling distressed and burdened by the secret of their sexual orientation.

Youth in Need of Parental Support

Some of these young people wanted to disclose their sexual orientation to their mothers and fathers because they believed that their parents could provide the support they needed to cope with the challenges of being gay. This finding was unexpected because, traditionally, the main sources of support for gays and lesbians have been friends rather than family (Blumstein and Schwartz 1983; Kimmel and Sang 1995; Kurdek 1988, 2004; Kurdek and Schmitt 1987; Tully 1989; Weston 1991). Gays and lesbians, historically, formed "families of choice" through networks of friends that made up for families who rejected them or from whom they distanced to avoid rejection. These chosen "families" provided the emotional, financial, and emergency support gays and lesbians needed.

However, times are changing. There have been slow but steady improvements in public attitudes towards lesbians and gays in the fifteen to twenty years that have passed since much of the family-of-choice research was undertaken. There are now more openly gay public figures, like Ellen DeGeneres, Rosie O'Donnell, and Elton John in entertainment and Congressman Barney Frank in government. Several situation comedies on television, including the popular *Will and Grace,* have featured openly gay characters. Furthermore, there is a growing presence of LGBT youth groups in high schools (Floyd and Bakeman 2006), something unheard of up until a short time ago. In the past fifteen years twenty states passed legislation prohibiting employment discrimination based on sexual orientation, with thirty-one passing laws that call for additional penalties for bias or hate crimes against lesbians and gays (Human Rights Coalition 2008). Furthermore, the ongoing debate about same-sex marriage has helped make gay issues a part of the national conversation.

While there is still a long way to go in terms of public attitudes, these changes reflect a society in which gay and lesbian people and their concerns are more public than ever before. This has probably led to young people realizing and disclosing their sexual orientations at younger and younger ages, often in their mid to late teens when they are still financially and emotionally dependent on their parents (Stone Fish and Harvey 2005; Wilber, Ryan, and Marksamer 2006). If young gays and lesbians are living at home with their parents and beginning to recognize and act on their sexual orientation, no doubt their homosexuality is more difficult to hide.

Most young people who realize and disclose their sexual orientation while still in high school do not have access to the range of social institutions, like gay bars, clubs, and gay urban neighborhoods, they would need to establish the familylike friendship networks described in the older studies. The average age of the young respondents when they came out to their parents was seventeen, and many were younger. Even though a number of the high schools the respondents attended had LGBT support groups, many others did not. In addition, many kids whose schools hosted support groups were too embarrassed or ashamed to attend and participate. They worried others would see them walk into the group meetings or that fellow attendees would tell the other students about them. So, unlike older gays who came out as adults in earlier decades, these young people had less opportunity to find and maintain social networks of lesbian and gay people. Thus it is understandable that they wanted to turn to their traditional source of support—their parents.

The wish for parental help was especially apparent among those who had enjoyed historically close relationships with their parents, like the following nineteen-year-old African American man:

RESPONDENT: I couldn't tell my mom about this cute guy I had met. . . . And I couldn't tell her about the clubs I was going to. I couldn't be me around my parents.

INTERVIEWER: That really mattered to you, why do you think it mattered?

RESPONDENT: Because they are my family, they played a big part in my life and in what was going on. I wanted them to be a part of everything that was going on, so it would be easy for me to talk to them.

The following African American young woman and her mother had a somewhat distant relationship before she came out, mostly due to the mother's history of drug addiction. Nevertheless, she still longed for her mother's comfort as she dealt with the trials and tribulations of coping with girlfriend problems: "I was having problems in the relationship, and [they were] just really, really bothering me, and I felt like I couldn't talk to nobody else. It's just like she could give me some encouragement, some words of wisdom; you know, maybe something that she could say to help me not feel like that at the time." What is interesting and also a bit sad is that her mother always yearned for a closer relationship but felt especially distant from her daughter during the time immediately prior to her coming out.

Other gay youth were agitated and anxious in anticipation of telling their parents and did not view them as potential sources of support. Despite the progress in societal attitudes, they knew their parents would have a hard time with their sexual orientation. Mom might watch the *Ellen DeGeneres Show* on television, but that did not mean she would be happy if her daughter was a lesbian or her son was gay. Nevertheless, a month or so before they disclosed their sexual orientation to their parents, these children felt they would inevitably have to do so because they could not deal with the pressure of hiding something so important from the people closest to them. However, they dreaded their reactions. This twenty-four-year-old Latino man, a gay activist, described:

I just didn't know what to do, I didn't know if my parents were going to disown me or there would be a lot of yelling and stuff like that. I also wondered about how other people would see me once they knew what was going on . . . and how I would see myself, because things were changing for me already. I didn't know if I would like the person I was turning into. So I got depressed a lot.

Perhaps the feelings of these respondents are best summed up by the following twenty-year-old woman: "I was just afraid of just losing everything, just being on my own." And this eighteen-year-old Latino gay male: "Well, because it's like every child obviously questions, 'Is my mother going to still love me?'"

Precoming-Out Subphase Summary and Clinical Implications: Proceed with Caution

Parent-Child Interaction

Families in the precoming-out subphase were typified by nervous, lonely youth and concerned but bewildered parents. As stated previously, late adolescence is a time when boundaries around the family system grow more flexible so children can develop independent ideas and relationships outside the family. In a reciprocal fashion, youth become increasingly autonomous and are assisted and supported by parents to do so. However, because they are not yet adults, they still need parental support. Adolescents and young adults may still look to parents to be sounding boards, confidants, and sources of advice. Parents are called upon to support their children's growing independence by allowing them more freedom, including more time away from the family, but are also expected to provide structure for and limits to their children's behavior.

What the findings of this study seem to suggest is that, like their heterosexual counterparts (and perhaps even more so), gay youth feel they need their parents' help and support through this tricky developmental phase—and this issue gets played out in the coming-out process. Even though we now take the presence of lesbians and gays for granted in our society, it is not the same as understanding and accepting a close friend, employee, or family member. It could be argued that to realize and admit one is gay in a society that still stigmatizes homosexuality takes a great deal of emotional strength, self-confidence, and an ability to think independently. However, the parent-child connection remains critical, and the anticipated risk of disrupting it is what makes this subphase of family adjustment so fraught with anxiety.

There are two ways therapists might encounter family members trying to cope with the challenges of the precoming-out subphase. Youth might seek out a mental health practitioner or school counselor for individual assistance. Parents who are disturbed by sudden changes in their children's behaviors and family relationships might also pursue professional help. In both cases the practitioner should take a cautious approach.

Individual Counseling with Youth

Immediately before the children came out to their parents, most of them were experiencing symptoms of anxiety and depression consequential to recognizing their sexual orientation and realizing they would eventually need to tell their parents. They anticipated that their parents would have a difficult time adjusting to this news, and some worried that they would be ejected from their homes. These combined worries and pressures contributed to their ongoing feelings of loneliness, isolation, depression, and anxiety.

It is possible that a gay adolescent in the precoming-out subphase who is considering coming out to her parents might approach a psychologist, social worker, counselor, teacher in a college, high school, or even a middle school seeking relief, support, and advice. She might choose to disclose her sexual orientation to the counselor, who will be called upon to be supportive and assist the youth in coping with sexual concerns, romantic attractions, and issues related to stigma, such as harassment from heterosexual peers. Under these circumstances, a professional helper might be the first adult to whom the young person has come out, so it is essential that he, first and foremost, communicate nonjudgmental acceptance of the client and her sexuality. Counselors need to validate the youth's feelings regarding actual or anticipated experiences of stigma, prejudice, and discrimination.

But what about the counselor or teacher's feelings? As stated before, therapists, teachers, and other human service professionals are products of a society that still does not fully understand or accept homosexuality. Some may feel that homosexuality is wrong, sinful, or believe gays and lesbians are destined for unhappy lives. Others may have a mature and comfortable understanding that normal sexuality takes many forms. They may accept that gays and lesbians are not sick and believe they can be happy—however, they still may harbor conscious or unconscious misgivings and prejudices.

When confronted with a real live gay child in their charge, therapists' unresolved feelings may come to the fore. For example, they might find themselves pushing uncertain clients to disclose to others without recognizing or addressing their ambivalence. Alternatively, the counselors' own fears and prejudices might lead them to discourage their clients from exploring their homosexuality or identifying as gay, telling them, instead, "You are too young to know what you are" or "How do you know unless you have sex with someone of the opposite sex?"

As I state at the end of chapter 1, helpers can't be blamed for having negative emotional reactions to homosexuality. However, professionals *are* expected to find ways to identify and examine these feelings as well as minimize or eradicate them so they do not interfere with their work with these vulnerable clients. At the end of the previous chapter, I described actions that therapists and professionals can take to try to identify and ameliorate their prejudices, and these methods can prove beneficial for therapists working with gay clients and their families in every stage of the adjustment process.

Although there is no available research that identifies the best therapeutic practices for this population, there is a growing body of clinical literature suggesting the utility of various individual psychotherapy models (e.g., Appleby and Anastas 1998; Davies and Neal 2000; Van Wormer, Wells, and Boes 2000). I have described elsewhere how the use of cognitive behavioral therapy might be beneficial for clients coping with the psychological effects of stigma (LaSala 2006). Whatever model therapists choose, they need to understand that lesbians and gays absorb societal prejudices, as we all do. For example, a young lesbian client might reveal to her therapist that she thinks her sexual orientation is sick or perverted or that, because she is a lesbian, she is destined for a lonely, unhappy life. Naturally, such thinking would lead a young gay woman to feel depressed and anxious.

The therapist or counselor's role is to help lesbian and gay clients see that such thoughts are inaccurate internalizations of societal messages, also showing them how to replace such negative self-talk with realistic ideas. For example, the practitioner could help the client understand that homosexuality is not a mental illness and that there are many gay and lesbian people who live happy, productive lives. As stated in the last chapter, people protect themselves emotionally from the damage of stigma by externalizing the cause of their mistreatment—"*They* have the problem not us, *they* are narrow minded bigots." One way to do this is for gays and lesbians to adopt values that protect against stigma, such as those articulated in queer theory in which society's restrictive norms governing sexuality and gender are rejected (Jagose 1996; Warner 1999). Whatever type of individual psychotherapy the clinician utilizes, the goals of treatment should include helping clients replace negative internalizations with more realistic ideas about lesbian and gay people and assisting them to find ways to cope and shield themselves psychologically from the ravages of stigma.

"SHOULD I TELL MY PARENTS?" In addition to pursuing symptom relief, young people might also seek guidance as to whether or not to tell their parents they are gay. Therapists and counselors might be tempted to believe that when parents are apprised of their clients' sexual orientation symptom relief inevitably follows. An unknowing practitioner might also underestimate client fear as well as potential parental disapproval and therefore encourage the client to come out before anyone in the family is prepared to deal with the possible fallout.

It is important to remember that despite recent signs of (slowly) growing societal acceptance, parents still react negatively when they first learn of their children's sexual orientation, and many gay and lesbian youth are still ejected from their homes by parents who cannot accept them (Wilber, Ryan, and Marksamer 2006). The not in my backyard (NIMBY) phenomenon might be evident, whereby parents may believe gays and lesbians deserve the same rights as anyone else, but would not easily accept gay members of their own families.

Professionals hoping to assist young people who are contemplating coming out to their parents face a difficult dilemma. On the one hand, if they prematurely encourage these vulnerable youth to come out, their clients might face potentially painful consequences such as parental rejection before they are ready. On the other hand, counselors who strongly discourage their clients from telling their parents, because they want to protect them from parental rejection, might inadvertently impart the message that their clients' sexual orientations are shameful and therefore must be kept hidden. This could perpetuate and even attenuate their feelings of anxiety, depression, and stigmatization.

Because of the possibility of parents' negative reactions and the likelihood of parental rejection, the counselor or therapist needs to proceed *slowly* and *cautiously* when working with a young man or woman who wishes to come out. Based on these (and other) findings, it is recommended she carefully explore the young person's options and help him prepare to face the likely consequences of any planned actions. For example, if the young gay male is contemplating coming out, is he prepared to deal with the most negative outcome?

As we have seen in the last chapter, youth might mistakenly overestimate their parents' suspicion that they are gay. Despite their belief that they have been giving off clear signals, once they come out, young lesbians and gays might be surprised to find that they have caught their parents completely off guard. How will they deal with negative parental reactions? What if the client is ejected from the home? Does she have a place to go? What if parents withdraw financial support for college—are alternative sources of aid available? Even if parents do not fully reject their children by ejecting them from their homes and cutting off financial support, it is likely they will be disappointed and disapproving, as we shall see. Does the young person have a network to rely on for physical and emotional support in case parents are rejecting, disapproving, or simply unavailable?

Counselors and other helpers need to help the young people anticipate these reactions, assess their available resources, and develop workable contingency plans and coping strategies. Before they come out, young gays and lesbians should have plans for an alternative place to live, at least temporarily, just in case, and they should also know where to get financial assistance in the event that their parents cut off financial support. They should also identify those they can rely on for emotional support as they weather the potentially stormy period immediately following disclosure to their parents.

A point that cannot be overemphasized is that counselors, as they explore these issues, need to be clear they are not discouraging children from being who they are. Young people who have been struggling to come to terms with their sexuality can be very sensitive to any communication that indicates their sexual orientation is sick or somehow wrong—particularly from the first adults to whom they disclose, which may be a therapist or school counselor. In fact, the clinician will want to make a point of praising and reinforcing their clients' efforts to come to terms with their sexuality to the extent of wanting to share such information with their parents.

However, it is helpful to balance such messages with practical advice about how the young gay men and women can cope with and even shield themselves from the disapproval of friends, family, and society. Throughout their lives, lesbians and gays must find ways to manage stigma and cope with disapproval. They must also continually assess their environments for safety and potential acceptance as they decide to whom to come out. It is perhaps never too soon for young lesbians and gays to begin to develop these important survival skills.

Family Therapy

Like parents in the family sensitization phase, parents at the precoming-out subphase might seek therapy for the child's difficult behavior or mental health symptoms. The parents may notice sudden changes in the child's behavior or mood, more dramatic and acute than they might see during the family sensitization phase. However, as during this last phase, parents might be ignorant as to its cause. They know something is wrong; they just don't know what. Of course, as in the family sensitization phase, it is virtually impossible to help the family cope with a problem whose scope and source is unknown.

However, it is also possible that the therapist who is seeing the family or the young person alone might know about the youth's sexual orientation when the parents do not. Of course, no ethically sensitive therapist would repeat what he is told in private, and this practice is particularly important in this situation. Nevertheless, the therapist who knows about the child's sexual orientation and has a good clinical relationship with the parents has several helpful advantages. First of all, the clinician might be sufficiently familiar with the family to have some idea how parents might react if they knew their son or daughter was gay. The practitioner can use this knowledge to decide whether the family is ready to know. Second, with a therapeutic relationship in place the parents will have a ready resource to turn to once they learn that their child is gay. The therapist can monitor the family reactions and be ready to assist parents if the family goes into an emotional crisis.

If parents suspect their child is gay, they might ask the therapist if she knows. In this circumstance it may be tempting for the therapist to encourage the parents to confront the child and ask. However, once again, caution is strongly advised. It is always a good first step to get a sense of the parents' feelings and ideas about their child's sexuality. What do they know about homosexuality? How would they handle the news that their daughter or son was lesbian or gay? The therapist should be able to predict with reasonable certainty how parents will react before encouraging them to move forward, because, as we shall see in the following section and in the next chapter, learning that one's son or daughter is gay or lesbian can be a devastating shock for parents, even if they have suspected it for some time.

Coming Out

Eventually, the pressure of having to single-handedly manage the challenges inherent in recognizing one is gay becomes too much—the balloon of secrecy is ready to burst and the time for waiting and hiding is over.

Coming Out in Distress

For many of the youth, their powerful feelings of distress, described in the first section of this chapter, propelled them to come out to their parents. Again, considering the average age of the young gays and lesbians in this sample when they came out (seventeen, ranging from fourteen to twenty-one), it is understandable that they were overwhelmed with the challenges inherent in realizing a gay identity. They also felt isolated handling such a big burden without their parents' help or support. As Joelle, the previously quoted nineteen year old, recalled:

> I was really struggling internally to kind of come to grips with what was going on and how I felt about everything and how that defined me and what I should do about it . . . and how to seek support because I felt very alone . . . I didn't know how to talk about it openly . . . I was really depressed because I felt very isolated. I wasn't quite sure that I wasn't the only one and I didn't have anyone to talk to. Kind of just the depression where you believe that you will always be alone and no one is going to love you so you feel a little hopeless in general . . . I was struggling so much that I just thought I would die if I had no one to share it with . . . if I didn't get any kind of reaction to know whether this was OK or not . . . I just couldn't handle it anymore inside of myself. I was just really going through a tough time. So, she [Mom] was the first person I said anything to about it.

Her mother remembers her daughter being upset when she told her, however she stated that Joelle came out to her as bisexual: "I guess when she . . . we were driving in the car, coming north on Route 27, and it was in the middle of one of her scenes, meaning the crying and the screaming, and she was upset about something, but she just kind of like turned to me and said, 'What would you say if you found out I am bisexual?' or something like that." The strategy of coming out first as bisexual and later as gay or lesbian, employed by Joelle and other respondents, is discussed in chapter 7.

Chauncey, the twenty-year-old Haitian man quoted in the previous chapter, experienced a great deal of peer harassment, but also enjoyed a close relationship with his mother, Marie. He came out to her a year prior to their interviews in a state of emotional upset: "At that time, all that grief and all that living a lie just accumulated, and I just felt heavy, you know, I just wanted to release and be myself." Marie remembered how distressed her son was when he came out. He told me, "Mommy, I cannot hide myself no more because sometimes, for a long time, since I was a teenager I've known I was gay. But I was pretending because I didn't know how you would react."

This twenty-two-year-old African American woman came out less than a year before the time of her interview:

> I was having problems in the relationship, and it was just really, really both-ering me, and I felt like I couldn't talk to nobody else, so I talked to her . . . like four months ago . . . She just said, "I know, stinker." She said, "I knew already." But she said, "That's your life, and, if that's how you choose to live it, I accept whatever you do. You're grown."

Her mother also recalled: "She was going through some kind of problems with the relationship, or whatever. And she was hurt, and I guess she felt like she needed somebody to talk to. I guess, you know, she finally decided to come and talk to me."

Not Wanting to Hide

As stated earlier, feeling anxious about hiding this important part of them-selves was a primary reason many chose to come out to their parents. How-ever, not all the young respondents came out in a desperate attempt to reduce their overwhelming distress. Some were calm and mostly adjusted to their sexual orientation along with the challenges it presented—they simply did not want to continue to hide their sexuality from their parents. These respondents believed that as they developed a lesbian or gay identity coming out was an important rite of passage. What is apparent in these coming-out stories are the young people's efforts to balance their growing autonomy with their desire to stay connected to parents while at the same time trying to figure how to man-age the parental distress they anticipated the disclosure would bring.

As recalled by this twenty-four-year-old woman:

> Well, I felt like I had been hiding it from her [Mom] for a good nine months, almost a year at that point. I didn't want to keep doing that. She had been someone I had always talked to about things . . . but I had never had something before that I felt I couldn't tell her. . . . This was something I felt that she should know, but I hadn't told her.

Tony (twenty-four), who was previously quoted, was apprehensive about telling his parents, but by no means did he feel compelled to do so because he felt distraught:

> And I told them because, despite all the complex give and take with my dad and everything, I've always been very close to my parents. And I didn't want to have this as something hidden from them. I wanted them to be a part of it. I wanted to be able to bring my boyfriend home. It was clearly something I was going to be trying. I didn't want them to not know about it.

This twenty-one-year-old lesbian who was a college student and worked as a bartender recalled:

> When I was away at college, you know, I was becoming more open about it and I still hadn't told everybody in my life, but I was telling more and more friends. And I had two close girlfriends there. They were straight, but we hung out with a lot of gay guys. And we were always talking about stuff and we'd go to meetings, and it was, I think it was National Coming Out Day . . . and I just decided I wanted to tell her. I was just getting upset that she didn't know because we were so close. So I called her from school and told her.

This next twenty-three-year-old man recalled:

> [It was] that August when I first went to college, the orientation for freshman, that's when I made the affirmation that I'm gay and I just told myself I'm not going back to faking it or, you know, putting up an act to myself . . . I am gay and that's it, and to me when I actually said it out loud, that affirmed it. And I told myself, "OK, now the hard part is telling her," because I know how she felt about it and how I was raised to think about that, so that was the hardest thing. So it took me three months, you know, to just get the courage and tell her.

Daughters were more likely than sons to come out to their parents because they were in a relationship, or about to begin one, and they wanted to share that information with their parents. As remembered by this twenty-three-year-old young woman: "So that happened because I had met someone who I had really strong feelings for at the time, and I really wanted to share that with my mom—I didn't want to make it a secret. I had a huge crush and wanted to share that." Also this twenty-one-year-old lesbian:

> I was always talking about the girl I worked with. And I felt like, since my mom always knows so much about me, I felt like I was hiding a part of myself from her. So we were actually on our way down to vacation. My mom and I were in one car and my dad was in his car following us, because we had luggage and my dog. So I told her first, and she told him. I was always talking about the girl and I just wanted to be open. I was seventeen then, after my junior year, the summer before senior year. I just felt like we have such a close relationship that I would just be open with her. It just kind of came up, I was talking about the girl. And I was like, "You know how I am always talking about her and all this stuff? Well, I have a crush on her."

Being in a new relationship and wanting to share it was particularly salient for lesbians, however, one young man also gave this as a reason to come out:

> I told her because my boyfriend at the time and my roommate at the time, who was also gay, were coming for Thanksgiving . . . I wanted her to know. I wanted her to meet him as my boyfriend, because she had met him before as a friend. It was important to me since I was moving to California with him . . . So I went with my mom to spend the day with her in Atlantic City and I told her on the way back.

Sometimes friends or knowledgeable relatives encouraged the young lesbian and gay respondents to tell their parents. This twenty-two year old became romantically involved with a young woman and wanted to come out. A relative gave her the push she needed:

> And my sister-in-law Julie would call me and say, "Listen. Your mom's getting real close to knowing. You should tell her, you know, unless you want her to find out some other way." So one day my mom and I had a fight, and during the argument, at the end, she was, "Well I just don't understand you!" and blah, blah. And I am like, "Yes, well, I'm a lesbian. Yes I am gay . . . and, another thing, stop bothering Julie. If you have a problem with it, well, too bad."

Soon after she told her mother, she felt quite strongly that her father, who had long been divorced from her mother, needed to know:

> I went to lunch with him. I couldn't figure out how to tell him. We were sitting at lunch, and I was sweating a little bit and I am like, "How the fuck am I going to tell him?" . . . It's not even so much about his reaction . . . I was like, I am not going to come out and be like, "So how is work? Good. I'm good. I'm gay." Like there was just no break in the conversation to even have me bring it up. So he was like, "So how are things with your mother?" and that sparked an idea in my head, and I said, "Well, she is kind of giving me a hard time about somebody I'm dating." And he was, "Well, what is the problem?" And I said, "I was dating this guy, but now I'm dating this new person that she kind of has a problem with." And he was like, "What is the guy's name?" And I said "Jen." And he didn't miss a beat. He was like, "All right, well, she's your mother and you have got to do your thing with her."

What is interesting is that, according to her father, she first told him she was bisexual. Several of the gay and lesbian youth respondents, including Joelle, reported initially telling their parents that they were bisexual as a way to try to break parents in slowly to the news they were gay. They then later informed their parents they were gay or lesbian. This did not seem to work as it was intended: the parents would get upset when they found out their children were bisexual, then once again when they found out they were gay for sure. Several of the youth in this study did self-identify as bisexual, and this topic is further discussed in chapter 7.

Suicide Attempts and Coming Out

Two of the youth had attempted to commit suicide immediately before they came out to their parents. For these respondents, their anxiety and stress over being gay and feeling the need to come out was too much to bear. Mike, the twenty-five year old who described the end of a friendship with a male crush earlier in this chapter, offers a compelling example of how the confusion and shame that comes with realizing one is gay could lead to thoughts of self-destruction:

RESPONDENT: I think I was going to do it on Valentine's Day originally because I was still a teenager and I had that little sense of drama going. I thought it would be a big "fuck you" protest to the whole heterosexual establishment. I got a knife at ShopRite first and then I went to church because I had long since lost my Catholic beliefs, and I had some type of very passive-aggressive behavior, but I was in lingering fear of hell happening—that was a very big part of it too. My religion teacher at school convinced us all that sex was going to get us into hell and we had to control ourselves and all that.

So I went to a priest because I wanted absolution before I did it, and I basically just confessed all this stuff. I was in complete turmoil. I think he was trying to comfort me . . . but he really wasn't in the position to help me out, and I just held the knife to my wrists and cut . . .

INTERVIEWER: What did you confess to him?

RESPONDENT: Oh God. I probably just confessed everything, I felt like a horrible person and like I was trying to change for the longest time and it just didn't work and . . . I don't know, I just felt like a pile of shit, basically. And I confessed to ever having offended God and being angry at God. So, I held it down to my wrists . . . I just kind of opened up. They were seeing, underneath the skin, the veins and a little blood and stuff. It was really weird. And he [the priest] kind of freaked, obviously. And he got a towel to hold on it and told me to put pressure on it. And I just kind of sat there and did what I was told. And then they drove me to the hospital . . . they stitched the wound and my parents came in and I just kind of lost it.

I had left a suicide note at home. Just basically saying I just didn't want to live . . . I told them why. I told them I had nothing left to lose at this point. I don't know, maybe I felt like I could only come out if there was so much else happening at the time that it seemed inconsequential. Maybe somewhere subconsciously that is really what I had in mind. Like I said, if I really wanted to die I could have died, but I didn't really want to. I wanted my life to change.

After an explosive family argument during which his brother called him a faggot, Jay took an overdose of pills and was hospitalized on an inpatient psychiatry unit. While in the hospital, he told his mother, Adele, who had previously suspected, "It's true; I am gay."

For the parents of these young people who had severe psychiatric symptoms, worry for their children's well-being overshadowed their disappointment over their children's homosexuality. Mike's mother Ann recalled yelling at her son in the hospital, "You were going to kill yourself over THAT? That's all?" Her main concern was that her son would recover both physically and emotionally, but she was also secretly mourning that she would not have grandchildren. Currently, Ann is a member of PFLAG, a support group for parents of lesbians and gays, and is a regular speaker at high schools throughout New Jersey. When audience members ask her how her son came out to her, she tells them he wrote a note. She never talks about her son's suicide attempt, as she does not want, in any way, to impart the idea that suicidal behavior before coming out to one's parents is a good strategy.

Fathers

A striking finding in this study is that, in a large proportion of these families, children did not come out directly to their fathers but rather mothers told fathers. Of the forty-seven children who had an ongoing relationship with their fathers, forty-one reported that their fathers knew of their sexuality, but only twenty-six had told them directly. In the rest of these families (fifteen), the children's mothers told their fathers. Randy, aged nineteen and a college student in a small city in New Jersey, remembered: "He found out a couple of days after—he said my mom had to tell him—that she couldn't keep it a secret and everything." When asked why he was reluctant to tell his father himself, he described his fear: "Because my dad is the nicest guy in the world, but when he wants to be strong and powerful, he can be." His mother described her son's reluctance to come out to his father:

> I said, "I know, I said I've suspected for quite some time," and then I said to him that he should tell his father, and he said, "Mom, I can't tell him," and he didn't want his brothers to know, and at that point I respected his wishes. I said to him, "I won't say anything, but you have to tell Daddy," and he said, "I can't, I can't, Mom." And I said well, "OK, I'll talk to Daddy first, but you're going to have to sit down and talk to Daddy." So I did tell my husband without Randy there.

This next young woman, Wanda, aged twenty-four, recalled:

> We never really talked about anything important, ever, so anything that went on was never between my father and I, it was always between my mother and my father, and then my mother would tell me what my father

said. And after I told her, she told me, "I mentioned this to your father, and he said, 'You're absolutely crazy—there's no way this could be going on.'"

Her father, Frank, a butcher, who was quoted in the last chapter, remembered: "My wife was in this mood because she wasn't saying anything. Then she just started one night in bed—she started crying and whimpering and weeping, and I'm like, 'Now what, now what?'"

One possible explanation of this not uncommon phenomenon was that the gay and lesbian respondents grew up feeling more distant from their fathers than their mothers. Because of this history of distance, youth were very unsure how their fathers would react, and being unsure made them anxious and afraid to come out to them. Furthermore, in some families, this distance was compounded by a history of father-child discord that left the young people even more reluctant to come out to their fathers.

In most of the families in which mothers told the fathers, there was little subsequent discussion between the youth and their fathers, leaving the youth anxious and unsure as to exactly how their fathers felt about their sexual orientation. Joelle recalled:

My father knows now. . . . I only became aware of that recently in that I never trusted him enough to tell him since age sixteen. At age probably like nineteen and a half I asked my mom whether he knew or not, and she just told me, "Yeah, I told him like a year and a half ago." And he had just never said anything to me about it.

This daughter, whose parents were divorced but who lived with her mother, recalled how frightened she was to tell her father and begged her mother to keep her sexual orientation a secret:

I was really afraid of how he would react, I am not really sure why. I can't give you a very good reason for it now. I think just largely because I hadn't shared anything personal with him in years—if ever. He and I did fight sometimes, and it was horrible, because he is very passive aggressive, and I inherited that from him or learned that from him. So the two of us fighting is just terrible. So, when I told my mom, I made her promise not to tell him, which was very hard on her. She kept the secret for several months and finally said, "I feel that I have to tell him." She told him, and he didn't acknowledge to me at all that he now knew. I am sure he knew all along because my girlfriend was sleeping over. Recently, he asked, "So Nora is your girlfriend?" I said yes, and that was it.

Women are traditionally in charge of the emotional climate of the family and are also often the ones who manage communication between members (Kirkman, Rosenthal, and Feldman 2002); thus it makes sense that the main discussion on this issue took place between mothers and children. However, perhaps because of the distance between fathers and their children, the fathers' reactions were an unknown for some of the youth. Not knowing might shield the children from facing paternal disapproval, which they feared, but also might make them more anxious.

Parents Confront Their Children

Though most of the youth in this study disclosed their sexuality to their parents without any prompting, in a third of the families parents confronted their children upon encountering clear evidence they were gay. It seemed as if the signs were so strong that parents could no longer ignore them.

Gay Porn

For several of the boys, the parents found gay porn on the family computers, which led them to confront their sons. Allen's wife Janet and son Robert were previously discussed in chapter 1. It should be noted that Allen, a civil engineer, had an older gay son from a previous marriage. He described his discovery:

> I was on a business trip. I had my laptop and I was on the Internet and it became clear to me that somebody had been on my laptop because there was gay pornography . . . and, you know, I understood the fascination with pornography. That didn't surprise me. Even that it was gay, that didn't even really register to me. I mean, look, he has a gay brother [from this father's previous marriage], he could be curious. I didn't have any real reaction to it. But I told Janet, and she basically confronted him that night, and after he initially denied it he came back to her that same night and said, "Yes, I am gay."

Janet recalled:

I learned because my husband was away on a business trip, and he had the laptop with him and he said that someone had been looking at gay pornography on the computer. And I knew that Nick [the father's gay son from a previous marriage] hadn't been around and I thought, "Well who could *that* be?" And I just felt my blood run cold. . . . Robert was here [at home at the time], so I went upstairs, he was watching television, and I said to him, "Robert, if you were gay would you tell me?" And he sort of started huffing and puffing and said, "Oh, now you want to know about my sexual orientation?" and then he closed the door and said, "Yes, Mommy, I'm gay."

And Robert:

So he [Dad] had found evidence on his computer or whatever. He was on a business trip and he told my mother on the phone, and she literally came into a room in which I was dancing around to the opening of the musical *Chicago,* so this is just emphasizing how strange it was that they really, I don't think, suspected . . . So I turned off the music, and she asked about it . . . and at first I was like . . . I mean it took maybe five minutes. What was I supposed to say? It was my sister's? She was eleven. There was really no way out of it, so I said, "Mom, I am gay." And that was quite a shock to both of us. The second I said that, I couldn't believe I had said that.

Immediately afterward he confirmed the news with his father:

That was a tough day. I think I was worried . . . I knew that he wouldn't react violently . . . I knew that neither of them would hurt me physically or that either of them would reject me or write me out of the will or whatever . . . but like . . . I guess I was sorry because I disappointed my mother. My dad already had one gay son. I didn't feel like he needed another. I was sorry that I couldn't be for them the kind of image that they had always seen me as when I grew up. That was the hardest part of coming out.

This next mother, Gloria, an actress and the mother of Noah, a twenty-two-year-old young man who was an aspiring actor as well, also found computer pornography before she confronted her son two years ago:

This is why I asked him. Because I was in his bedroom, the computer we had in the house at the time . . . I don't remember what I was trying to do, but a friend of mine was here who is much more computer knowledgeable than I, and we put on the computer and there was a disk of male nudity. And my friend said, "This doesn't mean anything. Kids go through all sorts of stages." But I thought, "I don't know." Anyway, I was going up to see him, and I said to him, sitting over pizza, thinking that my friend was right, "You know I found this disk in your room . . . " And he said with a very big smile, "Mom, I am gay." I said, "No, you are not gay. Some people think they are gay because there is a question of envy of people of the same sex and some people think they are gay because they are going through stages . . . " And he said, "No, Mom, I am gay."

It seems as if the computer has replaced "under the mattress" as a place for a young male to stash his pornography. It might be tempting and reasonable to wonder if these young men simply did not know where the delete button was on their computers or how to erase their search histories or where to hide their DVDs. Or perhaps they were just a bit careless—not an unheard of characteristic among adolescents and young adults.

Parents of lesbians also found indisputable evidence. Martha found out Jennifer was a lesbian by discovering her diary when she was fourteen years old:

It was a terrible way. Rules in the house were anything left downstairs was fair game. This was how I got them to pick up their Barbies and things when they were little. So I would confiscate things. Or, if one of the other girls took it, it was, "Well, it is not my fault, you didn't put it away." Well, she left her journal out and I read it.

Even though Martha was one of the rare parents who was very accepting right from the start, her daughter felt devastated and overexposed and distanced from her mother afterward, which is described in the next chapter.

The badly hidden evidence could be attributable to teen carelessness; however, another explanation is possible. Although no respondents reported doing so on purpose, failing to secure a diary or leaving a trail of naked men for parents to follow may have been the means to let their parents know "accidentally on purpose."

Consider the report of the son of the previously quoted mother who found the disk of male nudity:

> She found the all-reliable Internet porn (*laughing*). Which I am sure I wasn't trying too hard to cover up because I really wanted to come out to her and I am a total coward when it comes to coming out because I am not out to my father, as you may have noticed. So she asked about it, and I told her I was gay.

It is probable that young respondents think being discovered in this way takes the coming-out issue out of their hands. Being "caught" and confronted saves the young person the difficult task of having to plan when and how to tell his parents this potentially distressing information. In the end, for some respondents, admitting to something was easier than announcing it unprompted.

Risky Behavior

For other males, risky behavior led to parents worrying and then confronting their children. This next mother recalled becoming understandably terrified when she discovered that her teenage son Harry was leaving the house in the middle of the night to meet men. She stated:

> In the middle of the night he was leaving the townhouse. I found that out one night when I was sleeping, and it was like a spirit woke me up. I swear, this voice wakes me up and said, "Get up! Get up now and go downstairs." I got up and went downstairs and looked. The patio door was still open a crack, and I saw a car in the driveway. And we live next to St. Michael's Church with a big parking lot. And [my son] got into this car, and they drove off. I was insane. I woke up my husband. I said, "Quick, you have to go get him, he just got into a strange car, it is the middle of the night!"
>
> My husband went looking, and he couldn't find him. And then he came home. I got in bed and I prayed the rosary and asked the Blessed Virgin to keep him safe and bring him home safely to me. And, when he came back, I was in bed, my husband was in bed—we were sitting there waiting for him. He came up the steps, he walked in the room, looked at the two of us . . . and he said, "I am gay." And he turned around and he walked out. I

remember just turning to my husband and I started crying, and I remember exactly what I said. I just said, "This is not going to be an easy life for him." That was it. That was what my heart was breaking about, that it was not going to be an easy life for him. And he has not made it easy.

Harry, now twenty, did not remember his past behavior as dangerous:

> I was just chatting with people [online]. It was cool and something I didn't know about and I was having fun with it. I had made plans to meet someone. I think that night was when I was supposed to go out to meet someone, and she caught me trying to sneak out. And, of course, afterwards there was like a ton of questions. What were you doing, who were you with?

Eula, an African American mother living in an urban setting with her son Andrew (nineteen), discovered he was gay when she began to receive threatening phone calls from men in their neighborhood. Much to her shock and terror, she found out that her son was passing himself off as a pretty young woman and exchanging contact information with men on the street who thought they were getting the phone number of a beautiful girl. Once word got out that he was a male, these men became furious. Their threats pushed Eula to confront her son who then admitted he was gay.

Discovering a child is doing something dangerous or potentially risky is, arguably, the worst way a parent can learn a child is gay. Parents naturally worry about their children, even under the best of circumstances, so to see their children putting themselves in harm's way is not only excruciating but can also interfere with their acceptance of their children's sexual orientation, as we will see in subsequent chapters.

Intense Relationships

As stated earlier, some parents of lesbians noticed that their daughters were involved in particularly close friendships with other girls. However, once the relationship became so strong it was impossible to ignore, parents confronted their daughters. This mother recalled: "There was a girl from high school who kept calling who I knew was a lesbian. And she kept calling and calling the house, and Tina was talking to her and talking to her, like laughing and giggling and that kind of behavior. And, I don't know, all of sudden it just clicked, and I asked her." Her daughter Tina remembered:

> There's this girl Anna, and she was really nice, she's been friends with me, and this was, like, when I started, like, coming out to my closest friends and stuff and kind of testing the waters. And I would talk to her about it because she had been out. And it's really hard, because I was in high school so I really couldn't be out. And I would talk to her about it, and we got closer. And so she started calling my house—and I was thinking she was cool. And my mom and I were at the dermatologist, and she was like, "Who is this Anna girl who keeps calling? I'm like, "Oh, she's just a girl from school." and she's like, "Wait, isn't she the lesbian? And I'm like, "Yeah." And in the dermatologist's office my mother is like, "Is there something you want to tell me?" And I'm like, "No," because I was not ready at all.
>
> And then, like, I remember we were done at the office and she was, like, "Are you a lesbian?" And I'm like, "No, I'm bisexual." And then she became a big mess and started yelling at me. And she's like, "Well, how do you know?!"

As in many cases, this mother told the girl's father after she found out.

Confrontation in Distress

It breaks a parent's heart to see a child suffer—and, as previously described, during the precoming-out subphase many children are indeed suffering. Parents' worries over their children's emotional states led them to confront their children, pushing them to talk about what was troubling them. An African American mother, who at the time of her interview was a returning college student, remembered her daughter's extreme distress when she was a senior in high school. One day she finally confronted her:

> I got in the car. I was like, "Keshia, what's wrong?" "Oh, Mommy, I have something to tell you, and I don't know if I should." I said, "Whatever it is, you can tell me; I don't care whatever it is. If it's upsetting you this much, you have to tell me. And after you tell me, whatever it is, we will figure out how to deal with it." She said, "I'm gay." I guess I wasn't prepared for the "I'm gay." And I felt like the whole outside spun around . . .

Her daughter recalled her mother confronting her, even though she was planning to tell her:

I don't know why I felt like this is the time to tell her—it was just that if I don't say something I'm going to explode. I don't know what's going to happen to me. So she comes home from the library one day, and I just started crying, and she said, "Keshia, what's wrong with you?" . . . and then, at that moment, when she said that, I didn't want to tell her anymore, and I was like, "Nothing, nothing, I'm just going to go to work." And she was like, "No, what's wrong? Tell me!" So I was like, "Uh, Mom? I'm gay." And she was hugging me at the time because I was crying so much, and she grabbed my shoulders and she pushed me back like this and she just looked at me . . . I don't know if it was fear or shock or what, and she just looked at me and she hugged me again and she said; "No, no, no, it's just a phase, you know? We just moved here and you're going through all this different stuff. We'll talk about it when you get home from work . . . " So that's how she found out.

Charlotte, who described her close relationship with her twenty-five-year-old son M. C. in the previous chapter, recalled how she confronted him five years ago when he was still in college:

I was concerned because you know your child. You know they're unhappy. I thought perhaps it was loneliness, not having made a lot of friends at college. So I was aware for quite some time he was unhappy—often morose. We'd speak to him on the phone, and he never really indicated he had a specific problem, but he was just not happy. Anyway, he came for a visit. He was playing the piano. And it was just like a weekend of down and morbid music. And I had been asking him throughout the weekend, "Is there something bothering you? Let's talk about it." And then he started like making leading remarks. I don't remember what they were, but finally I remember I walked over to him. I said; "M. C., I want you to stop playing the piano. Something is troubling you. I can see you aren't happy." And he would make remarks, "Well, I'm miserable. I'm miserable." I said, "You have to tell me what it is. If you're in trouble, I'm here to help. I'm your mom. I love you. You're not going to go to bed tonight, you're not going to leave this house until you sit down and tell me what it is."

I had such a fear that he had some deep trouble. I could see he was deeply depressed. . . . I sat down. He sat down. He sort of indicated I might not like what he was going to talk about. And I, of course, reassured him. I did not think, "My son is gay, and he's going to tell me." I did not have that thought. Only like a fear that something was troubling him deeply and maybe he was in trouble. I didn't know. He tells me he's gay. Or he has reason to believe he's gay.

M. C. remembered his despair and his mother's confrontation:

I was in one of my depressed moods, to say the least. I was thinking about the future and feeling depressed that I could never really be open about my life. And it was one of those moments. I actually almost went into tears and she kind of forced it out of me. She kept asking me what was wrong. And she asked me, "Is it drugs?" I said no. I don't know if she asked me if I got a girl pregnant or not. If it was, I said no. "Is it grades?" She was pressing me on it . . . We were sitting down on the sofa, and she was like, "Tell me." I am like, "No! No!" And she keeps on, "Tell me! Tell me!" and kept on insisting on it. She was adamant about it, though not in an angry kind of way—a concerned kind of way, almost herself going to go into tears. Then I told her. I don't think I looked at her face when I told her.

Summary of the Coming-Out Subphase of Family Discovery

The findings of this study suggest that for some young gays the burdens of coping with stigma and loneliness can be overwhelming. Like the respondents in the study, lesbian and gay youth might feel deep and painful anguish and alienation—sometimes to the extent that they become suicidal. This maelstrom of angst can push children to come out to their parents in the hope of getting some relief. When upset children do not come out, parents who anxiously notice their children's suffering might confront them—knowing something is wrong, yet taken by surprise when they discover the source of their children's pain.

Other children might come out not because they are in distress but because they are tired of hiding something so important from the people they love and they believe it is the right thing to do. Most models of family development describe how the family of the young adult must find ways to balance their support of the child's blossoming autonomy with the need to maintain family connections. By coming out to their parents because they wanted more honesty in their relationships, lesbians and gays are offering their families an opportunity to find a new healthy balance based on honesty.

The distinctly different way mothers and fathers interact with their children was evident among the families in this study and especially conspicuous in the coming-out subphase of the discovery stage. It seems that the primary communication in the family about the child's sexual orientation occurred predominantly between the mother and child. In fact, many young respondents never told their fathers directly that they were gay or lesbian nor discussed their sexuality with them after they came out to their mothers. Do fathers first choose to be peripheral in the lives of their children, and the family then organizes itself around this choice? Or do families keep fathers distant—or is there a combination of both phenomena? Though this research never fully answers this question, evidence for a systemic explanation of the nature of father-child, mother-child relationships becomes apparent in later stages of the family adjustment trajectory. As we will see, this information will have implications for clinically engaging fathers and keeping them involved with their families.

How parents react and family relationships change following the discovery that a child is gay is the focus of the next chapter. Changes in the family due to the youth coming out as well as what helped or hurt parental adjustment will be described along with relevant clinical implications.

CHAPTER 3

Family Discovery

Parents React

Man is not imprisoned by habit. Great changes in him can be wrought by crisis—once that crisis can be recognized and understood.
—NORMAN COUSINS

IMAGINE HOW IT MUST FEEL TO BE A PARENT AND SUSPECT there is something horribly wrong with your child, something that is your fault that will rob you both of all your hopes and dreams. Because what you suspected was so awful, you tried desperately not to think of it and to talk yourself out of believing it—but it seemed to stay with you, always there in the back of your mind, like an ever present shadow.

Then imagine finding out that what you dreaded was actually true. Suddenly, your son or daughter is not who you think. You are feeling guilty that you ruined your child, sorrowful over the loss of a normal life, and afraid for her future. You try to shield your child from these feelings. You want to be supportive, but, still, this discovery and your feelings about it have overwhelmed you.

Now, imagine you are a young person who has just come out to your parents. You are relieved they finally know and grateful they did not throw you out of the house like other parents you've heard about. They are still your parents and, thank God, they still love you. Nevertheless, you feel ill at ease. You know they are distressed—you're not sure as to all the reasons why and you're not sure you want to know. You also feel overexposed—as if you had been stripped bare and are now being forced to walk around naked. It is far from easy to get used to the idea that someone so important now knows what has been your shameful secret for so long. To keep the peace as well as try and shield yourself—at least a little bit—you attempt to back off, keeping your distance.

In the precoming-out subphase the young respondents were the ones who were highly anxious and depressed. However, during the family discovery stage, which lasted anywhere from one to six months after the child came out, it was as if this emotional burden was suddenly removed from the child and thrust onto the parent. For the families in this study, the initial shock of learning that their child was gay was an event that at least temporarily, overwhelmed parents' coping abilities. Over half described symptoms of depression, which included insomnia, extreme sadness, hopelessness, and anxiety, in the one to twelve months following the child's coming out, while their daughters and sons experienced some combination of relief and discomfort.

Parents' attempts to cope with and protect their children from their guilt and loss combined with their children's wish to avoid overt conflict worked in tandem to create a temporary family distancing that typified parent-child relationships during the family discovery period.

Parental Reactions

Self-Blame

Unfortunately the idea that bad parenting makes a child gay has persisted in spite of all the evidence to the contrary. So it is sadly logical that parents who reported the most emotional distress during the family discovery phase were those who felt to blame for their child's homosexuality. In this sample of families, many mothers of sons worried that perhaps their children were gay because they loved them too much, and this idea is in keeping with traditional views of the genesis of homosexuality. In addition to feeling guilt, parents who struggled with self-blame were coping with an anticipatory courtesy stigma (Corrigan and Miller 2004)—they worried they would be blamed for their child's homosexuality and would become targets of social disapproval themselves.

Susan and her son Mitch, both of whom have been quoted previously, recalled having a very close relationship as he grew up. Susan experienced profound guilt, sorrow, hopelessness, and a sense of inferiority upon learning her son was gay.

I remember I would talk to friends and they would say something about their children and I would think, "I am just not as good as you. I messed up as a parent. I did this to my son." And again, I didn't do anything to him. What is is. But I was feeling pretty responsible . . . and my whole thing is that when I tell people they are going to say, "That is because he was your whole world for two years. That was all you cared about. Taking him out in his little stroller and dressing him up in his little short pants and his little knee socks." I was a little hopeless . . . I felt that I made lots of mistakes and I wasn't sure what they were. I thought crazy things like . . . I stayed home for twelve years raising my kids and I thought I mothered them too much. But that is crazy. But I thought, "It is all my fault. I did that to him." He was an only child till Jackie came along, which wasn't very long, it was only like twenty-six months, but all I did was play with him, I read to him, I changed his diaper four hundred times a day . . . I changed his outfit five to six times a day . . . I took him for walks. He was just like my little buddy. I was twenty-eight when I had him, so I was more than ready to have a child, and he was just my whole entire world. So, when I found out I thought, "I did it. I did all that to him." Crazy but that's what I was feeling.

Cynthia, a widow who had been quoted in the last chapter as knowing her son was gay before he told her, still felt sad and lonely and had problems sleeping right after she found out: "The fact [is] that I am the mother and I was told growing up that men become gay because their mothers are too mothering. I even heard that later after this all happened, and it was like, OK, how can you love your child too much?"

Mothers of lesbians feared that they had turned their daughters off to males by dating or marrying men who set poor examples. This mother, a nurse and midwife, grappled with feelings of anxiety and hopelessness when her daughter first came out: "Maybe it was my fault. What did I do wrong to cause this? Was it because of my husband, the fact that he wasn't a stable father, the fact that we had a bad marriage, alcoholism in the household? I was very sad." One African American mother who struggled with crying spells and anxiety-related stomach problems in the weeks after her daughter came out initially felt she was to blame for her daughter's homosexuality because of her own bad experiences with men: "Like my second husband, which is my son's father, he was very abusive, and she witnessed that. All of those things came into play. I thought, 'Oh God, She is looking at all the things that happened to me with men and now she doesn't want to be with men! That is why!'"

Several of the fathers initially thought they might have had something to do with their offspring's homosexuality, although their reasons tended to be vague. "I did feel guilty, although I didn't exactly know why. I was seeing a therapist. She was very quick to throw cold water on my guilt." Joe, a previously quoted father, always believed that he inadvertently gave off a "gay vibe" because gay men had approached him sexually several times during his life, and when he first learned about his son Tony he initially believed that this somehow influenced his son to be gay. As discussed previously, he also initially attributed Tony's homosexuality to his own desire for a daughter when this son was born. When Tony came out, Joe went to therapy to get help with his guilt.

Earlier studies of parents of gays and lesbians also identified guilt as a typical emotional reaction (Griffin, Wirth, and Wirth 1986; Herdt and Koff 2000; Robinson, Walters, and Skeen 1989). As stated earlier, parents have an almost automatic, innate tendency to blame themselves if their children become ill or troubled—mothers are prone to guilt even if their children seem to be fine.

However, it is curious that almost none of the youth in these families were aware that their parents blamed themselves. They might have known their parents were suffering, but they were unaware as to why. Somehow, the issue of parental guilt did not cross the parent-child boundary in these families. The same was true for parental mourning, which will be covered in the next section.

Of the seventy-six parents interviewed, there were a small handful who identified as lesbian, gay, or bisexual. It is noteworthy that none of these parents reported feelings of guilt when they learned their own children were gay. This is perhaps because, being gay themselves, they were better informed and therefore knew that homosexuality was not caused by poor parenting.

Loss and Mourning

From the moment a daughter or son is born, parents begin to dream about the child's future. Fueled by an initial flush of great pride and joy, some of these dreams are forgivably grandiose: "Maybe she will become president . . . find a cure for cancer—maybe both!" There are smaller dreams too, about future weddings, grandchildren—a "normal" happy family life with all the white picket fence trimmings—and it is the perceived loss of these aspirations that is particularly distressing for parents during the family discovery stage. The heterosexual family myth (Herdt and Koff 2000), that all kids will grow up to be heterosexual and will therefore get married and have children when they grow up, is abruptly dispelled, leaving parents shocked and confused.

For some parents the grief over these perceived losses was deep and profound. In keeping with the Hill (1971) framework, these parents perceived or defined their children's coming out to mean that their sons and daughters, as they knew them, were gone, along with the dreams they had for them.

Mike is the young man previously described who attempted suicide in the presence of a priest in church. Immediately afterward, while her son was in the hospital, his mother Ann was certainly concerned and did everything she could to aid his recovery—yet she couldn't shake her sense of loss: "I cried a little bit, but for selfish stuff or things that were conditioned for mothers. All of a sudden the wedding, the daughter-in-law—I don't have any daughters. So I am going to miss out on that. But, you know, they were my disappointments; he didn't disappoint me."

The following mother tearfully recalled a similar sense of loss that persisted even though her daughter had come out to her two years before the interview:

> Yeah. I wept like the first week [after I found out]. I just would find myself weeping. Just because of all the things that weren't going to be. I felt like my daughter had died. It sounds terrible, but not that I wanted to give up on her, but like all of a sudden I realized—I'm going to start crying—I had these very definitive dreams for her that now wouldn't come true.

Although gay and lesbian parents did not blame themselves when they found out their sons or daughters were lesbian or gay, they also felt a sense of loss. As stated by Mac, a retired firefighter who was gay himself, "I recall the moment she was born, just saying, "Oh, my God, I'll have somebody to walk down the aisle." You know, and, now, where does that play in? Will there ever be a moment to walk her down the aisle?" Similar to what was found for parents struggling with self-blame, the youth were largely unaware that parents were coping with a sense of mourning. Although the daughter of the last mother quoted was ignorant as to the exact reasons for her mother's suffering, she was aware of its depth and magnitude. She observed:

I think she [mother] was shocked, she was scared. She was like, "Oh, God, this is the mother of all things." She didn't know what to do. Like even now when she talks to me about stuff, she doesn't know what to tell me because she's not lesbian and she doesn't know the experience of a lesbian . . . and I understand that . . . She was like, "When did you know, how do you know, how are you sure, do you really know? This is just a phase—well, it's normal for, like, girls or people or teenagers to be attracted to the same sex, but it's just a phase." And that really hurt, because it's not. Like, why can't this be OK?

This father of a gay man recalled his initial feeling when he first found out his son was gay six years ago:

There was a loss. There's a loss of a dream, of an idea that you have for that child. So it's like when people are hoping for a boy and they get a girl. It's not that they don't love the child, or the child is born with Down's or something, you know? There's a loss in your head. There was the loss of his heterosexuality or just the fact that we would have to deal with this. And we realized that this was something we're going to have to deal with for the rest of our lives. You know, this is not something we can change or fix. . . . I just felt like, what I thought was my normal kid, you know, the easy one, the one who was going to just have the normal life, was not going to have a normal life.

However, his son was not aware of the cause or depth of his sorrow:

I didn't really know what his reaction was. I went in and gave him a hug, and that was pretty much it. He didn't really say anything. . . . The next day after I came out, he finally decided to talk to me, and it was a positive reaction actually. And he said that everything was going to be OK . . . And I remember him saying, "It must feel like the world was lifted off your shoulders," and I said, "Yes, it does."

Fear of Rejection

Some parents perceive that their children are rejecting them by choosing a gay lifestyle. They fear that as their sons and daughters enter the gay community, they will be excluded and abandoned. This worry has been found elsewhere among parents of lesbians and gays (Herdt and Koff 2000; Weinberg 1972) and was also discovered in this study. Janet, the previously quoted psychiatrist with a gay son, began treatment for depression after she discovered he was gay. She reported what initially concerned her most:

> I realize that this is really what I was left with . . . some feeling of being excluded from his world. And I still have trouble when I see him . . . with a group of gay men: I feel uncomfortable and like they are in this world that I am not a part of and I feel rejected in some way. And I think the feeling has to do with feeling excluded and rejected. Somehow my son has rejected women . . . me and my kind of sexuality or something like that. So there is that issue.

Once again, her son Robert was unaware of his mother's fears and concerns.

The children's lack of awareness of their parents' guilt suggests that parents might be protectively shielding their children from the full extent of their reactions. It would make sense that parents would want to do this because their guilt was at least partly driven by their belief that their children were damaged. So these parents might have known that if their children were aware they felt guilty, they would also know that their parents believed they were somehow ruined, hurting their feelings.

Parents might have shielded their children from their feelings of loss for similar reasons. The parents in this study may have been acutely aware that, if their children knew they were mourning a normal life for them, they would also be imparting the message to their children that they were abnormal. Such shielding is one component of the overall thickening of family subsystem boundaries that occurred during the family discovery stage.

Relieved Youth

Another explanation for the young respondents' lack of awareness emerged in the interviews and further suggests that family boundaries became stronger and less permeable through distancing during family discovery. Children might not have known about these reactions in their parents because they did not want to know them. Ignorance wasn't exactly bliss, but it was perhaps easier to deal with parents' feelings if they didn't allow themselves to fully recognize them. Bear in mind, finding ways to emotionally distance from other people's condemnation was a survival skill these children learned early in their lives as they became (or feared becoming) objects of their peers' jeering condemnation. Thus it makes sense that they were deploying this very skill to protect themselves from fully acknowledging or understanding their parents' most distressing feelings.

Furthermore, their relief may have further blinded them to what their parents were experiencing. Right before they came out to their mothers and fathers, young people worried that their parents would react violently and even reject them. So when their worst fears did not materialize, they might have been so overwhelmed with feelings of relief and gratitude that they did not see the full extent of their parents' struggles. These young lesbians and gays expected the sky to fall, and, when it didn't, they were too relieved to be concerned or even notice that there were still gray clouds overhead. Their parents didn't throw them out and still seemed to love them, so why pay any attention to those clouds?

Close to a third of the youth respondents reported that the depression and anxiety they experienced before coming out was replaced with profound feelings of relief and appreciation. This twenty-five-year-old biracial girl described what she felt after she came out to her mother three years ago: "I was feeling lots of relief, like I could breathe . . . [I felt] happy, proud: I actually have a life now." And this eighteen-year-old male who had come out two years earlier:

INTERVIEWER: How did you feel immediately after you came out to your parents?

RESPONDENT: Relief and some hope . . . hope that life would just keep getting better and there would be improvement . . . improvement of me being more comfortable and improvement as far as my parents . . . I would be able to bring people into my house, and I would be able to have a more open relationship in front of them.

It is worth noting that, after finding out their children were gay, the parents of each of these previously quoted respondents underwent significant emotional duress and described temporarily distancing from their children. Nevertheless, youth could feel relieved even if there was now some conflict or distance in the relationship because even though parents were struggling with the news, or did not really approve, they still didn't reject their children. As stated by Tyler, this twenty-three-year-old African American gay male college student:

I felt like a weight was off my chest. I feel like in life the only person I have to answer to is my mother. I don't have to answer to anyone else. As long as my mother sees me in a good light, I don't have to care about how anyone else sees me, because my mother is my best friend in my whole world. As long as she says "I don't care what you are doing, you are OK with me." And as long as I have my mother's approval, I don't care about anybody else. She is going to give it to me, she loves me. She is my mom.

However, his mother reported that she experienced severe symptoms of anxiety and depression after she found out her son was gay. She was profoundly worried for his safety because they lived in a blighted neighborhood whose inhabitants were known to be intolerant of gays. For several months after coming out she and Tyler frequently argued about his safety. Nevertheless, as can be seen by the previous quote, this young man experienced a profound sense of relief upon coming out.

The mother of this next youth felt profoundly sad and lonely immediately after she found out her son was gay and experienced frequent crying jags and insomnia. She worried that her son's homosexuality was her fault. Furthermore, she had sensed some distance in her relationship with her son both before and after he came out. Nevertheless, her son recalled:

I was always called names and stuff when I was young, I grew up in Texas . . . just a bunch of hicks. And so, because of that, I had a negative connotation of it [being gay], but I never really associated those things with me. But it was great to be able to discredit that by coming out to myself and my friends and mother . . . it wasn't a bad thing. It just allowed me to feel that I was normal.

Marie, the mother from a Haitian family, described her anxiety and depression when her son initially came out to her. Her son Chauncey recalled feeling wounded by some hurtful remarks his mother made when he told her he was gay, and he subsequently distanced from her, which is described later in this chapter. Nonetheless, he still felt a sense of relief once he came out to his mother.

Definitely I needed that validation from her . . . it was easier, it was an easier transition because I didn't know what I would have done—like I said, I was anticipating being thrown out, so I just knew that if that did happen I would have, like, you know, have to fend for myself. But it was definitely an easier transition for me. She did accept me.

Feeling Good About Being Gay

Several of the youth described how coming out to their parents even though their parents were having a difficult time, helped them somehow feel more positively about being gay. As described by this nineteen-year-old art student: "That was another part, the world must know now, because I've told my parents. Whether they like it or not, now that they are done, everyone else can know too. They are the hurdle, and now the rest of it I don't care about it." Or this young Latino man who worked in retail: "It made me more gay. Because it made me feel like, I don't know, like it made me show it more on purpose just to get her used to it. At times I act feminine just so she can see me act feminine and she could get used to the fact that I am not going to change." This young woman, a law student, said: "I was trying to deny that is what it was. So, once I actually came out to her, I realized that it wasn't such a bad thing." This sixteen-year-old daughter of the previously quoted midwife recalled her feelings immediately after coming out to her parents three years ago: "Yes, I mean coming out to your friends is totally different. But when you come out to your parents, it's like, 'Yeah, I am officially out now.' And I was like, 'Oh my God, I'm out. I don't have to worry about this any more . . . I'm done. That's it.'"

In each of these cases, parents had a hard time initially accepting their children's sexual orientation, yet coming out still helped the youth feel more confident about their sexuality and gay identity. If parents were initially accepting, it was especially helpful. As in the report of Franklin, whose father Norman was previously quoted, "Yes, it made me more positive about it. Knowing that at least one person, I mean my father of all people, was accepting. So that definitely made it better."

These positive feelings might have been attenuated by the young respondent's original expectations that their parents would reject them, which for youth in this study was largely unfounded. These feelings of relief along with feeling better about being gay or lesbian might have gotten in the way of the youth noticing (or wanting to notice) some of the distressing parental emotions that coming out left in its wake—feelings that perhaps were too much to handle during this time when they felt relieved but still vulnerable.

Not seeing or wanting to see the extent of parental distress is further evidence of a strong, thick parent-child boundary that was typical during family discovery and may in fact have been functional. I will further explicate these dynamics later in the chapter.

Parental Fear and Worry

Fear of Physical Harm

Parents, cognizant of the difficulties gays and lesbians face, worried for the well-being of their children. Even though sons and daughters were mostly oblivious to their parents' feelings of guilt and loss, the young respondents were indeed aware that their parents were worried for their safety.

Of course, HIV risk was a primary concern for parents of gay men. This African American mother of a gay son recalled her initial anxieties:

> I mean there are gay people in my family. I have a lot of friends who are gay. I read a lot. I live in New York City. The hospital that I work at, most of the physicians are gay. Most of our patients are HIV positive. So it is something I am very aware of, and I worry about James with hate crimes and I worry about him being in the city at night. There are so many people who are closed minded. I am just worried about that. And now he is starting to get a little muscular, but he has always been very small. So I have been worried about him being out and getting hurt. And he is out late at night at a lot of clubs. So I worry about that a lot.

And Norman, who was quoted previously, worried for the health and safety of his son: "I was concerned about his health . . . He was very young, and I was concerned about adult sexual activity . . . his activities with older and more experienced adults . . . and him not understanding hygiene." Like most of the young respondents, his son Franklin was aware of and understood his father's worries for his physical safety.

> He would always say, when he was talking to all of us, "You guys, I don't care who you bring home or who you do whatever with, just make sure to use a condom, make sure you don't do anything haphazard." He would say, "Be careful!" I remember him saying, "Franklin, you can be naive about

things, and just be careful, think about your own personal safety when you are having whatever experiences, whatever it is, if it is social or whatever. Be aware of your surroundings, be careful." Things like that.

Parents were also afraid their sons would be physically assaulted due to their sexual orientation. This mother described:

Really, my main concern right from the beginning was will there be some-body out there that will try to hurt him because of this, and that was my husband's biggest concern. That's something we've always been so worried about. He'll be out someplace and somebody will beat the hell out of him or something because of who he is...He's going away to college, and, you know, and he's not going far, but he's going to live on campus, and I'm wondering, like, how do the colleges handle it?

Her son knew about his parents' worries. When asked about their concerns when he first came out, he replied: "Oh, what would other people think? Like how they would react to me and how I would be treated by other people and things like that."

If there was any evidence that the gay male youth were engaging in risky behavior, this understandably frightened parents. Marta, a Latina mother, became severely depressed and anxious upon learning her seventeen-year-old son Carlos was gay a year ago. Her brother molested him as a young child, and she blamed herself for failing to protect him. She recalled her reactions upon first learning Carlos was gay after coming home from work early one day and finding him in bed with another young man:

I saw him dead. Because of the AIDS thing, all that was coming out at the time, I saw myself preparing for a funeral. I didn't see a future for my son, and that bothers me a lot. That is what I kept thinking—any day now. I didn't see him having much more time to live. I was preparing for his death. It was hard for me to deal with that.

Carlos was well aware of his mother's concerns, particularly in light of the fact that he had recently contracted a sexually transmitted disease (STD):

I think her worst fear was getting AIDS. I know because she actually told me that the other day. A few months ago, I caught an STD, chlamydia.

And she was like, "Oh, so you haven't been using protection!" I was like, "I have, but I'm only having sex with one person. He had chlamydia—he didn't know. But we both got tested and everything, and now it is all fine. I'm not having sex with anybody else." And she was like, "That is one of my worst fears, you have to be careful, think of this as a learning lesson." I am like, "I know."

This next mother was previously quoted discovering her son Harry was gay after she found him sneaking out in the middle of the night, when he was fifteen, to meet men. She described her (understandable) anxieties:

You know, back then, I must have suspected on some level because I wasn't shocked. But one of my first thoughts, truthfully, was that I knew to the day I went to my grave that I was going to be worried about this guy. There was never gonna be a moment's relaxation now. This changes so many things because it's a world where he'll forever be on the outside. And he's someone that always had trouble being accepted by people who didn't know. What would happen when they did know? I just felt like, "Oh, I'll always be worried, every day of my life now." Um, not because of me—I mean he's no less any of the things we knew and loved about him; it's just the intolerance because it's such a concern.

Joe was previously quoted as feeling guilty when he first suspected his son Tony was gay because when he was born he wished for a daughter. Even though his son came out to him nine years ago, he recalled his initial sadness with tears in his eyes: "I am kind of an emotional person. I just guess I certainly knew he was going to have a harder go through life. As a parent I wanted to try to make things easier. As a parent, we always want to try to make things easier for our children. I thought, 'Oh gosh, you are going to have such a hard time.'" Tony, like almost all the other respondents, was cognizant of his parents' fears for his well-being when he first came out: "He was very worried about disease and about people hurting me physically. He still is. He still sends me newspaper clippings, like if there was an article in the *Times* recently about the sort of indifference in the gay community towards condoms. If there is anything in the paper about that, he'll send that to me, just in case." Mac, the retired gay fireman, talked about his concerns for his daughter, who came out to him five months before his interview:

You know the bashing that goes on at school, the evil looks you get from people. The people who are willing to condemn you without even knowing you. There's still a lot of gay bashing that goes on. Especially right now. You know, gay bashing is the in thing again right now. And, you know, it makes me worry about her. I've created an environment here for her that she's very comfortable in. And she and her girlfriend are very comfortable with each other. I've seen them walking around holding hands and stuff like that. And, you know, you have to think about the evil side of what could happen to them.

Like Mac, parents of daughters were no less worried, although their fears focused less on HIV risk and more on discrimination and issues of physical harm. This African American mother of a lesbian, who struggled with self-blame, also admitted:

There's so much stigma attached to being a homosexual, I guess deep down inside, I do fear for her . . . I did tell her to be careful who she tells because I would hate to think that somebody would harm her because of it. I don't care who Nicole tells. I don't care who knows this about Nicole. Nicole is my daughter. She's the only thing that matters. But I wouldn't want somebody to harm her. And, because it's an issue, I told her be careful. So, in a sense, I guess I was a little scared, too.

This next African American mother talked about how a recent murder of a young lesbian contributed to her fears for her daughter:

You know. There was just a young girl murdered in Newark. See, Erica hangs in Newark. That's another thing I worry about. She always stays up there with her friend in Newark. You got these people with these issues behind this sort of thing and it's just—it's a fear that something might happen to her because of her sexual preference.

Fear of Discrimination

Earlier, vicarious courtesy stigma was defined as the angst parents empathically feel because their loved one is stigmatized (Corrigan and Miller 2004). During family sensitization, when parents suspected their children might be gay, they began to worry about how their sons and daughters would be affected by societal intolerance and discrimination. Once they knew for sure, their fears became more real and intense.

White middle- and upper-middle-class parents, particularly fathers, were especially concerned about discrimination in the workforce. This father was a wealthy businessman in New Jersey. He described his initial feelings upon learning of his daughter's lesbianism three years ago:

> Maybe there was some shame involved. In other words, do I want people to know my daughter is a lesbian? Even to this day, depending on the situation. And, I've even instructed her, because she's going into the workforce, I said, "You're going to have to be very, very careful . . . " Thank God she's chosen a field where it's acceptable.

Like other parents, he shielded his sense of self-blame from his daughter but not his concerns about life being more difficult for her. His daughter reported: "I think maybe he was worried about it being rough for me. I mean it is obviously not the easier path." Another mother had symptoms of depression, including profound sadness and insomnia, in the months after her daughter came out. She recalled:

> I was scared for her. I was afraid people would be mean and not love her any more. I have family members that are very cold, closed-minded people. Like my brother, who is a bitter angry man, who hates you if you are not like him, if you are not white. He is a jealous kind of person, if you have more than he has. I couldn't even really talk to anyone about it. I felt like, who can I tell? I thought about going to talk to someone, and I finally told my sister because we are so close, and she was pretty shocked.

Her daughter recalled,

> I think she was definitely worried about the whole family thing and what I would do about that. I don't think she thought I could ever have kids or anything like that and telling her brothers and sisters. They've never really had to deal with anything like this before, and I don't think she thought a couple of them would take it very well.

Once again, the youth were aware of their parents' feelings of worry for their well-being. Perhaps they had an easier time recognizing these concerns because parents in all families seem to have a natural tendency to worry about their children's safety; thus parental worry is a normal part of family life. So parents were able to be up-front with their children about these concerns, and their children were able to recognize them and take them in stride.

In addition, it might have been easier for the young people to acknowledge parental anxiety for their well-being because it was a sure sign that their parents still loved and cared for them. Parental worry, typical and expected, irritating but also perhaps a bit comforting, was proof that they would not be rejected as they had originally feared.

"What will people say?"

As stated earlier in this book, gay and lesbian youth have to find ways to cope with real or anticipated stigma. However, once parents knew, they suddenly found themselves in a crash course on this topic. *Public stigma* is the second type of courtesy stigma identified by Corrigan and Miller and describes the harsh judgment aimed directly at those associated with the stigmatized person. Once parents knew their child was lesbian or gay, they also knew they would have to deal with other people's criticism and prejudice, especially in light of the still commonly held belief that their own faulty parenting produced a lesbian or gay child. Parents learned what the young people already knew—where there is stigma, there is often shame. Once parents knew their children's sexual orientation, they worried about others' condemnation—of their children, but also of themselves. As Frank, who was quoted previously, recalled:

> I was probably more—I don't know—selfish with myself. What are my friends going to say or this or that? Is that selfish? I don't know . . . I'm not very good with words. Embarrassed? More worried about myself—you know what I'm saying? It was hard, I took my nephews to the side and I told them. They're like brothers, you know. Everybody accepted it. And Wanda is a great kid. Always was. My sister was OK. [I] never told my parents. Pop is gone, Mom is ninety years old and she's out in left field: Alzheimer's, you know. My father-in-law, forget it!

And this mother of an eighteen-year-old son:

> At that point [when the child comes out] you start thinking stupid things like, "What are people going to say? The family?" You start worrying, "Oh my God, my mom!" . . . thinking about my mom, his [husband's] mom, old-fashioned people. For them I think it is really hard, and I don't think we knew too much years ago. I remember my mother-in-law when she found out . . . she said you should take him to a doctor, maybe they will give him a pill and make him straight. So I knew that if they thought that, they are more ignorant about it, they don't have a clue.

This fear of stigma—what other people will think—becomes and remains increasingly important as families traverse the adjustment trajectory and is an ongoing issue to be addressed clinically, as will be described in subsequent sections of this chapter.

Religious Stigma

Of the seventy-six parents interviewed, five cited religious concerns as problematic when they first learned their children were gay. This mother described:

> When he told me he was gay, I was disappointed because, first of all, he used to go to Catholic school, that means he was baptized, had first Holy Communion, he had Confirmation, and now suddenly, you know, he doesn't have to go to church. He said he didn't believe in God . . . I was disappointed. I never expected that. That's not the way I raised him to be.

This father recalled:

> At the time [when their son came out], we were more religious than we are now, and we lived in the middle of a very Orthodox community. I mean, we lived two doors from our synagogue. All of a sudden, we have this whole situation about how do we deal with this whole problem—our son's gay, and we're living in a religious community.

Parents were also worried that their children's homosexuality would prevent their sons and daughters from getting into Heaven. "I worried because of the religious aspect because I would hate that she wouldn't get to Heaven because of that."

Considering that Catholicism and many fundamentalist Christian churches have been among the most outspoken opponents of gay rights, it is rather surprising that more parents did not identify religion as an important factor in their adjustment. Of course, I cannot know for sure, but I strongly suspect that parents having the most difficulty adjusting to the news that their child is gay are among those having the most trouble reconciling their religious beliefs with their children's sexual orientation. And, as I stated early, people who are struggling to come to terms with this issue are probably the least likely to talk to a gay researcher. However, in my clinical work as well as my other research, I have seen how parents' religious views could get in the way of their adjustment and can even impede parent-child relationships.

Sadly, the Catholic Church, the Evangelical Church, and some other fundamentalist Protestant and Jewish congregations use biblical justifications to deny gays civil rights and legal protections. I am no biblical scholar, but I think it is important to point out that doing this is simply wrongheaded. Church leaders and clergy have used Scripture, selectively interpreted and stripped of its historical context, to justify people's personal prejudices under the guise of strictly following the word of God.

From a historical perspective, this is nothing new. Leviticus states: "Thou shalt not lie with mankind as with womankind: it is abomination. Do not lie with a man as one lies with a woman; that is detestable" (Lev. 18:22), and this passage is the one most famously used to condemn homosexuality. However, the Bible includes all sorts of mandates that have no place in today's civilized world. Fundamentalist interpretations of the Bible have been used to justify slavery in the U.S. (Foner 1988, Gaustad and Noll 2003). In addition to its admonition against homosexuality, Leviticus also has passages that permit fathers to sell their daughters into slavery (21:7), prohibit men from shaving their beards (19:27), and Exodus calls for the death of anyone who works on the Sabbath (Exod. 35:2; *The New American Bible* 1991). Thus people who claim to adhere strictly to the Bible and use its teachings to justify denying lesbians and gays their rights are arbitrarily selecting certain teachings to follow while ignoring others.

If you are a fundamentalist Christian and object to homosexuality because of your religion, this line of reasoning has probably not changed your mind.

Despite having repeated these logical arguments over and over, I have yet to convince anyone to abandon such ideas, perhaps because such beliefs are not based on the principles of logic but rather what is believed to be (dare I say it?) a higher wisdom. Nevertheless, lesbian and gay youth and their parents must face the conflict between their religious beliefs and their children's homosexuality, and they may need the support of understanding professionals to help them reconcile their spiritual beliefs with love of their children in a way that maintains family connections. Not an easy task—but certainly a necessary one.

Changes in Relationships During Family Discovery

Parents do not react to their children's coming out in a vacuum. The interpersonal family context plays a role in parent-child relationships during family discovery and also later, as parents begin to adjust to the news that a son or daughter is gay. Even though the young lesbian and gay respondents might not have known the exact cause of their parent's suffering, some parents were so overwhelmed with guilt, grief, and worry that these feelings affected the parent-child relationship. As stated earlier, the task of families with older adolescents or young adults is to support them to feel confident enough to develop autonomy yet remain connected to family. During the family discovery phase, guilty, sad, anxious parents in this sample faced children who were seeking their understanding and acceptance, which inevitably led to family discord rather than the accepting, supportive interactions the youth sought and needed.

Conflict

In some families parental distress and disapproval sometimes created conflict. Like many other parents in this study, the mother of a gay male graduate student in this Italian/Puerto Rican family was initially ashamed. She feared for her son's safety and was concerned she would not have grandchildren. When asked what she thought about when her son first came out to her, she replied:

> AIDS definitely. Discrimination definitely, that is one of the worst. People see two men together and really they don't even know the person and they

make judgments. And, as a parent, you don't want your kid to go through all that. Yes, grandchildren is in it. And probably because we thought this kid at the time was this perfect kid, with school going so good and everything going for him. And then this came about, and I thought this is a big cross he has to carry now—and a little shameful for us. In my family we've heard comments already. And over the years, you know, you hear different things . . . just in general, like your hairdresser is a gay male, maybe, and they have a certain word for him. You hear that in conversation and then you find out your kid is like that. And you hear all these people talking about this, and now your kid is one of them. It was difficult and it still is.

Her feelings, along with her son's wish for her understanding and support, resulted in ongoing family conflict during the discovery phase. Both she and her son described angry, painful family arguments initially after he came out. The NIMBY effect was certainly an issue for this mother.

Like that first month was very difficult, the way I treated him, the words I said. So he was in shock, not expecting me to be saying such things. I think he would have expected me to be more understanding, because the funny part—was this lesbian cousin I am telling you about, I was very understanding and accepting of her. But when it hit home and it is your own kid, I flipped out. So, knowing him, he probably thought I was so accepting with her, and then him seeing this other side of me go crazy like that. It was very bad.

Her son, like most of the respondents, felt relieved right after he came out to his parents, but he also recalled the pressure he initially felt from his mother and father. Although his parents did not discuss this in their interviews, the son reported that they would have long talks with him to try to convince him that he was not gay, which, of course, resulted in conflict:

[At the time] when I went home, no matter what time I came home, they would be waiting and we would have to have a two-hour discussion about how I wasn't gay. I had to keep coming out. The frustration was that they were trying to deal with it and then subsuming me with their trying to deal with it; as I am too trying to deal with the fact that I was coming out. So I was frustrated and tense, I would walk home and I would walk into the

house and it was the same scene every day. That was like three months . . .
They were there in the living room and there was a discussion about me
not being gay going on. That was frustrating.

He recalled a particularly disturbing conversation he had with them:

When I came home one time from [college in] Delaware, they sat me down
for a talk. We never have talks like that. And they told me they were willing to
take a loan out, because they were watching a TV show [and learned that] for
$10,000 I could get a piece of my brain cut out and then I wouldn't be gay
any more. I sat at the table and I let them talk, and then I said to them, "All I
want you to do is think about what you just said to me. You want me to get
my head cut open, a piece of my brain cut out. I am going upstairs and I will
pretend that we never had this conversation. But I really want you to think
about what you just said, because it hurts me." And for like a day I just didn't
say anything. Didn't argue, didn't do anything but just let time go.

Distance

For other families, rather than overt conflict, the parent's initial shock and
struggle with the child's sexual orientation led to a simmering tension and
distance between parent and child. This mother of a lesbian recalled: "I think
we became more distant . . . or I should say distant because we never were
distant before . . . and it was, if we started to talk, I would start to cry. It was
never a good conversation . . . It was never anything but that; her, of course,
being upset that I wasn't accepting and me feeling like I was never going to
accept it." Her daughter recalled:

And within five minutes of me talking about it, she said, "I'm not OK with
this, you know?" In a nasty way in which . . . she made her point clear. So
we had a miniconversation, I got upset, and I definitely started withdrawing from her . . . staying at school and seeing friends and my girlfriend, and
that's it. You know, not wanting to bother with her so much . . . since she
didn't accept it . . . I felt, I couldn't talk to her about anything.

Susan was quoted earlier in this chapter as feeling guilty for being too
close to her son Mitch when he was a toddler, and she worried this closeness

made him gay. She remembered that when she first learned Mitch was gay a year ago she became so anxious that she experienced a bout of colitis. In recalling how the relationship changed, she described the initial distance: "Well we didn't ask him anything. We didn't ask him about young men in his life or any of that stuff. We just didn't. It wasn't like we were in denial, but we just didn't feel comfortable. And I don't think my husband feels comfortable yet." According to her son's report, she may have shielded him from some of her more intense feelings. However, her son recalled how the family members distanced from each other:

> She didn't cry. I was very shocked because I talk to a lot of people about coming out, because I find it to be really therapeutic to talk about it with people, and I am under the impression that most parents get really upset and cry . . . Still, it made it harder to talk . . . both of us found it harder to talk to each other, I would say, up until about several months ago.

With regard to his father, he recalled: "No contact basically. We would avoid each other at all costs, which we still pretty much do. It is just that I don't want to walk right in the home and be yelled at right away."

During his interview, Frank, the previously quoted butcher, tearfully recalled his early feelings of disappointment when he first learned of his daughter's lesbianism: "Well, you expect a wedding. You expect a son-in-law and to go fishing and get drunk, this is what I expected . . . Maybe I still want it to go away, I don't know. I accept it. I'm not going to make life miserable. But, yeah, what parent wouldn't want everything perfect, come on, if you can understand that." He recalled his relationship with his daughter, Wanda, during the first year after he found out: "She didn't kiss me for a year . . . We just like avoided. We were like two magnets flipped around . . . That's what it felt like. No arguments. You could feel that aura around us, if you know what I'm saying."

Frank's wife and Wanda's mother Donna recalled the distance and family strain:

> Well, we definitely weren't ourselves. I mean, you know, she wasn't her typical silly self—she'll act, like, silly at times, most of the times, that's when you know she's all right, but she wasn't. And I was just sitting on the couch all the time, basically. I definitely was upset—sad, not mad or anything, but just sad, being that she wouldn't get married and have grandchildren.

Wanda remembered the tension and distancing in her family. In talking about her relationship with her mother at the time, she recalled:

> I withdrew from her, and she definitely wanted to talk about it . . . and I just did not want to even think about it. No discussion. I didn't want to answer questions. I just wanted to pretend like it wasn't happening. I would see her eyes would be red. She wouldn't cry in front of me, but her eyes would be red. She would just be very quiet. We didn't talk much. Christmas was just like a big facade. It was horrible.

She did not say much about changes in her relationship with her father, perhaps because, like most of the respondents, she had been much closer to her mother, so the shift in the maternal relationship was more noticeable and more traumatic for her. "He didn't believe it at first. He was just shocked, stunned."

The distance and avoidance described in this section seemed to be a way for the families to prevent overt conflict or arguments about the children's sexual orientation. During this early stage, children' feelings were raw and parents were overwhelmed. Thus it seemed as if the family's circuits were too much in danger of overload for this topic to be discussed in any way that could be meaningful or productive.

DISTANCE INITIATED BY YOUTH. Even though the young respondents felt relief and gratitude for not being rejected, it doesn't mean that the kids were totally comfortable with the whole idea of their parents now knowing their secret. Try to imagine you have a disfiguring mark on your face that has been there since you were born. You have walked around your whole life wearing a veil to hide it and protect yourself from other people's stares and reactions of disgust. However, as time goes on, you learn there are people who have a similar facial blemish who, instead of being ashamed, are proud to show it. As a matter of fact, you come to learn to your surprise that they do not consider the mark a disfigurement but, instead, a type of badge of honor. Your weariness with hiding, along with the example set by these people, inspires you to shed your veil. You would probably feel liberated—but you still might also feel rather naked. After years of hiding, the residual shame is much harder to discard than that veil.

In about half of the families in which there was distance during the family discovery phase, it was the gay sons or lesbian daughters who initiated it—often because they felt ashamed or embarrassed—despite their relief at not being rejected. In this next African American family, the mother discovered her daughter was a lesbian and, unlike most parents in this study, was very accepting right from the start. She worked hard to show her daughter that she had no problem with her sexual orientation. She affirmed, "I tried to get closer." Nevertheless, even though her daughter felt relieved, she also felt embarrassed:

> I did kind of pull away. Because, like I said, when I told her about it, it just felt wrong, and I was embarrassed every time I saw her. It was like, "Well she knows about you now. She's thinking about this." I don't know why . . . to this day I don't know why, it just felt wrong for her to know . . . I felt relieved, but, again, it was also embarrassing. I don't know why, but it was just embarrassing talking about that aspect. Like I said, I had kept it to myself, it was a personal thing that I shared only with myself, and it felt really weird, like she was intruding in on a part of me that she wasn't supposed to be in . . . even though I invited her into that space.

This sense of embarrassment was particularly acute for youth who came out as a result of being confronted by their parents, rather than on their own initiative. As described in the previous chapter, Martha discovered her adolescent daughter Jennifer was a lesbian by finding and reading her diary. Martha tried hard to be accepting of her daughter. She told the interviewer: "I wanted to have contact and Jennifer didn't." However, her daughter felt exposed and embarrassed that her mother found out before she was ready to tell her. Jennifer recalled:

> Oh my God, I screamed at her. I remember when I came back, that night she came in to my room and she handed [the diary] to me, and I was like, "Did you read it? Did you read it?" And then she told me that she read it, and I just started screaming at her, "GET OUT OF MY ROOM!" I was screaming at her, and she was like, "Jennifer, it's OK! Jennifer, it's OK!" She just wanted to get close to me like, because that was all she wanted from me. But I was screaming, "GET OUT OF MY ROOM! I HATE YOU!" I think I pushed her aside and ran out. I wasn't ready for her to know, even though she was accepting, which is rare and any kid would die for . . . I just could not bear to see her—because someone so close to me knew something so personal. The way that she was willing to accept me made my life

easier. But, since she had found out so much personal information, I was so mad. I feel like I went silently crazy about it. Because of the very private nature of everything . . . everything was relating to this one issue, and she was finding out everything about it. I had no privacy after that.

Two different but related ideas might explain the tendency for some youth to feel embarrassed during the family discovery phase. First of all, the boundaries separating parent and child subsystems are meant to keep information about parental sexuality from children and vice versa. The common reluctance of families to discuss youth or parental sexual behavior is evidence of the importance of family boundaries regarding sexuality. When parents find out their children are gay, these boundaries are breached, whereby the typically taboo subject of the child's sexuality suddenly becomes a topic for open discussion. This understandably creates anxiety in the child, which no doubt makes him want to self-protectively distance.

Moreover, the anxiety around this breach of boundaries is compounded by the inescapable reality that, by coming out, gay youth admit that they are engaging in, or planning to engage in, sexual activities that are outside the mainstream. Those who are known to engage in nontraditional, nonprocreative sexual behaviors have long been targets of ridicule, discrimination, and punishment (Graff 2004). Fellatio, cunnilingus, and anal sex, particularly between members of the same sex, have long been considered sinful, particularly by Judeo-Christian religions, and have historically been criminalized in Western European and American culture. Until a U.S. Supreme Court decision in 2003, many states had laws on the books that made such practices illegal (Lawrence v. Texas 2003).

Goffman (1963) describes how some manage the effects of stigma by "passing," or concealing the part of themselves that is stigmatized. Hiding one's homosexuality by remaining "in the closet" is a common way of protecting oneself from the painful effects of stigma. As discussed in chapter 1, gay and lesbian youth who were realizing their sexuality were also learning that it was wrong and needed to be kept hidden for self-protection. Keeping a stigmatized identity hidden and then revealing it (by choice or by force) to someone as close as one's father or mother is perhaps akin to ripping a scab off a wound that has not fully healed. The person feels sore and overexposed.

These feelings of embarrassment and shame left these young people feeling vulnerable to the negative effects of parental disapproval, guilt, and worry. Thus they distanced to avoid facing their parents' feelings. Vicente, a Latino gay man, described how, after his mother told his father he was gay, Vicente distanced from him, fearing his disapproval. Nevertheless, the father, who was divorced from Vicente's mother and living in a separate home nearby, seemed to be reaching out to his son during this time.

> I just stopped talking to him. My fault, not his, because he did try to talk to me . . . I'm just afraid of him disapproving. I just didn't talk to him. He would call and I wouldn't pick up. There would be voice mail, I wouldn't answer them. Although I've never really lived with my father, I still care for him a lot. I don't want him to say something or do something that will hurt my feelings more. After Mom told him, I went over to spend like a week with him, and we didn't mention anything—not once. That was fine. But I still feel uncomfortable . . . after he found out I just ignored him, I didn't want to talk to him for like two years. I think I was more, like, shy to talk to him. I didn't know how to approach him. Even today I just don't want to, I am not comfortable talking to him about it. I know he wants a Mr. Macho son and I think I am pretty macho, but I still have sex with guys, and to him I think that is always going to be wrong.

Unfortunately, Vicente's father did not agree to be interviewed. However, by his son's report, he showed no overt signs of disapproving or rejecting Vicente, either during the discovery phase or anytime thereafter. It is unclear how much this was a function of not having the chance to express his disapproval because his son cut off communication with him. Nevertheless, what the recollections of this young man and others in this study suggest is that the need for self-protection from anticipated or imagined parental disapproval could be another reason for withdrawal.

Divergent Perceptions of Parent and Child

In several families, daughters and sons recalled distance during the discovery phase when their parents did not. Norman, the father from Guyana, said his relationship with his son stayed the same after Franklin came out, however, his son recalled that right after he told his father "he didn't really talk to me. He would say 'Hi' less than usual . . . He withdrew . . . Like he was in denial—he didn't want to believe it." Franklin also recalled tension with his mother, but her view on this could not be confirmed; she was deceased at the time of the interview.

As stated earlier, the young people would withdraw from parents when they saw actual signs of disapproval. This young woman recalled:

> No, [there was] no talk about it. And then when I finally did tell my mother there was still no talk about it. I would mention it, I would say, "I have a crush on someone." And she would be like . . . it would be really awkward. Really, we haven't talked about it at all until probably a year [after I came out]. I might have mentioned it again the spring of my sophomore year, which is twelve months later, because I had my first girlfriend.

However, her mother did not recall any changes in her relationship with her daughter after she came out. When asked specifically about this, she replied: "No. I still had the same basic emotional response to her. You know, basically I love her, so that stayed the same." Even though Chauncey felt relieved, there was distance between him and his mother after he came out:

> It was less talking. Because I felt she wasn't ready. Yes, she would say stuff. She definitely uttered a disparaging remark to me that was really hurtful, and I'd rather not repeat it. I was really hurt by it. She said it out of anger, but I forgot what we were fighting about. But that was like immediately after . . . I would say less than six months after it happened. Yeah, I pulled away from her big time. I started not coming home.

However, his mother Marie felt the relationship remained unchanged throughout the family discovery phase.

In the following family, there was a significant discrepancy between parent and child. This mother recalled some awkward hesitation on the part of her twenty-three-year-old daughter initially after she came out:

> I would kid her and say, "You know, a hug a day." And she would kind of back off a little bit and not want to be hugged. But now it is like, "Hey, I am home," and she is much more open in that way . . . Maybe I am a little more loving too—I am trying to listen. I will ask her about her relationship, which she really doesn't want to talk about.

Her daughter perceived the relationship during the discovery phase very differently:

> I think I wanted to talk about it with her more than she wanted to talk about it with me. I wanted to tell her stuff, and she kind of just pushed it away. I would call her a lot from work, because it would be easier for me to talk about it on the phone than face to face. And she would try to push it away. Yeah, she kind of would blow it off or block it out. Like I had told her a couple of times that I was seeing someone, and she would kind of push that off. If it would come up, like if she [girlfriend] would call me at my house, my mom was like, "Oh, I didn't know you were seeing anyone." I was like, "I told you a couple of times."

Tara, the previously quoted eighteen-year-old chemistry student, and both her parents participated in the study. Both her mother and her father denied there was any difference in the interactions with their daughter during the discovery phase. However, in remembering her relationship with her mother and father right after she came out, she recalled:

TARA: It was still bad mostly. We didn't talk at all. Not until a couple of years, like two years ago, that I actually could sit down and have a conversation with my mother. . . . We would just get into fights.
INTERVIEWER: OK. How about with your dad?
TARA: I avoided him.

Though more research in this area is needed, there are several plausible explanations for why parents were less likely to recall or report deterioration in the relationship with their children. First of all, parents may have perceived their love and commitment to their children to be unwavering and unconditional. Therefore, in their minds, this basic relationship stayed the same, despite whatever arguments or distancing occurred during this period.

It is also possible that parents did not want to admit to themselves that there was parent-child distancing. *Dissonance reduction* might have some relevance here. This theory holds that when people's behavior is at odds with what they know or believe, they will change their ways of thinking to decrease the inconsistency (Festinger 1962). In order to maintain their self-images as good parents, despite negative or distancing reactions to their children, parents may have been more invested in remembering their relationships with their children during family discovery as more positive than they actually were.

Furthermore, social desirability or the wish to maintain a good image (or at least not embarrass oneself) in the presence of the interviewer may also have been at work. As stated earlier, the interviewer team for this study consisted of a lesbian woman, a mother of a lesbian who is clearly well-adjusted to her daughter's sexuality, and the author, an openly gay man. We reassured parents that we would not be shocked by their responses and that we had either witnessed or experienced firsthand a variety of parent reactions, which we believed were understandable. However, in spite of our continued reassurances that we wanted the honest truth and would not be judgmental, it is quite possible that parent respondents worried that their interviewers would think they were uncaring parents or might be offended by honest parental responses that could be interpreted as antigay. Certainly wanting to look good in the presence of a researcher is not uncommon during interview research (LaSala 2003; Laslett and Rapoport 1975; Padgett 2008).

An additional explanation is also possible. Perhaps the young people *wanted* more closeness with their parents than they were able to get at this time, so they were more likely to perceive parent-child distance whether or not it actually increased during family discovery. Vulnerable young people wanted reassurance and comforting from parents who themselves were having difficulty coping with their initial reactions. Bob, the successful stockbroker quoted in previous sections of this book, tearfully described his sense of loss right around the time his daughter came out:

> You know, I went through the blame, anger, grief, blah, blah, blah . . . and recognized that much of my anger and grief was because of the destruction of my future for her. You know the picket fence, the two grandchildren, the dog, the wonderful husband . . . etc. You have your children's whole future laid out for them in your mind, you know, living happily ever after. I was angry at God . . . at life . . . for giving me a lesbian daughter. All the problems . . . all the challenges . . . all the loss of these picket fence images and so forth . . . Why am I stuck with this burden? Why couldn't it be somebody else?

His daughter, Ellie recalled:

> He called me [soon after coming out]. And he was crying and upset and scared and he went through the entire grief process of dealing with accepting things. He said to me that he was mourning the loss of the daughter he thought he had and the life that he thought I would have. He was fearing

my future and how that would affect me. In retrospect, I felt hurt by the process that he was going through. I wanted him to just say, "I accept you no matter what," which he did in those conversations, but he also said a lot of "But I am scared. But I am worried. But I am angry." I just wanted the blanket "That's OK." But nobody gets the blanket in that situation.

Interestingly, this respondent's mother did not participate, yet this young woman claimed her mother still had initial and ongoing problems because of her inability to accept or adjust to her daughter's lesbianism. Nevertheless, this father-daughter relationship illustrates how family members' divergent perspectives and needs can create frustration and conflict during the family discovery phase. Different recollections of the parents and children following the child's coming out is a finding somewhat unique to this study and further research of the relationships of parents and their children could help confirm, clarify, or suggest additional reasons for this phenomenon.

Shielding Fragile Youth

As stated earlier, youth had been unaware of the extent parents blamed themselves for their homosexuality. They were also not conscious of how their parents mourned the loss of the image of them as heterosexual. Parents at times were perhaps shielding their children from the reasons for these feelings, keeping them to themselves and fortifying family boundaries that had been breached when the child came out.

However, for some of the families in this study, this type of shielding took on an even more protective function. Several parents believed their children to be emotionally frail when they came out, and in these cases their protective instincts took over. They shielded their children from their most troubling feelings and reactions during the discovery phase and instead worked hard to appear supportive. This was especially true for parents of children who were suicidal around the time they came out. Fred, whose son Mike had cut his wrists in church immediately before coming out, described: "Well, in that situation where he has attempted suicide you are kind of walking on eggshells. You don't want to be too hard. You don't want to be too easy. You are kind of playing it by ear. You are trying to feel things out. Sticking your toe in the water to see how hot or cold it is." Ann, Mike's mother became clinically depressed during the family discovery phase as she mourned the loss of a future daughter-in-law and grandchildren. She described a similar perception of the experience of the family atmosphere around the time she and her husband learned their son was gay:

> We kind of had to feel our way because, with the house being small, Mike can hear the TV out here, and it was right around the time that Ellen came out, and I was very aware that I might have been laughing at things and I wasn't sure if it was OK. I didn't want to offend him. And there were other shows where something would be presented and I wasn't sure, you know . . . should I leave it on? So I asked him, "Does it bother you?"

Mike seemed unaware that his mother was struggling to adjust to the news that he was gay and that his parents felt they needed to be extra cautious around him. Perhaps his parents' protectiveness, along with his relief over not being rejected, worked together to prevent him from noticing any changes in his parents' behavior: "They didn't care, they just wanted me to be happy . . . I never felt persecuted."

In this next family, we also see the tendency for parents to shield their children from their self-blame in an effort to maintain connections with their children. Nancy, the African American school administrator and mother of Joelle, recalled feeling very sad, lonely, and inferior as a parent and wondered: "Is there some failing in my nurturing that somehow she is looking to other women to nurture her in a way that I didn't nurture her?" Nancy's daughter Joelle had severe anxiety and depression at the time of her interview and was having trouble adjusting to her first year away at college. This mother recalled that, during the discovery phase, Joelle also seemed emotionally fragile, so she was very careful to try to shield her daughter from her reactions in an effort to protect her feelings: "I think that . . . maybe I was more unsure of myself—I never really thought about this—because I didn't want to damage her . . . maybe any further than I already had or something. You know, it was like walking on eggshells." Joelle had no idea of her mother's initial self-blame or worries about hurting her. In recalling her relationship with her mother during this time: "I think the relationships just in general continued to grow as I, like, got older and we talked more openly. We continued to talk openly just like I would have as a child."

In some families it wasn't the child who was emotionally fragile *but the relationship between parent and child* that was vulnerable during the family discovery period. Parents tried to protect or shield their children from their feelings because they wanted to preserve their relationships with them.

Gloria, a previously quoted mother, spoke during her interview of how she felt distant from her twenty-two-year-old son Noah. But, ever since he left the house to live in an apartment on his own, she yearned for a closer relationship with him, and after our interview she sought my advice about how to get him to call her more often. She recalled how, two years ago, when she realized her son was gay after finding gay porn on his computer, she felt very much to blame: "I thought: 'What had I done?' My friends had nice straight children and I didn't. I had this abomination. I am being very frank. I had this abomination in my house arising out of my parenting." However, she put aside her feelings to try to be a support to her son: "Well, I was resolved to be helped . . . to get information and education. I was resolved not to take those first worries and impressions and then let this separate me from my son." Her son understood that his mother was thinking of family factors, yet seemed unaware of the extent to which she was experiencing self-blame. He described his mother's initial reaction as follows:

NOAH: OK. So even though she cried a little bit at the beginning she was still basically supportive.
INTERVIEWER: Did she say anything in particular?
NOAH: I don't remember. I am sure there was some asking of "Are you sure about this?" I think there was some talk of how it "happened." Which is to say that it didn't happen, it just is. It wasn't having a bad father or being an only child or the water. It is just like genetic. So nothing either of us could do about it except be happy.

In these families we see the important role of protective family boundaries. Fear of disapproval or rejection from family members as well as the breach of the taboo subject of sexuality led youth to distance from their parents: in effect, establishing self-protective boundaries. For families in which children seemed emotionally vulnerable because of mental illness, or where parent-child relationship seemed tenuous, parents strengthened and maintained these protective boundaries. Based on these findings, clinicians would be advised to find ways to acknowledge and at times fortify these boundaries for families in the discovery stage, and this will be further discussed later in this chapter.

Improved Family Relationships

There were a small handful of families in which parents and children reported their relationships immediately improved following the child coming out. For these families, something seemed to give way once parents knew their child was gay. Like a clogged pipe that is suddenly cleared, communication was now able to flow freely.

This next quoted respondent, Adele, was the mother of Jay, the young man who developed colitis as a result of the bullying he experienced at school. She suspected her son might be gay for several years before finding out for sure following his suicide attempt four years ago. At that time she was very anxious and worried for her son. However, when asked how, if at all, her relationship with her son changed immediately after she learned he was gay, she said:

> If anything I think maybe it was a little bit closer . . . The one thing I am thinking of, which is so silly, is going up to our cottage in Maine that summer . . . and finding a really neat wind spinner that was a rainbow and hanging that outside. That's what popped into my head . . . Jay and I found it together in a store and thought this would be something nice to hang on the cottage.

It seemed as if Jay's relief and belief that he could finally be honest with his mother helped enhance their relationship. Jay recalled feeling as if he and his mother were close again after the period of tension and distance that preceded his coming out:

> We would joke. We were friendly again. It was almost as if I was five again. She was Mommy and I was Jay and everything was happy. . . . And I just went from being evil psycho teenager to happy young adult like that (*smacks hands together*). And she is the one who got me involved with High-tops and 1st and 3rd (support groups for LGBT youth). She is the one who researched it all. . . . There was less fighting, less crap. There was nothing in the way of us being normal people. There was no tension in the air. And it got better and better. It was, very quickly, within that summer, I would say, we became just as close as we are now.

Even his relationship with his father improved immediately after he came out to him: "I was nice to him . . . Because I didn't hate him anymore . . . I didn't have any of that angst. I didn't have any of that anger built up inside of me that I was taking out on him. And I became a nice person again. Relationships with just about everyone I knew improved."

Feelings of relief played a major role in the improvement in family relationships. Parents who had long suspected or who had noticed something seemed to be wrong with their child—that she seemed distant or unhappy—were relieved to finally know for sure what was going on, even though they might themselves be struggling with feelings of guilt, loss, and fear. As stated before, even though they felt overexposed, the young people in this study still experienced a great deal of relief and gratitude toward their parents because they did not reject them.

An additional factor that seemed to improve family relationships during family discovery was the new honesty that was possible. Despite parents feeling distressed and youth feeling exposed, it must have been a relief for these families to finally be able to talk about what had been a secret for so long. This mother of a twenty-three-year-old gay man, who herself was a social worker, described how good it felt to relate to her son after she knew about his sexual orientation:

> I felt a relief. I felt that our interactions became honest. I wasn't pretending, like if he would say he went out with Bill and Sue, you know, "Oh, who are they?" And it was like I didn't ask any more who Bill and Sue were, I didn't care. I interacted more with him then to make sure he was OK and that he knew I was OK. I needed him to know that I was truly OK, that I was the same mom.

Her son also noticed the improvement in the relationship with his mother right after he came out to her:

> Yes, there was a change. Because we had pretty much talked about everything that was going on in my life, so after I told her then it allowed me to talk about my relationship with my boyfriend at the time and things like that. It was actually a lot of fun having her to talk to about that . . . kind of cool to be able to include her.

He also mentioned some minor improvement in his relationship with his father:

I don't know if it is related or not, but, after he found out, it did seem we started talking a little bit more. He seemed a little bit more interested in what was going on with me in California. He would ask more questions about how I was doing, what I was doing. Before he was kind of curious, but it just seemed like he actually cared more about it.

Wolf (1991) and Garcia-Preto (1999) describe how the onset of sexuality, along with the adolescent mandate to move away from parents and child-hood, can strain communication in heterosexual families. When families are launching (or preparing to launch) their sons and daughters, the challenge is to give the children the "roots" of family connection and security that enables them to use their "wings" to explore their own freedom sufficiently to establish independence. A family in which parents leave room for a child to be openly lesbian or gay but where strong parent-child relationships are maintained is manifesting a good balance between supporting autonomy and connectedness.

In two additional families both the mother and the child agreed that their relationship improved even though the ongoing distance in children's relationships with their fathers remained the same. When asked how, if at all, their relationship changed after her seventeen-year-old daughter came out, this African American mother recalled: "Our relationship got better. Once I gave her space, it got better, so her being gay or lesbian had nothing to do with me against her because of that. And like I said, it was the same, my feelings didn't change." Her seventeen-year-old daughter agreed: "Yeah, [after I came out our relationship changed] for the bet-ter. Like I said, before we weren't able to talk about anything. and when I say anything, I mean anything. After I told her I was gay, things got much better." Her father never lived with the family, and her relationship with him had always been distant. Coming out to him did nothing to change this.

Candace attributed some of the improvement in her relationship with her twenty-four-year-old son Ryan to the new honesty that was possible between them along with his growing emotional maturity.

Well, again, his age had a lot to do with it too. He had been in the mode of not talking to me for a couple of years. So now he was very understanding and would talk to me when I would ask him questions. So I initiated the conversation, and he would talk to me, so long as he wasn't in a bad mood or late for school or something.

Ryan recalled the relationship becoming increasingly open after he came out to her: "I think things got better, our relationship was open. Like she wanted to know if my friend Zach and I were dating, and I told her no, we were just friends. So that was a good thing. I don't know if she believed me, but I did tell her. So now she could know things that she didn't know before." Clearly, things got better between them during the family discovery phase.

However, with regard to his father who was divorced from Candace and whom Ryan only saw twice a year, he stated: "I don't think things changed. We were never really that communicative anyway." As discussed previously, father-child relationships are generally more distant than their mother-child counterparts. This was certainly true among families in this sample, so in some ways it is not surprising that if paternal relationships were distant or strained before the children came out they remained so afterward.

Sometime gay and lesbian children saw improvements in their relationships with their parents during family discovery even if their parents believed things stayed the same. For example, Toshi's mother stated that her relationship with her son did not change immediately after coming out. It remained as strong as it had always been, even though she began to worry for his safety once he came out to her. However, Toshi insisted that his relationship with both his mother and father improved immediately after coming out:

> It got closer. It just happened that way. I mean, when you can be honest about something which was a major issue for you that definitely makes it closer, especially when your parents actually help you out, instead of like, "No! We hate you!" . . . We definitely talk. I don't feel uncomfortable at all. I don't have to lie to them as much. I guess the whole honesty type of thing really strengthened the relationship.

As stated in a previous section of this chapter, in some families youth had a tendency to see parent-child relationships deteriorate while the parents believed they stayed the same, and this could be explained by parents' efforts to maintain (and project) their self-images as good, all-accepting parents. A similar explanation might apply to families in which youth believed their relationships improved when parents thought they stayed the same. Parents might prefer to believe and/or report no improvement in their relationship with their children because such a report might suggest a time when their relationships with their children were less than optimal. Such parents might have been unwilling to admit, either to themselves or an outside researcher, that their relationship with their children had been anything but invariably strong in order to maintain their self-images as good parents.

However, the reports of Gloria and Noah suggest another explanation. Gloria remembered the relationship with her twenty-two-year-old son Noah as being distant right after he came out because she put so much energy into shielding her son from her feelings of profound self-blame, which she experienced immediately after Noah told her he was gay. Nevertheless, her son recalled:

> I really just remember it improving. I think it took time and I think it took her reading those books and joining PFLAG, but I just remember it improving, and the only really significant difference in terms of our conversation was she would ask about boys and if I was seeing anyone. I felt now she knew everything about me, so I could keep telling her things. We talked more. I was more open with her.

Apparently, Gloria did such a good job shielding her son from her reactions that Noah believed the relationship improved. The importance of protective family boundaries that emerged during family discovery has clinical implications that I will return to later in this chapter.

Fathers and Closeness

According to the extensive literature available, mothers are generally closer to their children than fathers. As stated repeatedly in this book, compared to fathers, mothers have more contact with their children, are more likely to talk with their children about emotional issues, and are more likely to discuss sex with them (Craig 2006; Finley and Schwartz 2006; Kirkman, Rosenthal, and Feldman 2002; Rosen 1999). Even though sex role socialization is a common explanation for these differences, some of the findings of this study suggest that *systemic* factors may play a part in maintaining these differences.

Among these parents, there was a small handful of fathers who were historically, emotionally distant from their children but who then became closer to them initially after they came out. Invariably, in these families, the mothers, who had traditionally enjoyed intimate relationships with their sons and daughters, were having a difficult time coping with their children's newly disclosed sexual orientation. As can be seen by the quoted responses that follow, the new mother-child distance opened up an opportunity for some fathers and youth to develop closer connections, often to the children's surprise. This new closeness was an unexpected silver lining in the coming-out process.

Remember Bob, the successful stockbroker? His daughter, Ellie, spoke of how historically she had been closer to her mother. However, things changed dramatically when this young woman began to befriend openly gay people *before* she came out. Her religiously Episcopalian mother vehemently disapproved of her friendship choices, and when she made her feelings known to her daughter this, unsurprisingly, led to arguments. Immediately after Ellie told her parents, she felt relieved to finally be more honest with her family, even though coming out seemed to aggravate the already thorny relationship she had with her mother (who, perhaps for this reason, declined to be interviewed for this study). However, Ellie identified positive postcoming-out changes in her relationship with her father.

> I felt like I could be honest with her about my life. The door was open, whether she wanted it open or not. It improved my relationship with my father greatly. The number one biggest improvement was in our relationship. If someone would have asked me when I was younger if this would happen . . . I would have said, "No. There is no way in hell my dad would accept something like this." But it is by far the catalyst to my relationship with my father. I am closer to him now then I ever have been in my entire life.

Bob agreed that he and his daughter became closer right after she came out:

> I think it was that the two of us were dealing with a subject that intersected both of us as opposed to most subjects between a father and his twenty-something-year-old daughter. There aren't that many things that we are both involved in or concerned about and now we [father and daughter] are both involved and concerned with her well-being and her relationship with her parents and her parents' well-being and education about being gay and what it all meant in the world.

This report of Tony's father Joe also demonstrates how coming out can improve father-son relationships.

I think, if anything, I felt a much stronger attachment to him, because he had chosen to come out to me. And I think vice versa—I think it worked very positively from both our standpoints. I just felt better about him—I really did. I felt like I was dealing with him as I should be, accepting him for who he was. I felt very good about myself over that fact, that I wasn't having really any problems doing that. Internally, I was struggling, but externally, with him, I felt very confident in how I was dealing with it. I felt as confident in dealing with him for the first time in my life as I probably ever had.

His son Tony described how his mother, from whom his father recently divorced, had a very hard time coping with his sexual orientation when she initially found out.

I told her, and it was awful. And Mom was the one I was sure would be on my side . . . It definitely affected our relationship. I pulled back a lot. Because hers was the support I had really counted on and had counted on my entire life. She certainly wasn't unsupportive—the whole thing just made her so upset. She kind of withdrew . . . I did withdraw a little bit too. We both kind of withdrew. I would make periodic forays towards my mom. Like when it was just the two of us in the house, "I would say how are you feeling about things? How are you feeling about me?" And often her response would be, "I love you and I need to work through this, I need to get used to this." Just something sort of like the issue is not up for discussion at the moment.

This distance with his mother seemed to throw open a window that allowed a closer relationship between Joe and Tony to develop:

TONY: Dad and I kind of engaged. We started talking a lot more, about this and other things. Like I said, he joined PFLAG and he would invite me to come with him to the meetings. He was very curious about where David [my partner] and I went, not in a nosey way, just like, "Do you go out dancing? Where do you go?" He became just more accessible.

INTERVIEWER: And it didn't feel like he was being intrusive?

TONY: No. It didn't at all. Sometimes my mom would ask these things, and when she did it would feel like that, even if she was asking the same thing.

INTERVIEWER: What was the difference, the thing that told you OK, this is nosey, versus this feels like he is being accessible?

TONY: A lot of it is just the dynamic of my relationship. Mom and I, because we are on so much the same wavelength, we can say many more things with a single statement. By simply asking me where it was that David and I went dancing, Mom could also be asking, "Are you being safe?" She could be asking, "Are you going to some den of sin and having sex with forty people?" And it was hard for me to figure out which of those questions she was asking, whereas, with Dad, what he asked was what he was asking.

It is interesting and important to note that improvements among families in which coming out led to more positive relationships between fathers and children continued beyond the family discovery phase right up to the time the family members were interviewed. As a matter of fact, in all the families in which there were improvements in parent-child relationships during family discovery, they continued throughout the family adjustment trajectory—and these families were joined by others who experienced family relationship enhancement later on, after parents had the time and opportunity to adjust.

Summary of the Family Discovery Phase

When a family finds out for sure that a daughter or son is gay, it has an immediate, disruptive impact on the family and its members, particularly parents. Well-meaning parents who do not reject their children may grapple with feelings of self-blame, grief, and worry, and, in this study, such feelings carried many parents into an emotional crisis as they struggled with anxiety and depression. In some families these feelings spilled over to create conflict. However, in others, family members were able to avoid overt conflict by distancing—and the experiences of these families suggest a possible coping strategy for families wrestling with the challenges of the discovery stage.

Parent-Child Interaction During Family Discovery: Boundaries and Mutual Distancing

After an explosion, a cloud of smoke engulfs the area in a dark, tense silence, and, until it clears, nobody knows how the landscape will be changed. A version of this edgy quiet was present in the families in this study whereby distance seemed to be the defining characteristic of family relationships during the family discovery stage immediately after the child had come out.

From a structural perspective, these findings underscore how parents and children can mutually act in ways to modify parent-child boundaries during the family discovery stage, making them thicker, stronger, and more protective. None of the parents in this study rejected their children because they were lesbian or gay, however, after discovery, parents struggled with feelings of surprise, guilt, grief, and fear. In an effort to avoid conflict and protect their children, many parents seemed to emotionally retreat to their corners. Although there was tension in many of these families, and the children knew they were upset, the distance that occurred during family discovery seemed to allow parents to deal with their feelings of guilt and mourning on their own without inciting overt family conflict.

Children may also play a role in creating these thick boundaries. First of all, in this study, once their parents knew about their homosexuality, children initially felt exposed and anxious. After years of hiding, it can be unsettling and embarrassing that parents are now aware of this very personal and, for some, shameful information. Therefore, some children may need to distance from their parents in an effort to restore their bearings and get accustomed to the idea that their parents now know what they have long kept a secret.

Second, these findings suggest that a child's relief over not being rejected can create a smokescreen behind which they cannot see or can avoid seeing their parents' guilt and mourning. Knowing their parents were coping with feelings of self-blame and loss would put them face to face with their parent's thinking that they were abnormal. Because, during family discovery, children are so afraid of rejection or extreme parental disapproval, they may be unwilling or unable to cope with any of their parents' strong negative feelings.

In order to avoid facing their parents' disapproval and also to prevent family conflict, young people found ways to distance from their parents by avoiding certain topics of discussion, at times creating a situation where there was less contact with parents—in effect reinforcing these boundaries in an effort to maintain some kind of fragile peace in the family during this difficult time. Although there was tension in many of these families, and the children knew they were upset, this seemed to allow parents to deal with their guilt and feelings of loss without inciting overt family conflict. This tentative and somewhat uneasy calm may be an important component of family adjustment

Therapists put a premium on close family communication, so it is hard to think of family distancing as a good thing, even though, for the families described herein, it was. Nevertheless, thick, mutually reinforced family boundaries are not without their problems. Many families in this study described a nervous tension as an unpleasant component of this distance. Furthermore, as stated by Ellie, children who came out to their parents were seeking a blanket of comfort. However, parents who were initially overwhelmed by the news were unavailable to offer this to their children.

Nevertheless, this distance can be a way family members maintain themselves and their relationships, at least until the dust settles and the family can get used to the idea that the secret is out. Thus some temporary disengagement, rather than being problematic, might indeed be functional and could even be recommended by therapists working with families in the throes of the discovery phase.

Treatment During the Family Discovery Crisis

The prevailing wisdom in family therapy is that clinicians need to bring everyone together to talk openly about their concerns. However, if undertaken at the wrong time, particularly too early in the family adjustment trajectory, this can be counterproductive. Clinicians approached by anguished families in the discovery phase might find themselves in the perplexing cross fire of distraught parents and offspring who are feeling overexposed and embarrassed. Or, instead of fighting (or to prevent them from doing so), family members may have retreated behind their own walls of cold silence. Based on the findings of this study, it would be fruitless to push family members to talk everything out when they are too hurt and angry to listen and understand one anothers' perspectives. Thus individual sessions with parents and children might be the best place to start.

Parents

SEPARATE SESSIONS. Protective parents might not want to share their feelings of self-blame and loss with their children, and young people might be distancing or shutting down in the presence of their parents to protect themselves from their disapproval and avoid conflict. Based on these findings, mutual distancing is something family therapists might want to support, particularly during the period immediately after the child has come out. Thus, when therapists are sought out by a family that is struggling with a daughter or son coming out, family sessions may not be what's called for. Instead, it is probably a better idea to routinely meet with family members individually, at least initially, to first assess how they are doing and whether or not they are emotionally able to participate in a productive family session.

Parents seeking therapy at this time will need help coping with guilt, loss, and anxiety. The therapist is advised to assess parents for guilt and grief as these feelings were frequent sources of mental health symptoms in this sample during the family discovery phase. If parents are extremely depressed and anxious because they are blaming themselves or overwhelmed with feelings of loss, they may need to be seen alone for a while.

Some family therapists have suggested that traumatized family members need to first get a chance to express their intense feelings to the therapist alone. If distressed parents who are newly aware of their children's sexual orientation feel sufficiently heard and understood by the clinician, they will experience the emotional relief necessary to be receptive to referrals for education and support. Subsequently, once they are calmer and better informed, they will also be better able to productively discuss issues in a family session (Guerin and Pendagast 1976; LaSala 2000).

A cornerstone of good clinical practice is the establishment of an empathic, supportive relationship with clients. As anyone in the helping professions knows, this kind of relationship is easier to describe than it is to establish and maintain. Like the interviewers in this study, practitioners need to find ways to break through the walls of parental reluctance and assure mothers and fathers that they can discuss all of their feelings, including their guilt and shame, without fear of being judged.

But what if the therapist *is* judgmental? Working with these families can inspire a maelstrom of feelings, some of them contradictory. We might think that parents who don't immediately accept their coming-out sons and daughters are bad parents and, at the same time, wonder if there isn't something wrong with these people for having gay children in the first place. Unfortunately, family therapists do not spring from the soil, fully formed, as nonjudgmental adults; they grow up in the same society as their clients and are exposed to the same homophobic, oppressive messages about gays and lesbians. Rachel, one of the mothers in this study, talked about how homophobia and heterosexism "has to be burnt out of you." At the end of chapter 1 I advised therapists and other human service workers to make ongoing efforts to look inward, examine their ideas and feelings, and seek information and exposure to lesbians and gays. It is my sincerest hope that readers follow this advice.

TOLERATING INTOLERANCE. Those who enter human service professions do so because they care deeply about human suffering and hope to help eradicate it. Seeing a vulnerable person in pain not only breaks our hearts but makes us want to do something to help. Thus it is understandable for human service professionals to want to protect children, even, at times, from their own parents. It may be hard not to negatively judge parents who are not accepting of their children, particularly fathers and mothers who say ugly things to them when they first learn they are gay. I knew of several parents who told their coming-out children that they would rather have learned their sons or daughters were murderers. Of course, it is understandably difficult for most therapists to hear such a thing and yet remain neutral.

However, we must remember that attempting to rescue these children by defending them and attacking their parents is not the best way to help them. Instead, we must find ways to help their parents express, understand, and cope with their feelings so that family relationships can be preserved and strengthened. Keeping this in mind, therapists might need to show parents that, even though they themselves are gay positive, they will not be intolerant of their clients' intolerance. The therapist can demonstrate that many different feelings are understandable and acceptable by talking about what other parents go through. For understandable reasons, it would be too difficult for newly out gay and lesbian youth to hear this, so, of course, this needs to be done in parents-only sessions.

What scissors are for hairstylists, open, nondirective questions are for therapists, and it is a good idea to use them liberally in interactions with clients. However, some parents of gay children are ashamed of their feelings. In their minds, good parents should never be rejecting or ashamed of their kids, so they might hold back such feelings from their therapists. It is also difficult for people to recognize and face their own shame (Nichols 1995b), therefore it is possible that parent-clients will not fully realize all that they are experiencing and may not recognize certain feelings until their therapists identify them. Nevertheless, the practitioner does not want to give the impression that a client *should* have certain feelings or that something is wrong if he does not.

Perhaps clinicians should think of themselves as playing the position of catcher in a baseball game. Catchers, of course, don't control the motion of the ball coming toward them. However, even before the pitch, they have a general idea of its path. When the ball comes their way, they're crouching, they have their mitts on, and they're ready to catch it, whether it is a wild pitch or one that sails through the strike zone.

Not all parents experience their feelings in the same way, but clinicians need to communicate to their parent-clients that if they are experiencing certain feelings, such as guilt, shame, anger, mourning, disgust, despair, or fear, they have their catcher's mitt on and are prepared to hear about them. Therefore, it might be a good idea to invite clients to talk about specific feelings they might be experiencing by saying something like "I know of some parents who feel guilty that they made their children gay. I know others who feel ashamed of themselves and their children when they find out. Others feel disgusted, yet others have none of these feelings. What are you experiencing right now?" Trusting someone with our shameful feelings is not something that happens right away—it takes time before we know we can tell someone our most embarrassing secrets without being judged. Thus, if parents initially deny these feelings, practitioners should be prepared to gently ask about them again in future sessions.

If, like me, you are an openly gay man or a lesbian, you may have to work harder at convincing parents that you are receptive to hearing their most negative feelings. I often tell parents, "I have worked with many parents like you and I know that parents have a variety of reactions, some of which they are ashamed of. I've heard it all, so nothing you say will shock me." Sometimes I find some limited self-disclosure is helpful: "My parents and I are OK now, but when they first found out they had a terrible time and said some pretty awful, hurtful things to me—so there is nothing you can say to me that I will find shocking or offensive."

Once parents start expressing their feelings, I have three suggestions: 1. normalize, 2. normalize, 3. normalize. Based on the responses of the participants in this research, a variety of feelings are possible, and parents need to know that what they are feeling is not out of the ordinary. When relevant, it might be helpful to use examples from the reports of the parents in this book to help clients see they are not the only ones who feel the way they do.

Considering these findings, it might be a good idea for practitioners to assess parents carefully for depression and anxiety and consider at least a short course of medication if their symptoms are debilitating. Once these feelings are examined and discussed, and parents feel that the clinician truly understands them, parents might then be open to hearing information about gays and lesbians and their lifestyles.

It is a tricky task to offer education and advice to clients without conveying the idea that their feelings are wrong. Clinicians need to empathize with their clients and show they understand their feelings. They need to wait for signs that their parent-clients really know they are understood, such as when their clients vigorously agree with the therapist's reflections and also when they seem relieved that someone finally, truly understands them. Eventually the clients' discussion of their feelings will slow down and they will seem as if they have exhausted the topic, with nothing new to add. When therapists think their clients believe that their feelings have been heard, it might be time to suggest they get information on gay and lesbian people and perhaps offer a referral.

Sometimes a bit of trial and error is called for. Carl Whitaker used to advise family therapists to "learn to retreat and advance from every position that you take." If parents seem unwilling to accept referrals for information when offered, back off and return to exploring and empathizing with their feelings.

SIGNS OF HOPE. In addition to offering support and empathy, it would also be helpful for practitioners to communicate a realistic sense of hope to parents during this phase. As a matter of fact, the therapist should not let even the first session end without giving a message of optimism. Parents in this study described feeling relieved when they learned through PFLAG or from their understanding friends and relatives that they would eventually feel better about their children's homosexuality. Some even identified benefits to having a lesbian daughter or gay son, such as increased honesty in family relationships. Parents at the beginning of the discovery stage might not be ready to hear this message, but clinicians can tell them that, based on the experiences of other parents, it is unlikely they will feel very badly for a long time.

The good news is that if parents are seeking help from a therapist after learning their child is gay it is likely their intent is to find ways to adjust to this information as well as to maintain the family. Thus the therapist should align with this positive component of the parents' motivation by offering them hope that they will eventually feel better. This hope is realistic—the stories of these families strongly suggest that it is indeed possible for families not only to survive but to flourish after a child comes out—as we shall see.

Youth

It would also be a good idea to assess children separately, at least initially. Sometimes, because they are feeling so raw, exposed, and reactive, they may have distanced from their parents or shut down in an effort to get some breathing space to protect themselves. In addition, the blanket of parental reassurance Ellie mentioned is often just not available at this time, and children are feeling angry and confused that their parents are not able to offer the support they need.

During family discovery it might be the professional helpers in the child's life who offer that comforting blanket. Like their parents, gay sons and daughters also need a place, away from the family, to vent their complex mix of emotions including fear, relief, anger, frustration, and sadness. The relationship with the therapist or counselor is an ideal place for this.

Like their parents, once they feel heard, young lesbians and gays might be more amenable to education about their parent's reactions and more receptive to potential reframes of their parents' seemingly insensitive behavior. Young people may need to be reminded how difficult it was and how much time it took for *them* to come to terms with their sexual orientations. Therapists can then point out that their parents also need time to get through their own processes. Reframing parental reactions as part of a normal and progressive process, similar to their own adjustment, can go a long way in helping young people not to personalize their family reactions and to avoid participating in hostile interchanges that will only make things worse.

Clinicians need to make sure that their young clients are not trying to get reassurance by demanding immediate approval and acceptance. I know of no children who have won parental acceptance in an argument. As will be described in the next chapter, sometimes, in certain circumstances, mild pushing on the part of the child can be helpful. However, bitter verbal warfare, initiated by children, can backfire and is, in fact, unnecessary in circumstances where parents are already making some effort to adjust by seeking therapy.

Finally, young gays, particularly those whose parents are seeking therapy to help them adjust, have good reason to be hopeful, and clinicians can point this out. If a parent is in any way taking an active role in trying to adjust, such as reading books or researching online, the prognosis is good, and it is likely that parents' feelings will improve. The seventy-six mothers and fathers in this study found ways to eventually adjust to the news that their daughter or son was gay, so, even though it is not a sure thing, recovery is indeed possible for parents, particularly for those who are seeking help and information.

Getting Outside Support

No man or woman is an island—nor should anyone try to be during a crisis. It is of utmost importance that people access social support during difficult times, and the coming-out period is no exception. Speaking structurally, the boundaries around family systems in crises must loosen up to allow members to receive necessary assistance outside the family walls.

This is particularly important for young, coming-out gays and lesbians who are vulnerable during a difficult time, in need of reassurance and support, but feel distant from their parents. It is advised that therapists and counselors work with their young clients to take an inventory of the people they can lean on during this period. With whom can they talk about their anger at and disappointment with their parents and their fears that they will never be accepted? As we know, for people coping with the emotional ravages of stigma there is something healing about finding a group of others like themselves (Corrigan and Watson 2002). Do the young clients have gay and lesbian or even understanding straight friends they can rely on?

If not, they can be connected to a community of LGBT young people through helpful Web sites. Out proud (http://www.outproud.org/) and the Gay, Lesbian, Straight Education Network (www.glsen.org) are excellent sites where youth not only can get information but can also join online chats with others like themselves.

However, a word of caution is in order. Children must be made aware of Web-related safety issues. They need to understand that some people online are not who they say they are, and sexual predators, unfortunately, are not unheard of on these Web sites. So, if they decide to meet an online acquaintance in person for the first time, it should be done in a public place, preferably with a known friend or, depending on the child's age, a trusted adult.

Parents who are struggling with the news that a son or daughter is gay and don't know where to turn need a lifeline—something or someone to assist them in coping with their feelings of guilt, self-blame, and isolation as well as help them deal with the prospect of their own stigmatization as parents of lesbians and gays. For such parents, Parents, Families, and Friends of Lesbians and Gays (PFLAG) can be an invaluable source of needed information and sustenance. PFLAG (www.pflag.org/) is a national organization that provides information about lesbian, gay, bisexual, and transgender (LGBT) people and sponsors support groups for their parents. Support groups are held at local chapters throughout the country where fathers and mothers can receive guidance and emotional support from a community of parents who, for the most part, have grown to accept their gay children.

Thus clinicians might want to refer parents of families in the discovery (and subsequent) stages of family adjustment to PFLAG as an adjunct to psychotherapy. An excellent, brief, easy-to-read booklet is available on their Web site, which addresses many of the concerns parents typically experience when they first learn a daughter or son is gay, http://www.pflag.org/fileadmin/user_upload/Publications/Daughters_Sons.pdf.

It is worth noting that even though PFLAG has helped many parents, reports of a small number of mothers and fathers in this study suggest that PFLAG might not be for everyone. Such exceptions are discussed in the next chapter.

With regard to information and education, several excellent books that parents might find helpful are available and these include (but are not limited to): *Love Ellen: A Mother-Daughter Journey* by Betty DeGeneres (DeGeneres 1999). Also, *Beyond Acceptance: Parents of Lesbians and Gays Talk About Their Experiences* by Carolyn Griffin, Marian Wirth, and Arthur Wirth (1997), *Straight Parents, Gay Children* by Robert Bernstein (2007), and *Fortunate Families: Catholic Families with Lesbian Daughters and Gay Sons* by Mary Ellen Lopata (2003).

Therapists are also advised to encourage parents to seek other sources of social support from nonjudgmental friends, relatives, and colleagues. As we will see in chapter 4, parents were greatly assisted by supportive, enlightened, nonjudgmental confidants, not necessarily therapists or PFLAG members, who helped them cope with their feelings of mourning and self-blame.

Based on the findings of this study, clinicians might want to normalize and even prescribe some family distance during the family discovery crisis. Temporarily retreating from each other emotionally can take pressure off relationships during this difficult time and give parents the space they need to work through their most difficult feelings, including their guilt. It can also give youth a much needed opportunity to adjust to the fact that their secret is out. Elsewhere I describe how deliberate, short-term, emotional distancing along with brief, superficial interactions can help family members stay connected, at the same time allowing them the emotional space to work through their feelings (LaSala 2000), and I recommend this for families who are struggling with the challenges of the family discovery phase. Once parents work through their most intense initial emotional reactions, and youth feel less embarrassed and exposed, the family will be ready for family sessions.

Working with Fathers

As we have seen in this chapter as well as in chapters 1 and 2, young respondents were particularly nervous about telling their fathers they were gay or lesbian. This could be related to the distance the youth experienced with their fathers as they grew up. It was not unusual for children to tell mothers they were gay and then for the mothers to tell fathers. In some families, children and fathers never directly discussed the youth's homosexuality. As stated repeatedly, it is not uncommon in American families for fathers to be more distant from their children than mothers, and this could at least partially explain these findings. However, from a family therapy viewpoint, relaying such important information indirectly through a third party could be seen as an indicator of an emotional triangle in the family—typically not a good thing (Nichols and Schwartz 2008). Under such circumstances, not only do mothers run the risk of becoming exhausted, but the father-child distance is perpetuated as both miss the opportunity for honest, satisfying communication.

Based on these findings, it is recommended that therapists pay special attention to fathers in their work with these families. Whenever possible, fathers need to be included in treatment and encouraged to talk directly about their feelings regarding their children's sexual orientation. Distant or relatively silent fathers might be harboring deep distress or, conversely, might be less disapproving than expected. Either way, fathers need to be brought into the fold, included as much as possible in the family work.

Furthermore, the therapist must be careful to avoid taking sides against distant or hostile fathers. Jay talked about how easy it was to make his father a scapegoat, and he might as well be speaking for the many frustrated mothers, children, and therapists who find themselves doing just that. Practitioners must resist this tendency and help the family do so as well. Instead, clinicians should facilitate open dialogue between fathers and children without interference from the mother or the therapist. Keep in mind, even a father who presents as an ogrelike bigot can be hiding considerable worry for his child along with shame that he was not man enough to raise children who are all entirely heterosexual. Furthermore, as the findings from some of the families in this study suggest, family members may collude in ways that keep fathers distant. Active engagement and careful assessment could help determine if fathers are suffering in silence and/or are potential, newly discovered resources for the youth as well as the mother who is having difficulty accepting the news that her daughter or son is gay. More tips on engaging fathers of gay and lesbian children are offered at the end of chapter 4.

Family Therapy

So how is the clinician to know when the family is ready for conjoint family therapy? Sadly, there is no fail-safe formula to offer that will work in each and every situation. There is no substitute for careful, sensitive, thoughtful assessment, and this is especially true when working with these families.

Having said that, a general guideline for family therapy to be productive is that family members, particularly parents, need to at least be open to understanding each other's perspectives. In the midst of their feelings of guilt and mourning, can parents begin to see that their child is seeking honest communication along with acceptance and reassurance? Children might react to parent's feelings with some version of "You just don't understand!" and they would be right—parents probably don't fully understand. That's why they need their children and the therapist to help them do so.

Can children recognize that their parents need time to adapt to the news of their sexual orientation and their reactions are most likely temporary? One indication that family therapy is appropriate is if at least one member of the family can speak to the others in a calm, rational manner and can be coached to use "I" statements about what she is thinking or how he is feeling, such as "I am worried about you getting HIV" or "I told you I was gay because I wanted us to have an honest relationship."

The previously mentioned advice from Carl Whitaker about knowing when to retreat is also relevant to this situation. I always tell my students who are nervous about bringing angry, anxious family members together, exposing children to family conflict, that whatever happens when they are together in session is no worse than what they experience at home—so it is extremely unlikely that a premature family therapy session will do any additional, permanent damage. As a matter of fact, even if things go awry, it might be important and validating for a clinician to witness and then point out the family's damaging interactions. If discussions deteriorate into destructive criticism, contempt, defensiveness, hostility, and withdrawal that cannot be stopped, then the therapist can orchestrate a mutual "retreat" by stopping the session and postponing future family sessions until people are calmer and less reactive.

POSITIVE REFRAMES. Throughout the family adjustment trajectory, but especially during family discovery, there are two important truths for the family therapist to remember: 1. Parents want their children to be happy, healthy, and make them proud, 2. Children want their parents to love, support, and be proud of them. Almost all family communication, no matter how combative, have these wishes driving them, and, like a scuba diver excavating sunken treasure from the ocean floor, it is the therapist's job to help the family reach through their anxiety, anger, guilt, loss, and conflict and bring these unspoken wishes to the surface.

A lot of this work will be a combination of reframing and encouraging people to "go deeper" and discuss whatever feelings lie beneath the surface of their anger and combativeness. Instead of attacking surprised or intolerant parents, children can be coached to try to understand their points of view and find effective ways to ask for what they need. A statement such as "You are such a bigot—being gay is natural and normal—why can't you see that?" is translatable into "Please love me and accept me for who I am. I need you to help me feel stronger." Therapists might reframe the young person's statement with a comment such as "You care very much what your parents think about you and you want their help and support. Can you find a better way to ask them for what you really need?" By hearing this intervention, even if the child cannot find a better way to ask for help, parents can gain an understanding of what their angry children are really seeking from them.

In the same vein, parents who exclaim "How can you choose this lifestyle? Don't you know what two men do together?" are in fact saying, in a disguised version, "I would hate to see you get hurt or do something that will cause you humiliation or make you the target of prejudice—especially if it is something I caused. I am afraid that being gay will prevent you from living a happy life, and this fear breaks my heart." In this case, the therapist can encourage the parents to share these fears with their children in a way that can open up a needed discussion about what it means to be gay, that it does not preclude a happy and healthy life.

During their interviews, several parents told me that, besides me and their child, they had never known any other gay people. Parents of newly out gay children heard me speak at a PFLAG meeting or some other function in which I was recruiting respondents and were fascinated (and relieved) to learn of a gay man who had a successful career, a long-term relationship, and who seemed happy—so they wanted contact with me up close. Thus it cannot be underestimated how isolated and uninformed these families can be and how worried they are for the future of their children. Successful therapy during this phase—perhaps all family therapy—is about getting family members to understand the ways in which their conflicts and distance hide deep yearnings for love, reassurance, acceptance, and relief from fear.

There is much more to say about family sessions, and further suggestions will be presented in later chapters. As the respondent families traversed the family adjustment trajectory, particularly as they progressed from family discovery to recovery, they recalled experiences that suggest what can help and what can impede family adjustment, and these findings have important implications for therapy with gay and lesbian families.

CHAPTER 4

Family Recovery

Close scrutiny will show that most crisis situations are opportunities to either advance or stay where you are.
— MAXWELL MALTZ

NYONE WHO HAS EVER BEEN CAUGHT IN A VIOLENT STORM knows what it is like to be pummeled by pounding rain and roaring wind as the skies crackle with lightning and explode with thunder. Fortunately, there always comes a point when the skies start to lighten, the thunder begins to sound a little more distant, and the downpour slows ever so slightly—the storm is not yet over, but soon it will pass.

Virtually all models of family crisis identify a stage in the process during which the family is just beginning to recover. As described earlier, a family crisis is an interaction between the distressing event, how the family defines the event, and the family's coping ability. To pull through, families mobilize existing and new resources, restructure themselves, and redefine the meaning of the crisis event, making it less overwhelming and more manageable (Hill 1971; McCubbin and Patterson 1983). The family enters the recovery stage once parents begin to adjust to the news that a son is gay or a daughter is lesbian.

About half the parents described how their feelings about their children's homosexuality improved with time. Parental self-blame and mourning seemed to decrease within six months from the time the child came out. By the end of the family discovery period, which lasted anywhere from one month to twelve months after the child came out, parents were less likely to be clinically depressed and anxious. Parents continued to worry about their children's future, but, for the most part, their guilt and grief seemed to dissipate.

So what is it that led to this upturn in parental emotional states and subsequent improvements in parent-child interactions? Getting educated was one factor that helped, finding empathic and positive-thinking confidants was another. However, it is too simplistic to consider parental improvement as solely a function of educational activities such as reading books and visiting helpful Web sites. The interactions parents experienced both inside and outside the family were important contributors to family recovery. In particular, the child's behavior, emotional state, and appearance along with parent-child interactions also played significant roles in parental (and therefore family) resolution.

Parental Adjustment: What Helped?

Sharing and Support

As stated earlier, when a family is in crises, the boundary around the family system needs to loosen up, becoming more permeable to allow the family to get outside help (Carter and McGoldrick 1999; Hill 1971). Anyone who has ever had a difficult personal problem and found someone empathic to talk to knows the soothing relief that occurs when you get things off your chest—and therapists have long known the healing power of attentive listening (Nichols 1995a: Rogers 1951; Teyber 2000).

However, the majority of parents in this study did not enroll in professional psychotherapy. Instead, they turned to members of a support group, understanding friends, coworkers, their hairstylists, nonjudgmental relatives, and lesbian or gay people they already knew. These confidants normalized not only the parents' feelings but offered them a sense of hope. A nonjudgmental listener or a support group served as a sounding board to which parents could vent their feelings of guilt and sadness. Through these relationships, parents learned that their children's homosexuality was not their fault and that happy, productive futures for their sons and daughters were still entirely possible.

Parents, Families and Friends of Lesbians and Gays (PFLAG)

Suppose you are struggling with something so emotionally painful, you can barely stand it. You can't sleep, you can't eat, you are tearful and worried most of the time, and things are made worse by the feeling that you must hide your problem because, if others knew, you would be ostracized. You don't know what to do with yourself. It seems as if you are the only one experiencing these problems—so you feel very, very alone. Then, to your relief, you find a group of people, some just like yourself, experiencing the same difficulties yet finding ways to cope.

In this study fifteen families were recruited from PFLAG chapters in New York City, Philadelphia, and throughout the state of New Jersey. Like most of the parent respondents, the mothers and fathers in these families recalled feeling distressed, isolated, and alone when they initially learned that their daughters and sons were gay. At PFLAG group meetings they found, to their enormous relief, that there were other parents who had been through the same experiences and who had survived to eventually adjust and even become proud of their lesbian and gay children.

Jay's mother Adele described how, four years ago, she initially felt anxious and even panicky when her son told her he was gay. After several months of nervous worry, she went on the Internet to search for information and discovered PFLAG. She found a local chapter within driving distance from her home. At her first few meetings she experienced a great sense of relief as she discussed her grief, fears, and regrets with other people who had wrestled with the same feelings. In the depths of her despair she began to see a flicker of hope as she listened to the stories of others who had pulled through such difficult times. When asked what was so helpful about PFLAG, Adele remarked, "Just being able to share with people going through the same thing that you have gone through. And being able to hear that you come out on the other side of the tunnel, eventually, and that it takes time."

Janet, the previously quoted psychiatrist who became very depressed upon learning that her son Robert was gay, described how the healing power of the passage of time, combined with participating in PFLAG meetings to share her feelings, contributed to her adjustment.

> Well, first of all, it is nice to just have a place to spill whatever you want to say . . . the angry, horrible thoughts. I really felt relaxed about expressing them there. I really think time is, frankly, the most important thing.

I think there is some process that happens with any emotional trauma. I don't know what it is that the human being does, but I think we come to grips with things. But also for me it is helpful to talk . . . it is helpful just to be able to not feel like I have to hold things in. So it was important for me to talk about it to whomever I could. I do think PFLAG helps because it is an opportunity to talk with people who want to hear you. So you go there and you know that it is OK to talk about this.

Upon learning of her twenty-year-old daughter's lesbianism, Rachel, a divorced museum curator living in a wealthy suburb feared that her daughter Beth was destined for a life of loneliness and depression. When she first learned Beth was gay, she struggled with self-blame and worry to the extent that she began a course of antidepressant medication. However, at the time of her interview, which was four years after learning of her daughter's sexual orientation, Rachel observed:

Beth once said to me, "Are you disappointed, Mom?" And I remember I said, "I don't feel disappointed . . . " What I felt was . . . how do I explain this? I felt disappointed because I thought maybe she wouldn't have a home or children or a kind of life I imagined . . . initially because I was ignorant. And PFLAG helped me more with this than anything. Unless you want to live in a small town in a conservative state, gay people who are productive can have any life that they want. You might have to walk on eggshells here and there, but in general the world is open. At the beginning I was disappointed only in that I would have liked a son-in-law, because I never had a son. But I don't think about that anymore. I love Beth's girlfriend, and, in fact, we were just talking today. Yeah, I was disappointed that there wouldn't be a son-in-law and I was disappointed because of the clichés in my head and the ignorance. Ignorance is a pervasive problem for parents of gay children.

PFLAG meetings had a normalizing influence that was comforting and reassuring for attendees. At PFLAG meetings Rachel met other parents who appeared to be "normal," and this helped her a great deal. Rachel was quoted in the previous chapter as saying homophobia "has got to be burnt out of you" and her full response is found here:

Well, I walked into a room, and who did I meet? I met my friend Carol from Short Hills and my friend Lois from Montclair . . . and all these other middle- and upper-class people . . . and, this is going to sound horrible . . . I thought I would meet crazy people . . . that all the parents of gay children would be crazy people. Now, am I a crazy person? No. Instead I met all these educated people who are lovely . . . who have become my friends . . . who have lovely kids who are gay. And I met people who I can identify with who had the same questions, some of whom were far down the road . . . and they were laughing about us. . . . They told me, "You are not alone." They make you realize it's not a tragedy to have a gay child. It is just something you need to learn about. So it is an extraordinary tool . . . because I don't think there are many of us out there who aren't brought up in homophobia, including gay people, and it has got to be burnt out of you.

Scholars have recognized the healing power of group affiliation for stigmatized people (Corrigan and Watson 2002; Frable, Wortmen, and Joseph 1997). Persons who face censure, such as the mentally ill or lesbians and gays, can develop a positive self-identity by finding others who share their stigmatizing characteristic. From others they can learn the important skill of externalizing the cause of their emotional distress—that it is not that there is something wrong with *them*, but rather that those who persecute them are misinformed or ignorant. A positive group experience that helps them avoid the psychological ravages of stigmatization and the attendant self-loathing can serve as a vehicle through which persecuted people can bolster their self-esteem.

At PFLAG meetings parents learn two important lessons: that there is nothing wrong with being gay and that their children's homosexuality isn't their fault. Parents learn to recognize that society's norms regarding sexuality and gender are overly narrow and restrictive; they also develop the ability to be critical of society—an essential skill for family members of gays and lesbians (and also bisexual and transgender persons) to survive in a world that marginalizes and oppresses them.

THE DOWNSIDE OF PFLAG. By now you're probably thinking that PFLAG is the perfect referral for parents who are struggling with the news that their child is gay, and you're ready to refer all parents of gay kids to the local chapter. This is understandable, considering the experiences of the previously quoted respondents along with countless others who have benefited from participating in these support groups. However, whether it be shoes or support groups, one size never fits all. Despite its many potential benefits, the PFLAG experience could be less than positive for some people.

Clara, a devout Catholic mother, whose daughter Daria was a graduate student, attended only two meetings because she felt that she could not talk about how her deep faith conflicted with her feelings about homosexuality lest she be judged by other group participants as small-minded. Joe, a previously quoted father, who had been active in the local PFLAG chapter, stopped attending meetings when political advocacy and lobbying eclipsed discussions of parental support. A third woman described the way in which her PFLAG experience overwhelmed her by "throwing too much at me at once." She came to her first PFLAG meeting in an emotional crisis and was nonplussed by the information other parents were discussing, namely, same-sex marriage and gay adoption, things she was far from ready to think about in terms of her son.

Thus it is important to recognize that, despite its potential benefits, some parents might be intimidated by PFLAG's unambiguously positive and, at times, activist approach. Members of PFLAG need to be mindful of this when new parents approach their chapters for help. Moreover, human service professionals ought to carefully assess parents to determine if they are prepared for (and will be able to benefit from) PFLAG's uniformly gay-positive approach. Like most interventions, accurate assessment as well as good timing is essential.

The Support of Trusted Confidants

When we decide to share our secrets, particularly those that carry shame, we need to find someone we can trust, not only to keep our confidences but also respect our feelings without condemning us. Most of the other parents recruited for this study did not attend PFLAG meetings, and many were unaware of its existence. As a matter of fact, several times during the study, the interviewers referred distressed parents to local chapters. There were other parents who were familiar with PFLAG but shied away from discussing such a distressing and personal matter with a group of strangers. Nevertheless, many of the parent respondents found it enormously helpful to share their painful secret with at least one nonjudgmental, tolerant, informed person. There was something about being able to talk openly to a friend or family member who would not judge them that helped allay their self-blame, grieve their dreams of heterosexuality for their children, and calm their fears.

This mother's twenty-two-year-old son came out to her two years ago. She recalled feeling deeply sad upon learning that her son was gay, but she also remembered the helpful assistance she received from her friends:

> I know I talked to Barbara, and I have another good friend, Ellen. Barbara is my age, Ellen is ten years younger. These are all generations that are very accepting. Ellen has a seven-year-old son, and I remember her saying to me, "It would be fine if my son was gay. That would be fine as long as everything else is good. He is healthy and all." You know this deep down, but to have someone tell you this is good too.

What seemed to help most was that these confidants demonstrated acceptance, knowledge of gay and lesbian issues, and had open-minded attitudes. As stated by this mother of an eighteen year old who came out two years ago:

> I have a real good friend who is ten years younger than me and she's the one person I would talk to about it and I would be falling to pieces about how she's going to face prejudice and all. And my friend said, "No, you don't understand . . . maybe people your age feel that way, but at my age it's very accepted." She said it's not a big deal. So, fortunately, that's what I did, talk to a friend [who] just had a completely different perspective. That helped a lot.

Mothers weren't the only ones who found relief in compassionate, positive-thinking friends or family members. This next father, Frank, the previously quoted butcher, talked about how upset he was when he first found out his daughter was a lesbian because he so wished for a "normal" life for her, complete with husband and children. At the time of the interview, which was a year after his daughter Wanda came out to him, he still became tearful thinking back on those difficult times. Frank said that his friend's problems with his own daughter led him to reflect on his behavior:

> I remember one incident . . . she had a friend over the house and I wasn't very nice, I wasn't very pleasant. I ruined her evening, let's put it that way. And that made me feel like shit . . . And then my buddy was over and his daughter got pregnant at seventeen. We were downstairs talking, and I guess he's a little stricter than me—not as open. I think he's Puerto Rican [the baby's father], and he [my buddy] didn't even like her dating him.

Now she's pregnant, seventeen, in high school, senior year, and I'm giving him advice. "You can't turn your back on your daughter, you gotta help your daughter." And I knew it was going to bite me in the ass because here I am giving him advice and I'm turning my back on my daughter through denial. She didn't kiss me and I didn't kiss her for a year. I never even realized it, but the time does go. Then one thing led to another, and we did have it out, we had our peace. I told her I would not interfere with her life, and that was about after a year. And then everything seemed better.

When asked if anything else helped him with those difficult initial feelings, he described how telling his nephews, with whom he frequently went fishing, also helped him get over his feelings of sadness and anger:

RESPONDENT: Well, I first told my nephews. It was just like a big weight off your shoulders. And that helped.
INTERVIEWER: How did they react?
RESPONDENT: They had no problem with it.
INTERVIEWER: Why was that so important? Why was it so helpful?
RESPONDENT: Because I respect them and they had to know. I didn't want them to hear it from someone else . . . I wanted them to hear it from me.

Some of these important people in whom parents confided warned them they risked losing their children if they didn't accept them, and they gave these parents a kind of tough-love perspective. This next woman was grieving the heterosexual image of her daughter when she first found out, but found solace in speaking to a wise older woman with whom she enjoyed a close relationship:

I talked to her "grandmother" . . . I met this woman in Linden; her daughter started watching my daughter when she was little. I got very close to her and she adopted my daughter like a grandmother. We became very close, and my kids started calling her Grandmother. She has three daughters of her own, they are all hetero. But she is so open-minded—more so than I am. She is a grandmother and she still goes to these go-go bars and things. She said, "You can't disown her." I said, "I am not going to disown her, but I said this is wrong." She would sit and tell me, "No, there is something inside of them—they know. You can't tell them they are not that way and try to change them. It is not going to happen." So she helped a lot.

For other parents, the confidant they chose was not necessarily a close friend or family member but a gay person they knew would offer helpful advice. When she first learned her son was gay, this Latina mother of a twenty-one year old was very worried that he would be facing a difficult life marked by discrimination and abuse. However, she recalled how useful it was to talk to someone else she knew was gay:

> I did [tell it] to my hairdresser, and one of the things he said to me is the best thing I can do for him is be supportive and let him know I love him. He said to me that is the best thing, especially for teenagers. I remember him telling me it is really good the way I am accepting him and showing him love, because he knew of kids killing themselves. If the parents don't accept it, that is the worst thing for the kids. So I figured that is what I had to focus myself to do. And then I started losing the fear about what people would say. I made myself just get stronger about it, if anybody would ask me, I would just tell them. I just figure that people would accept it better if they know that you accept it. This kid is still going to school and work; he is not a bad kid. I have friends they have teenagers who have more problems with accidents, driving, drugs, or things. So to me it is just what kind of person you are.

A small minority of parents sought therapy to help them with their feelings about their children's sexual orientation. Rachel, the previously quoted museum curator who initially struggled with depression, said, "Absolutely I believe people need counseling. Counseling helps. PFLAG helps. . . . Also finding one friend who you have total trust in or your partner if you have one, where you can talk to someone who will be accepting."

"They're Born That Way and Can't Change"

There are many myths we are taught about homosexuality and parents in this study needed to find a way to unlearn them. To that end, parents sought education through PFLAG meetings and talking to others, as described in the previous section. They also pursued information through Internet sources and television programs like the *Oprah Winfrey Show*. Like the previously quoted respondent who confided in her daughter's "grandmother," parents felt it was helpful to learn that sexual orientation was innate and unchangeable. This disabled, unemployed mother of a twenty-five-year-old lesbian experienced self-blame and suffered with symptoms of anxiety and insomnia when her daughter Chrissy came out to her five years ago. It should be noted that Chrissy's uncle molested her when she was a younger child:

> I was thinking at the time that it was maybe because her father was never in her life. Or because of what my brother did to her that she turned on men. I was trying to blame it on that. But later I found out that wasn't it. I used to watch the *Rosie O'Donnell Show* a lot then. I would see her with her significant other, and Ellen DeGeneres. I love Ellen. She's great. But I also see that they have certain sides to them that remind me of Chrissy . . . I am like, "OK, this is not going to change, she is going to stay this way . . . they are not going to change, they are going to stick up for what they are, they are this way, and nobody is going to tell them any different." Ellen came out, and she had this show, I don't know if you've seen it . . . she called this girl a man's name, and actually it was a girl. And the girl started crying, saying, "Because of you I came out, now I can be happy." So I am like, OK, Chrissy is more calm, she is happy now. Everybody knows. She doesn't care any more. She knows this is who she is. She is not going to change.

The son of this next mother came out two years ago. When she first learned her son was gay, she worried for his well-being and she was particularly worried about AIDS. However, through talking with her friends, she came to the realization that being gay was inborn: "I don't think anybody has a choice about that. I think it's something that's innate in you; it's not something you're choosing to do. And I felt bad for him that he wasn't going to have the opportunity to have a child, a biological child really, and he still says he wants to have children . . . because I think he would make a good parent, but I just know it's going to be tough for him."

As you may recall from previous chapters, Bob, a stockbroker, experienced profound sadness and grief when he learned his daughter Ellie was gay. He went online, read books, joined PFLAG, and came to the following conclusions, which were helpful to his adjustment:

> There are two or three basic facts. Number one was that neither she nor I have any control over her sexual orientation . . . other than hiding it, maybe. And the second fact was if I didn't continue to love her and care for her, notwithstanding this, that I would lose her. I think that something

in her, maybe genetic isn't the right word, but something in her physical being, whether it is a particular wire or chemical, says, "I am attracted to women as opposed to men." . . . It was there at birth and had nothing to do with environment or upbringing or anything like that. It happens to be the way she was hardwired, and you either accept it that way or you lose a child.

IS IT REALLY INNATE? When something bad happens to us, in the midst of our pain and suffering there is something comforting in knowing that there was nothing we could have done to avert the misfortune and its consequences. What's happened is beyond our control; we must accept our fate and move forward. Indeed, most adjusted parents in this study came to the conclusion that their child's homosexuality was biologically based. Their child was simply born gay, and this could not be changed. This finding is consonant with available research, which suggests that people who believe homosexuality is biologically determined, rather than a choice, are more likely to be tolerant and accepting of gay people (Sheldon et al. 2007). This makes sense, because if people believe that it is impossible to change someone's sexual orientation then intolerance toward homosexuality would be as illogical and as cruel as mistreatment of someone because of the color of their skin or their left-handedness. However, even though some research findings suggest biological or genetic determinants (Blanchard 2001; Brown et al. 2002; LeVay 1991), the available evidence is far from conclusive (Sheldon et al. 2007).

Conversely, some therapists, religious leaders, and academics believe homosexuality is a psychological or moral choice that can be altered and indeed should be. There are several conservative religious organizations like Exodus International (http://www.exodus-international.org/) and Homosexuals Anonymous (http://www.ha-fs.org/) who claim to have helped people change their sexual orientation through prayer, counseling, or a combination of both. Moreover, there are mental health professionals who practice what are called reparative or conversion therapies designed to make gay people straight. The best-known group of such clinicians is the National Association for Research and Therapy of Homosexuality (NARTH), led by psychologist Joseph Nicolosi. He and his followers claim that gays and lesbians suffer from a damaging blend of childhood trauma, shaming in their families of origin, and chronic unmet needs for love and affection from their same-sex parents. Reparative therapy is designed to help gay clients become heterosexual by working with them to ameliorate the toxic feelings stemming from their damaged childhoods (http://www.narth.com/docs/niconew.html).

Spitzer (2003) has undertaken research with two hundred women and men who underwent reparative therapy and believed themselves to be "cured" of homosexuality, as evidenced by their ability to engage in sexual relations with the opposite sex, marry heterosexually, and conceive children. Many in the psychotherapy community argue vociferously that such "treatment" is unethical because homosexuality is not an illness—rather the "illness" is societal intolerance of sexual and gender behaviors falling outside restrictive societal norms (Jenkins and Johnson 2004; also see the debate in Drescher and Zucker 2006). It is also important to note that, despite reports like Spitzer's of individuals undergoing reparative therapy and subsequently getting married and conceiving children (considered a "cure"), there is no evidence that this treatment permanently changes people's attractions to their own sex. In fact, there are many reports of people undergoing this "treatment" or others offered by ex-gay ministries who not only return to homosexuality but have also been traumatized by this so-called therapy (Besen 2003; Jenkins and Johnston 2004).

Challenges to the notion that homosexuality is innate and immutable also come from a vastly different camp. Some progressive, free-thinking scholars are also questioning the assumption that homosexuality is a permanent, central part of an individual's being. Taking a social constructionist view, they cast doubt on the idea that there is something such as a gay identity that is centered in a person's sexuality (Chauncey 1994; Jagose 1996; Stone Fish and Harvey 2005). Labeling oneself as gay or having a gay identity is a modern phenomenon in Western society. It is only in the past one hundred years or so that people with sexual attractions toward members of their own sex were defined or defined themselves as lesbian or gay. This label has operated as a way for people to organize their self-concept, identities, and social behavior. Constructionist thinkers argue that without social pressure many of us would be much less rigid about our sexual identities and behaviors and more likely to be sexually active with *both* sexes (Chauncey 1994; Jagose 1996). We might find that our sexual attractions change over time, based on life experiences, environment, mood, and emotional and physical attractiveness of potential partners. It bears emphasizing that these writers do not argue that same-sex attractions should be altered because they are wrong or sinful; rather, social forces have pushed people to develop primary and static identities as homosexuals, which would not happen if society accepted the full array of sexual expression.

Research and clinical literature suggests that sexual attractions and preferences, at least for lesbians and bisexual women, may change over time (Diamond 1998, 2008; Stone Fish and Harvey 2005). There is also evidence that some adolescents and young adults with same-sex attractions are refusing to label themselves or identify as gay because they do not center their identities on their current sexual feelings and behavior (Savin-Williams 2005).

The issue whether sexual orientation is permanent is made murkier when we consider bisexuality. Generally, sexual orientation is seen as dichotomous: one is either gay or straight. Social pressures have led some people to deny their attractions to members of both sexes. Unfortunately, for a long time, many people, including gays and lesbians, did not believe such a thing as bisexuality existed. Bisexuals were thought to be 1. people whose sex drives were so excessive that it didn't matter who they had sex with or 2. lesbian and gay people who were trying to avoid stigma by claiming to still be attracted to the opposite sex. Some also believed (and still believe) that bisexuality is a prelude to later announcing one's true gay sexual orientation, as indicated by the expression "bi now, gay later." Nevertheless, it is important to recognize that some people who later identify as gay identify themselves initially as bisexual. A small handful of the gay and lesbian youth in this study first told their parents they were bisexual in an effort to "test the waters" and see how parents would react before they told them the truth. However, it is inaccurate to believe that everyone who identifies as bisexual is really gay. Misrepresentations of true bisexual people have no doubt led to misunderstanding within and outside the lesbian and gay community and have perhaps contributed to keeping bisexual persons "in the closet." Therefore, some are confused when Anne Heche and Julie Cypher, ex-partners of Ellen DeGeneres and Melissa Etheridge respectively, embark on relationships with men. How could sexual orientation not be a choice if these women can switch their sexual and romantic interests?

Furthermore, if it is possible to swap sexual attractions, it is not surprising that parents might wonder if it would be feasible for their lesbian daughters to "change" and settle down with husbands. Having sat through a PFLAG meeting in which a woman announced that her "gay" daughter had begun a relationship with a man, I can tell you this information is disturbing for parents, particularly those who have accepted their child's sexual orientation based on the assumption that it is unchangeable. Sexual behavior and sexual orientation are complex topics, still shrouded in ambiguity and mystery, and current knowledge barely scratches the surface in terms of explaining sexuality and how it is influenced by social and biological factors.

Nevertheless, it is important to recognize that some (but not all) people who are in same-sex relationships—even some who identify as lesbian or gay—are sexually and at times emotionally attracted to members of both sexes (Diamond 2008). This could also explain why some who undergo reparative or conversion therapy are able to function heterosexually. Questions about the fluidity of sexual orientation are too complex to be settled in this book. However, it is important to be knowledgeable about what we know (and do not know) about bisexuality, social pressure, and ex-gay and reparative therapies in order to be prepared for parents' questions.

DOES IT REALLY MATTER? If we truly believe that it is acceptable to have sexual and romantic relationships with the same sex, then it shouldn't matter whether or not sexual orientation is changeable. If it is really OK, we should be as accepting of a person who has a relationship with a man and then a woman as we would of someone who usually eats vanilla ice cream and then decides to start eating pistachio. So what? Sex between two consenting adults, like eating ice cream, should be about pleasure, personal preferences, or expressions of love and affection, not about social rules and definitions.

However, in order to help our clients, we must (with understandable reluctance) leave Utopia and remember that the families who come to us for help live in a world that puts limitations and sanctions on people's sexual inclinations and behavior and exacts a price for those who don't follow the rules. Parents and their children need to find ways to cope with living in a world that stigmatizes same-sex attractions and relationships, and we need to understand this if we are to be helpful.

The Influence of the Child

As stated in the preface, the traditional way of thinking of parental adjustment goes something like this: 1. the parents get upset or angry when they learn their kid is gay; 2. their frightened, helpless children, who are only looking for love and acceptance, are victims of their parents' disapproval; 3. the parents get educated and become enlightened; 4. the parents feel better; 5. their attitudes toward their children improve; 6. the end. However, the findings of this study suggest that this story is too simple. Parental reaction and adjustment to the news that a child is gay or lesbian does not occur in isolation. The child's personal characteristics and the relationship she maintains with the family play a significant role in parental recovery, suggesting that this is, indeed, a *family* process.

Many parents (*n* = 17) mentioned how the personal characteristics of their sons and daughters helped them adjust to the news of their children's homosexuality. Parents reported that, if the child seemed mature, emotionally stable, happy, and confident, this helped them adjust. Parents who described their daughters and sons as "straight acting," meaning they did not manifest cross-gendered mannerisms, and indicated that their children were not sexually promiscuous were also likely to report that their adjustment was relatively quick. It is noteworthy that parents whose children's personal characteristics helped them adjust were the least likely to recall experiencing psychiatric symptoms when they first learned their children were gay.

As you might recall, Mike was the young man who attempted suicide after confessing to a priest in church. His father spoke of how his son's positive personal characteristics helped him adjust: "Well he is a good kid. So you could not help but like him. . . . If he were a head-banging, acid-dropping criminal, you would have a tougher time with it. . . . He has always been decent, honest, kind. He has moral values and ethics."

This next father, Allen, an engineer whose wife Janet was the psychiatrist quoted previously, claimed to have almost no problem adjusting to the news that his son Robert was gay. As you might recall, Allen has an older son from a previous marriage who is also gay. When asked why he had no trouble coping with Robert's sexuality, he proudly described his son's intelligence, creativity, and accomplishments.

> I look forward to you meeting Robert . . . he is a lovely kid, and of all the kids I worry least about him . . . He has just blossomed and has gained this part of what has enabled him to just be who he is. He is just so comfortable in his own skin. He knows who he is and he has just got so much promise. He can do whatever he wants to do and he will do well. He is smart and he is creative. And he is so far ahead of me at that stage in terms of his self-knowledge—it is just incredible. . . . Yes, I am sure that I really wouldn't have as easy of a time if either of my sons were flamboyantly effeminate. . . . My kids are anything but an embarrassment to me. They are really a source of pride.

Even parents who felt depressed or anxious when they learned their child was gay were helped to feel better by noticing and realizing the special qualities of their children. Frank became depressed and frequently tearful when he first learned that his daughter Wanda was a lesbian. However, he took comfort in the fact that she was honest and respectful: "She's a good kid. I just couldn't hold it against her. She never did anything to me. Always up-front. Yes, she didn't change. [She was] always respectful, helpful, the perfect kid. I'm not saying that because she's my daughter. If she was a bastard, I'd tell you."

Clara, the previously quoted devout Catholic who felt alienated at PFLAG, was depressed and anxious upon learning of her twenty-two-year-old daughter Daria's lesbianism because homosexuality went against her Church's teachings. However, in the two years since her daughter came out to her, her feelings improved, largely because of her daughter's qualities.

INTERVIEWER: How, if at all, have your feelings about your daughter's homosexuality changed over time?

CLARA: Yes, they have lessened. And that has a lot to do with how she is. Not so much me changing my mind with things. It is more Daria. I mean I read all this stuff, and it helps me a little bit, but what helps me the most is to see how she is growing up and to see that she is not a wild child. All the good things she does reassure me. . . . She has demonstrated that she is quite a capable person. She has traveled all around the world by herself and managed that. She has chosen a friend who is the most lovely person I have ever met. All these things say to me that she is on her own path, she is OK, and the signs look good. You know, to choose a friend who is so wonderful . . . looks good to me. I feel better.

If a child, particularly a son, did not appear to have many sexual partners, this also seemed to help. This mother reported:

Well, let's just say that my son has exhibited a very monogamous way of relating sexually. So he doesn't have multiple partners; he is always looking to have a committed relationship. He has just started out, but he has indicated that he is a very discriminating person. . . . OK, so the fact that he and his current boyfriend are monogamous and my son seems to be very discriminating would lead me to believe that they are going to be very responsible sexual adults. . . . We are surrounded by this conversation that gays are promiscuous, and you can't be in the world and hear it and not be influenced by it. But they [my son and his partner] have not exhibited that at all.

This is not to say that parents with well-adjusted, responsible "straight-acting" children did not still harbor concerns for them. This father, a construction worker, described his twenty-one-year-old daughter, who had come out three years ago:

Well, she seems to get along with just about anybody. She has her head on straight, and I think she is a mature individual. I listen to her when we do have conversations, and everything makes a lot of sense. She does talk to me about her relationships. She says she doesn't want to get really serious right now. I think that is mature the way she does that. That makes me feel a little better as far as her interaction with other people. How it is going to be in the business world is another story. I just don't know how that will be.

At the time of the interview, this next mother's eyes still welled up when she talked about how she felt three years ago when she first learned that her daughter was gay. During that period, she became depressed and began a course of Prozac. Nevertheless, her affection for her daughter and her desire to assist her helped this mother adjust:

RESPONDENT: She's adorable. It's hard criticize her or not to love her. If I feel bad, she feels bad. And it's hard to do that to her.
INTERVIEWER: OK. So, you try to feel better in some ways for her sake?
RESPONDENT: Perhaps. I don't do it consciously. But now I'm seeing that that might be.

Herdt and Koff (2000) found that if children seemed contented and adjusted when they came out, parents felt reassured, and the same was found in this study. This makes sense, whereby if one's gay or lesbian child seems happy, this contradicts the idea that lesbians and gays live sad, desperate, lonely lives in which they are constantly dodging persecution. This mother, who initially experienced pangs of sadness over the loss of a "normal" life for her son, reported: "I think his personality is very outgoing and he's charming and he can schmooze well and he seems comfortable with himself most of the time. And so the fact that he wasn't totally ripped apart by this made it easier for me. Had he been really sad about it, it would have made me, of course, sad."

Thus, seeing their children as likeable, adjusted, and happy and not engaging in stereotypical behaviors seemed to help parents adjust. It must be kept in mind that these parents were learning of their children's sexuality when they were becoming increasingly independent and autonomous. Therefore it is likely that if parents perceived their children as bright and confident and capable of handling the world, they were reassured that their children would be OK and, as a result, felt somewhat less troubled by their homosexuality.

It is possible that parents who felt guilt, grief, and worry but acknowledged their children were happy and healthy faced a kind of cognitive dissonance (Festinger 1962) in which they carried two contradictory perspectives: "Oh my God! Being gay is terrible—but my child seems happy." As stated in chapter 3, when people behave or experience something that is at odds with what they know or believe, they will change their way of thinking to decrease the inconsistency or dissonance. Needing to find a way to resolve the contradiction of a happy gay child may have pushed parents forward in terms of coping and adjusting. A means of reconciling the dissonance might be thinking that "if my kid is happy, how bad can it be?"

This does not mean that resolving the contradiction between their feelings and what they observed was a smooth process, or that parents did not still harbor worries for their children's futures. As a matter of fact, parental fears and worries seemed to persist no matter how adjusted and accepting parents eventually became. As we shall see later in this chapter, children's high-risk or cross-gendered behavior could aggravate parents' fears that their children would be targeted for mistreatment.

Improvement in the Family Relationship: Relief and Reciprocity

Another major factor contributing to the parents' adjustment was that they perceived improvement in their relationships with their children following the family discovery phase. As described in the previous chapter, a small number of families experienced parent-child relationship improvements immediately after the parents found out. However, close to a third of the parents described how, after a period of strain and distance, parent-child relationships improved, and this improvement was the primary factor that helped them adjust to the news that their daughter or son was gay. Once again, these enhanced family relationships seemed to have contributed to a cognitive dissonance for the parents in this study ("I hate that my child is gay! How awful!—But . . . not only does my child seem happier—our relationship is better!"), and the effort to reconcile this contradiction seemed to help parents move toward adjustment.

To further clarify what contributed to the relationships improving, it is important to remember how, during the family sensitization and family discovery periods, many of the children distanced to protect themselves. Speaking in structural terms, family subsystem boundaries became thicker, more rigid, and impermeable as distressed children distanced from their families, resulting in strained parent-child relationships. Then, burdened by the stress of hiding, isolation, peer harassment, difficulties in relationships with romantic partners, or worries for the future, children felt enormous pressure—enough to risk breaching this assumed boundary to come out. Like pent-up steam escaping from a valve, the youth were relieved of the pressure of having to hide, and grateful not to be rejected and thrown out of their homes, even if parents were clearly not happy with the news.

Perhaps all of us know what it feels like when someone with whom we have been close suddenly, and without explanation, distances from us. We might feel confused, insecure, even a little paranoid, thinking, "What have I done?" "Does this person hate me now?" When we learn that the strain had nothing to do with us, we feel relieved.

Now imagine what it feels like when the person who previously distanced from us starts demonstrating his gratitude for having us in his life. Once they got used to the idea that their parents knew their secret, and also realized they weren't going to be rejected, many of the children felt relieved, and this in turn led some to interact with their parents in more positive ways. For parents who were struggling, such interaction must have been like the spring sun melting a late winter snow. Even if they were feeling guilty and mournful and had distanced from their children right after the discovery, it must have been difficult to resist a newly appreciative child who had once been distant and irritable. Thus it makes sense that they began to interact more amicably with their children. Following the distancing and parental upset of the family discovery period, this parental warmth might have signaled acceptance—at least a little bit—of the child, who, in a circular pattern, responded with even more appreciation, which encouraged more positive parental response and so on.

Cynthia, an interior designer, initially felt depressed and struggled with self-blame when she learned her son Kenneth was gay several years ago. She recalled that, in the middle of his adolescence and before he came out, Kenneth grew distant and at times antagonistic. When asked what helped her adjust, Cynthia said talking to a gay friend allowed her to understand that her son's sexual orientation was not her fault. She also spoke of how the improved parent-child interaction in the months following her son's disclosure also helped her adjust to her son's sexual orientation. "He went back to his old self . . . where he was funny again, and he would call me and we would laugh and cut up and act silly. And we would talk again . . . His help was that he was very understanding and would talk to me when I asked questions. That all helped."

Kenneth, twenty-three years old, agreed that the relationship with his mother improved a couple of months after he came out, and, like many of the young respondents in this study, he perceived that his parents became more interested in his life:

> I think I must have felt liberated. Just because, finally, our relationship was open again, I wasn't really hiding anything else . . . I was returning to the relationship that I had before with my mother where we could talk about anything . . . I think things got better, our relationship was open. Like she wanted to know if my friend Jonathan and I were dating. . . . So now she could know things that she didn't know before.

Susan, a previously quoted mother, was devastated when she learned a year prior to our interview that her nineteen-year-old son Mitch was gay. When asked what helped her adjust, she offered: "The few months leading up to before we found out he was gay he was not a nice person. He was not pleasant to be around. He had a nasty streak. Then, once he told us he was gay, he went back to being this wonderful person. PFLAG also helped. Also meeting you [the interviewer—who spoke at a recent PFLAG meeting] helped."

Her son Mitch, it may be recalled, described his relationship with his mother as somewhat distant immediately after he came out. However, he would agree that his relationship with his mother became stronger once she got over the initial crisis of learning he was gay. He stated, "We are now pretty close . . . Well, yeah, because prior to coming out it was pretty strong. Coming out it was awful and also right after that. Where we are now is pretty good. So, yeah, it has fluctuated."

Tara, the eighteen-year-old chemistry student whose father was also a chemist, recalled her relationship with her mother and father right after coming out to them two years earlier: "It was still bad mostly. We didn't talk at all. Not until a couple of years, like two years ago, that I actually could sit down and have a conversation with my mother. . . . We would just get into fights." Her mother Dora had a terrible time with grief and depression immediately after she found out about Tara; she "felt as if my daughter had died." Now, two years after coming out, her daughter admitted, "Yes. My relationship with my mother is so wonderful. I can talk to her about anything and she'll be understanding about it. And I think that was like the one big hurdle I needed to get over." When asked what if anything helped her adjust, Dora stated, "Just time, that's all. Time and the fact that we got closer. I think once that barrier was down . . . then she became a lot more open. We get along a lot better now."

Her father Luke remembered how, immediately after his daughter came out, "I withdrew from her and I just did not want to even think about it. No discussion . . . I didn't want to answer questions. I just wanted to pretend it wasn't happening." Tara remembered it the same way. "He withdrew. I probably withdrew even more and I'm sure he did as well." And now, as she describes her relationship with her father, "It's gotten much better. . . . Oh, God, yes. I mean, it's much more comfortable to talk to him about almost anything now." Luke would agree: "I'd have to say we're closer. . . . We joke around more now than we ever did."

This next mother, Rena, recalled feeling depressed and experiencing frequent crying jags after she found out her daughter Lily was a lesbian about eight months before their interview. She also described how tearful and afraid her daughter was to tell her she was gay. After a difficult initial few weeks, this mother could say that she and her daughter had grown closer because Lily seemed happier and this helped Rena adjust.

> I got more involved with her. I'd seen her walking around the house and laughing a couple of times. She used to do that when she was little, like she would be thinking about something funny and she would laugh out loud. I hadn't seen her giggle or laugh in a while . . . a long time, I will say a couple of years. But, by herself, she just seemed more at peace with herself. She even made a remark to me that we are paying the price for her having some peace of mind. That made me feel bad. I said, "I don't feel like that."

Rocky, Rena's husband and Lily's father, stated:

All I can tell you is, since she told us—at least initially—she was much happier. And she does look much better. She goes and gets her hair done in a
nice butch cut, she looks a little gayer. And her face looks a little nicer, takes
care of her skin better. She wears nicer outfits. I think initially it was also she
felt good about it too, telling us. . . . Believe it or not, I think we are a little
closer. I told you, she was hard to hug, I think I've hugged her, physically
touched her more, since she told us. I think we are both relieved, and maybe
Daddy is a little bit more thinking that she needs it. . . . [now] yes, she lets
me do it [hug her]. It was obvious that she was an unhappy child.

Remember Jennifer, introduced in chapter 4, who was so appalled and
embarrassed when her mother Martha found her diary and discovered she
was gay, even though her mother expressed nothing but support and acceptance? A few months after Martha found out, Jennifer got used to the idea
that her mother knew, and the relationship between them improved to the
extent that Jennifer now said, "There is no hiding, no secrets. We can talk
about anything. 'Cause she knows my girlfriend and she knows a lot about
me and my lifestyle. I don't have to hide anything."

An additional factor that may have contributed to this type of reciprocity in the family was that some children saw their parents working hard to
understand their sexual orientations. Children were grateful to see parents
making an effort, which in turn led them to feel and act positively toward
their parents. Lily, whose mother and father were quoted earlier in this chapter, remarked that, even though there was still some strain, things were better
since she had come out, and she attributed the improvement to her mother's
efforts, for which she was appreciative:

I still feel that there is a lot about me that she doesn't get, she doesn't know.
But we are trying, she is trying, so I'll give her that. She kind of has all these
ideas that you need to get through. I mean she was always there for me, but
my life was never really like the topic of conversation. Now my life is the
topic of conversation, so it is extra attention. I feel like I am back in junior
high again where the parents are over you, kind of, watching everything
you do, asking questions. But it is a good thing, because they need to get
to know me a little bit better.

Mitch recognized and was grateful for his mother's attempts to become more informed:

> Yes. At first, it made it harder to talk . . . both of us found it harder to talk to each other. I would say things were bad up until like three months ago when my mom finally started, like, reading up on homosexuality and educating herself by, like, going to the library and reading everything she possibly could while trying to go to work and being a mom. Then I started to realize, "Wow, she really is trying." And things started to get better. . . . We had a little bit of fighting but overall we definitely strengthened our relationship if not exceeded the prior expectations.

This next mother felt as if her daughter had died when she told her she was gay two years ago, but described how the relationship improvement that followed helped her cope and become less distressed: "Because she's more open to me. She talks to me more . . . Because I accepted her for what she was. I mean, she thought I wasn't going to accept her, and I did, and she talks to me more about it, about herself and everything. She's more open to me." Her daughter agreed:

> And I don't know how to explain it, but that's when my relationship with my mom started growing a little bit more. Things started, I guess, blossoming, in a sense. She just wanted to know what was going on, and I told her. She was like, "Well, you know, if you ever want to, like, go walking around in the city with me . . . go in that little gay area you guys call the Village, we can . . . "—she's aware of this stuff. And I'm like, "Sure." She's like, "You know, you could always go with me into the city because I don't know if you met any friends that are gay yet." I'm like, "Oh, my God!"

Like dancers in a ballet, family members do not act in isolation; their behaviors are connected and coordinated. Based on these reports, it is possible to see how circular interactions created relationship improvements that, in turn, helped parents feel better. More specifically, children felt relief and some level of acceptance from their parents, even if it was a tiny bit, and their moods lightened. This was reflected in a new warmth and gratitude toward their fathers and mothers. Parents, even if they were distressed, were happy to see their children feeling better. They communicated their pleasure to their children, and this also improved their relationships, which again helped parents begin to feel a bit better about their children's homosexuality.

This pattern was further enhanced when children saw that their parents were trying to learn and understand more about lesbian and gay people. This led children to have better attitudes toward their parents, which then must have resulted in positive responses from their parents and improved parent-child relationships, and so on. Which came first, the chicken or the egg? Family therapists, trained to think systemically, usually don't care as long as the complementary patterns are understood and—when healthy and helpful—encouraged and amplified.

Fathers

It is no mistake that few fathers were mentioned in the previous section. One reason for the disparity is that not many fathers participated in this study. Another was that fathers and their children were less likely than mothers and children to report that parental adjustment was enhanced by improved family relationships. I have emphasized that the main action in most of these families occurred between mothers and children, and this is in line with how, in our society, the emotional, interactive components of parenting are relegated to mothers. In a complementary pattern, children and their mothers interacted while fathers remained on the sidelines. An exception to this was when an emotional void left by disapproving mothers was filled by some fathers, as in the cases of Tony and Joe, also Bob and Ellie described in chapter 3. When asked what helped him adjust to the news that his son Tony was gay, Joe recalled feeling gratitude, which fueled a reciprocal pattern of positive feelings and interactions between him and his son. Bob also described how his improving relationship with his daughter Ellie helped him adjust. Although there was no such case in this research, I recently was consulted by a therapist about a family in which the father had been more accepting of his son's sexual orientation than the mother, but, out of loyalty to his wife, the father communicated nothing but disapproval. This couple would refuse to talk to their son about his homosexuality and would not allow him to bring his partner home to join the family for holidays. Tragically, the mother died suddenly when the young man was in his early thirties. However, almost immediately following her death, the father began to reach out to the son's partner, inviting him to family events including the family's first Christmas after the mother's death. Although this is only one case, it demonstrates yet another way fathers might respond to disapproval, distance, and tension between a mother and her child.

A Negative Case Example

Another individual case is also revealing. During the course of this study, a woman called to talk about the research. She said that after her twenty-one-year-old daughter came out to her she threw her out of the house. She spoke of how difficult a child her daughter had been to raise, how bitterly the two fought during the daughter's childhood. Her daughter experienced academic and behavioral problems through much of her school career. During adolescence her daughter used and sold cocaine, frequently ran away from home, and was arrested several times. This mother angrily explained that her daughter's coming out to her as a lesbian was the last straw—she had had enough! She also stated that she might have been able to accept her daughter if she had been a well-behaved, well-adjusted child all along, but "This was just too much."

Before ending the call, I expressed the hope that someday this woman and her daughter would reunite and enjoy the type of relationship experienced by many of the parents in this study. But, since this woman did not give me her contact information, I will never know if she and her daughter ever experienced or will experience such a reunion. Nevertheless, this unfortunately negative case example is further evidence that who the child is and the relationship she has with the parent can play a significant role, positive or negative, in the parent's adjustment.

What Didn't Help?

When it came to children's influence on their parents' adjustment, there was good news and not so good news. As the report of this last mother suggests, not only could children be helpful to their parent's adjustment, they could also act in ways that might impede it.

Appearing Gay

The norms governing behavior and appearances in our society are so firmly entrenched that their violation can be deeply troubling. We are uncomfortable with short-haired women with deep voices who wear masculine clothing and work in construction. We are perhaps even more disturbed by males who sway their hips when they walk and wear cosmetics and feminine clothing. It is particularly upsetting for parents to see such behaviors in their children.

A few words are in order regarding the definition of cross-gendered behavior. First of all, it is common but incorrect to confound homosexuality and transgenderism. Even though many gays and lesbians manifest cross-gendered behavior and interests, transgender persons believe there is a mismatch between their physical sex and psychological gender. Transgender does not in any way indicate a person's sexual orientation: trans people can be heterosexual, homosexual, or bisexual. Thus it is important to recognize that transgenderism and homosexuality are separate and distinctly different phenomena.

Moreover, it is difficult to consistently define feminine and masculine behavior and define what constitutes effeminate mannerisms in a boy or what makes a girl a "tomboy." Femininity and masculinity tend to be subjective and, like beauty, are in the eyes of the beholder. Different people's eyes see different things, depending on their individual perspectives, which can be informed by their ethnicity and even the decades in which they were raised. Nevertheless, gender scholars agree that we expect men and women to act according to their prescribed roles and we become uncomfortable when people step outside them (Coltrane and Adams 2008; Kimmel 2004; Sandnabba and Ahlberg 1999).

Tomboy behavior in girls is generally considered acceptable, even charming, until puberty, and then such girls are pressured by parents and peers to abandon masculine pursuits such as climbing trees, rough contact sports, and dressing like a boy. Feminine or "sissy" behavior in boys is never acceptable, not even when boys are young (Bergling 2001). Such behavior invites stigma whereby it is perceived to be an indication of future homosexuality as well as a repudiation of maleness, which is seen as normal, healthy, and strong in contrast to what is perceived by many to be the dreaded alternative—homosexual—which signifies weakness, depravity, and shame.

It is important to recognize that there are indigenous cultures in which cross-gendered behaviors are respected or even revered as indications of intellectual and spiritual superiority (Carrier 1995; Gilley 2006; Herdt 1999). For certain Native American tribes, a man who acts like a woman or a woman with manly characteristics is seen as having "two spirits." Such persons are believed to be blessed by God, imbued with mystical holy powers (Gilley 2006). This is clearly not the case in Western cultures.

Like most of us, the parents who participated in this study were raised to believe that there are clear distinctions between the ways men and women were meant to act, and this may have contributed to the discomfort they felt when they observed cross-gendered behavior in their daughters, sons, and friends. As mentioned earlier, if children did not act in ways that made them recognizable as gay or lesbian, this seemed to assist and enhance parental adjustment. However, the converse was also true: parental adjustment was hindered if children behaved or groomed themselves in ways that were cross-gendered and corresponded to the prevailing stereotypes. Understandably, many of the parents felt that their children who chose to appear identifiably gay were putting themselves in harm's way. As a result, parents suffered a vicarious courtesy stigma, anticipating and feeling the suffering their children would experience at the hands of others.

When asked what, if anything, got in the way of her adjusting to the news that her daughter was a lesbian, this mother, who herself was a teacher, worried that her daughter would be assaulted or discriminated against because of her sexual orientation. "I fear for her financially. And I fear for the discrimination of others who look at her and her partner and go, 'You two are so gross. We have to blot you off the face of the earth.'" She had difficulty with her daughter's plain clothing, which she perceived to be unfeminine, and, like many parents of lesbians in this study, she was particularly disturbed by her daughter's adopted hairstyle. "I hate her ugly clothes. The hair she has grown out a little, but when she shaves it off completely it's hard."

Like many parents, this next father, a successful attorney, had practical concerns regarding his daughter's physical appearance: "The only thing that [my wife] and I both talked about was that, when Ally goes for a job, she is probably going to have to let her hair grow a little bit. She has a short haircut . . . and she'll probably have to dress a little bit more feminine for the job interview."

All the young people in this study were asked what, if anything, they did that impeded their parents' adjustment. Like most of the youth, Ally did not report that her appearance was in any way an obstacle to her parents' acceptance. Instead she believed that having her girlfriends sleep over was what made her parents uncomfortable.

For parents of gay men, if their sons acted feminine, this got in the way of their adjustment because they worried their boys would be targets of discrimination and harassment. They correctly understood that, among certain segments of our society, presenting oneself as a feminine man is like waving a red flag in front of an angry bull. In June 2006, Kevin Aviance, a gay performance artist who sported a feminine appearance, was brutally beaten on the Lower East Side of Manhattan, a neighborhood that is usually quite tolerant of LGBT persons.

Cynthia, the previously quoted widowed mother of Kenneth, described elsewhere in her interview that her adjustment to her son's homosexuality was helped by the improved communication and closeness between them after he came out. However, when asked if there was anything that got in the way of her acceptance, she admitted that his mannerisms troubled her: "His flamboyancy is hindering because I do get concerned about that sometimes. It seems to me that he is saying out loud, 'Somebody bother me!' You know how heterosexuals are so mean—some of them are horrible—and when you act flamboyant, to me you are just saying, 'Here I am.' And that worries me."

As in previous examples, her son, Kenneth had no idea that his appearance was an issue for his mother. It is curious that young gay respondents were not fully aware that their behavior and mannerisms could interfere with their parents' acceptance. There are several possible explanations for this. First of all, it could be once again that parents were protecting their children from their own fears. Parents might be aware that calling attention to such behavior in their children might resemble the harassment lesbians and gays experience in general society, and they didn't want to replicate it in their interactions with their children. A parent respondent in this study reported that she did not talk to her son about his effeminate behaviors: "I could have said something, but I knew it would hurt him."

A second explanation is that the children were unaware or did not want to recognize that there might be things they did to contribute to their parents' adjustment difficulties. This next mother threw her twenty-two-year-old daughter out of the house for a few days after she got what her mother perceived to be a particularly masculine haircut. Though the daughter currently lives back home, this mother is still very much disturbed by her clothing and hairstyle choices. It should be noted that, when I interviewed this mother, I sported obviously bleached-blond hair. This is not necessarily a gay hairstyle, but it is certainly considered untraditional and attention grabbing. Such a look could be a disturbing reminder to nervous parents of gay children (as it was to mine!) that their child was "out of the mainstream."

> Well, her hair right now is almost precisely like yours, with the bleaching, everything. And it's, I mean I don't like it at all. . . . But sometimes, she's gotten it cut, like, really close. You know? Like really close haircuts that I really couldn't handle. I made her wear a hat for a while, I mean—it's just too in my face. And some clothing . . . she basically only wears male clothing.

Her daughter was aware that her mother was bothered by her hair and clothing, but did not report that this got in the way of either parent's adjustment, despite the fact that she had been temporarily ejected from the home after she got a buzz cut.

Parents who did not perceive their children as presenting themselves in a cross-gendered manner might be disturbed by such behavior in their children's friends. For example, even if a son was not particularly feminine, if he associated with effeminate males this could make a parent uncomfortable. Susan, the previously quoted mother of a gay man, Mitch, explained her discomfort around one of her son's friends: "I found [one of his boyfriends] to be feminine. Mitchell said that he didn't think he was, but I even said to him, 'I think this young man is kind of feminine, Mitch. I don't care if you are homosexual or not, I just like men who look like men and act like men.'"

Other parents felt grateful that their sons were not effeminate, perhaps because such behavior in their children would make the parents themselves targets of stigma. Allen, the previously quoted father with two gay sons, felt lucky that his sons did not act feminine, but he talked about how shameful it must be if parents had an effeminate son:

> I am sure that I really wouldn't have as easy of a time if either of my sons were flamboyantly effeminate. My kids are anything but an embarrassment to me. They are really a source of pride. I think it takes a remarkable parent to really be able to be so accepting when the kids do stuff [like]that . . . it is a call for attention I think on their part. It's hard for me to imagine that a kid is not aware that there are ramifications for their family when

they do this and to be indifferent about it. . . . They must realize the way their parents might be affected by their own behavior. . . . And the fact is that my kids made it incredibly easy for me because they never did present themselves that way.

Janet, his wife, and the mother of the younger gay son, laughingly stated, "Once you have accepted that your child is gay then you want them to be gay but act straight . . . have a partner . . . adopt children. . . . It is all right if he is gay—just don't really *act* gay."

Failure to Launch

For parents, a child who grows into a happy, independent, successful adult is proof of a job well-done. It might be bittersweet to watch adult children leave the nest, but few American parents wish for the alternative. A child whose anxiety and depression interferes with his ability to hold a job or stay in school is a source of deep worry for a parent. In this study, parents' feelings about their children's homosexuality hinged on how well their children were doing when they found out.

Just as parents were reassured that being gay might not be so bad if their children seemed happy and confident, if their daughters or sons abused drugs or alcohol or suffered from depression or anxiety that interfered with their ability to attend school, work, or establish an autonomous social life, the parents' adjustment was impeded. They attributed such problems to their child's struggle with their homosexuality, and, more often than not, they were correct. Young respondents who were experiencing developmental problems had suffered the effects of stigmatization, harassment, and abuse by peers. These cases demonstrate how such experiences can affect children emotionally to the extent that they could develop debilitating emotional problems as adults. Parents perceived these difficulties as directly related to their children's homosexuality and, therefore, they interfered with their own ability to adjust as they continued to worry for their children.

Marie, the mother from Haiti, expressed a great deal of anxiety over her twenty-year-old son Chauncey's deep depression. When she first found out her son was gay, her anxiety escalated to the point where her blood pressure became dangerously high. At the time of our interview, one year after her son came out to her, she was struggling with insomnia, weight loss, and chronic anxiety out of concern for her son as well as guilt. She fretted that her son was gay because she left his father and raised him as a single parent.

The family lived in a section of New York City that is heavily populated by West Indian people who Marie and Chauncey described as extremely homophobic, harassing Chauncey continually since childhood. The men in their community noticed Chauncey's effeminate behavior and tight clothing, which contrasted with the oversized hip-hop styles usually worn in the neighborhood. They would yell "batty boy," an antigay slur used by West Indians, and kick and punch Chauncey when he walked down the street. Chauncey attributed his depression to this ongoing harassment.

Since graduating from high school, Chauncey had dropped out of two college programs, failed to hold a job, and was periodically suicidal. During their interviews, he and his mother were given referrals for low-cost, gay-friendly mental health services, and I contacted him several times afterward to persuade him to follow through. His mother loved and supported her son and clearly would not reject him because he was gay:

> He thought that I would disown him. But, when he told me, I said, "OK. Now I understand that you tell me the truth. Because I am your mother I will never hate you for that. This is your life, this is what you choose. . . . So instead of hating you, I have to support you." But, for me, no matter what I try to do to help him out, it doesn't work.

She attributed his problems to his struggles with his sexual orientation, for which she felt to blame and therefore, understandably, had a difficult time accepting.

Remember Adele's son Jay, who developed school phobia and a serious case of colitis when he was harassed by his peers? At age nineteen he came out to his mother and then, two years later, dropped out of college because he was experiencing a debilitating depression. At the time of the interview he was unemployed and living at home, not doing much of anything. Even though Adele supported Jay and was an active member of the local PFLAG chapter, she saw his homosexuality as the primary cause for his problems. When asked what, if anything, about her son helped or hindered her adjustment to Jay's homosexuality, Adele replied, "Well I think his medical issues contribute to my worry. Both the depression and the irritable bowl because they are so closely tied together."

A third young man, Harry, who, at fifteen had been sneaking out of the home in the middle of the night to meet men, was twenty years old at the time of our interview. He recalled how he developed school phobia in the sixth grade as a result of being bullied by other kids who perceived him to be feminine. His parents watched helplessly as their intelligent, promising son dropped out of high school at seventeen and moved into the home of a fifty-year-old man, which was where he was living when I interviewed him.

Ironically, living with this older man seemed to help Harry settle down. With his encouragement and support, Harry had enrolled in a local community college, and, by the time of our interview, he had successfully completed his first year. Nevertheless, shortly before her interview, his mother found pornographic pictures of her son posted online, and her anguish became almost intolerable. Though she loved her son deeply and would never reject him, she believed his homosexuality was at the root of his problems.

When a troubled person is a member of an oppressed minority, it is not easy to untangle the extent to which her difficulties are the result of oppression or other causes such as childhood trauma, family background, and genetics. In this study, young respondents might still experience emotional and developmental problems whose causes would not necessarily be related to sexual orientation, but would incite parental worry that could, in turn, interfere with parental adjustment. This mother of a twenty-four-year-old lesbian college student was extremely concerned about her daughter's excessive drinking:

RESPONDENT: She is not a happy person. She tells me she is completely happy, and she is relating this to her sexuality. "I am completely happy, Mom." But to me she is not. She is depressed. She has gained a lot of weight. I told her, "You know I've always had a weight problem myself. I understand it. I feel I can talk to you because I've been there." I don't put her down, but anything I say she takes personally. She knows the alcohol puts weight on, but after she drinks she will go and eat junk. So this is another issue. . . . But she is busy telling me how happy she is, but yet she is not. She is eating the same way I do when I get depressed or anxious. She would like to think she has it all figured out and everything is perfect, but it is not. She doesn't want to admit that . . .

INTERVIEWER: And this all gets in the way of you adjusting to the idea that she is lesbian?

RESPONDENT: Yeah, but I definitely have more fears about her drinking than anything. But my fears of her going out to these bars and people waiting for them—that is gay-related. That hasn't changed since I found out. I like her friends, too, [so] I worry about all of them.

For other parents, it was less clear that their children's problems were related to being gay or not. Yet they still worried for children who seemed to be struggling with becoming independent from their families. Charlotte, the mother of M. C., the previously quoted twenty-five-year-old gay man who, as a child, enjoyed playing Scrabble and watching political shows with her, worried about her son's isolation and loneliness:

> I'm very concerned about the loneliness. He has no friends, other than the one friend, who is not gay, and that is the young man we've spoken of. He works, he comes home, he lives with us [his parents] here. I guess this is his safe haven . . . his hideout. Initially, when he came back home, it was economics. But I could see now it's serving other purposes and I don't know whether that's good for him or what.
>
> I am very much concerned about the fact that he is not within a sphere where he's out to people. I mean he's out to his friend. He told one of his cousins. The one he thought would be accepting and is. He hasn't told the others. He told my sister because he's crazy about her and loves her dearly. He wanted her to know and so he came out to her. But he doesn't have any gay friends. He doesn't move in a circle where he's ever going to meet anybody. And I'm very concerned about that.
>
> I feel we're getting older; we're not always going to be here for him. He's got to be out there making a life for himself. Those are my concerns. His future, his friendships, of course I would like him to find someone that will care for him about whom he could care for and set up a home.
>
> He's very family oriented. That's what he wants, I'm sure. He would want children. I told you, the day he told me, he cried because he saw that was probably the one thing he never would have. But, to personalize it, I'm just concerned about him and I see him very lonely. And I just wish something would happen to help him change that.

Some parents described worries and concerns they had for their children that they did not perceive to be at all related to their homosexuality. As stated by this mother of a nineteen-year-old lesbian: "She does all these weird things. She pierced her tongue, pierced her nose. The tattoos that she has—they don't bother me in the least. My husband doesn't like them, but I don't mind tattoos. It is the piercing . . . in the nose and the tongue. But it's done. But that could have been anybody, that didn't have anything to do with the fact that she is a lesbian." However, other parents were not always clear which problems were gay-related and which weren't. When asked what if anything about her son helped or impeded her adjustment, this mother of a nineteen-year-old gay man responded:

> Impeded—yeah because he has had some crazy college behavior . . . staying out all night and drinking . . . he started smoking cigarettes. I am not happy about any of those things. But that, I'm thinking, well his health is going to overcome the cigarette smoking maybe. He did some crazy things. He took some diet pills because he just can't be thin enough. And that impedes everything because I would think, "Is he just doing that because he is a crazy nineteen year old or is he doing that because he is a homosexual male?" And I would confuse the two. I don't know. He was nineteen before he started smoking cigarettes. So then I am like, "Well, do all gay men smoke cigarettes?" I don't know (*laughing*), but that could be stuff that would just piss me off no matter what . . . because of where he is in his developmental stage.

It is interesting to note that none of the children of these parents was aware that their own behaviors interfered with their parents' ability to adjust to their homosexuality. Once again, it is possible that protective boundaries, discussed in chapter 4, were at work whereby parents shielded their children from worries about their behavior in an effort to protect them or at least not add to the burdens the children were coping with, and gay and lesbian respondents may have been self-protectively shielding themselves from fully acknowledging their parents' feelings. Add to this mix the idea that, in general, adolescents and young adults who are coping with the many challenges and rewards of becoming their own persons and developing their own identities are notoriously self-involved. Putting all this together, it is perhaps easy to see how children were so preoccupied with their own lives and difficulties that they were not always aware of their parents' distress over them.

Boys' Sexual Behavior

Anyone who has lived through the beginning of the AIDS epidemic in the U.S. knows the terrifying damage it has wrought, especially in the gay male community. Right before our eyes, men in their prime began to waste away and die as the rest of the world watched helplessly. Artists, movie stars, authors, young men, married men, eventually even women and children—it seemed no group was spared. Thanks to developments in pharmacology, HIV is no longer an immediate death sentence. However, AIDS remains a serious and eventually fatal disease, and it is particularly disturbing that, despite years of ambitious education and prevention efforts, young men who have sex with men (MSM) are still getting HIV at alarming rates.

Among a large multicultural sample of young gay men followed from 2001–2004, it was found that HIV diagnosis rates were increasing 14 percent per year for the entire sample and 23.5 percent for African American youth (Hall et al. 2007). In another recent large-scale survey, over half a sample of 3,492 young MSM aged fifteen to twenty-two reported engaging in unprotected anal intercourse (Celentano et al. 2006). So it is no small wonder that almost all of the parents of the thirty gay men who were interviewed for this study were particularly worried that their sons might contract HIV, and this fear got in the way of adjusting to the news of their sons' sexual orientation. These fears were heightened if they knew their sons engaged in sexual activity with multiple sexual partners.

When asked what, if anything, impeded her adjustment to her son's homosexuality, this African American mother who worked as a clerk in an urban hospital responded: "In the hospital that I work at, most of our patients are HIV positive. So it is something I am very aware of and I worry about." This next mother was a social worker, and she confessed:

> AIDS scares me and I've talked to him many times about that and about being careful about what he's doing, and not only just about AIDS, but any sexually transmitted disease. I know that he's also twenty-three, and, whether you're homosexual or heterosexual, you're going to be more exposed to something than you would if you were older or married or whatever, so that is something that worried me.

This next Latina mother also expressed her fears:

> I think he is promiscuous. . . . I am afraid of him getting AIDS. . . . He wants to have a close relationship but he doesn't seem to mind having these casual relationships until that happens. I don't think there is such a thing as safe sex unless you are having sex with someone who you know to be HIV negative. And there are a few other diseases floating around too. So I worry a lot about that.

Her son, like most of the boys in this study, was aware of his mother's fear of AIDS and the role her anxiety played in her feelings about his sexual orientation. Unlike most of the young respondents, he understood his mother's grief:

> She was crying because she lost the image of what I was going to be like when I grew up . . . an image that she had been harboring for fourteen years . . . and that I might not have kids. Even though, of course, things are different now . . . but, you know . . . no grandkids, probably going to die of AIDS—that's what she was thinking.

This next African American mother struggled with feelings of guilt and anxiety when she learned her son was gay. Like many parents of gay men, she was aware of the stereotype that they are sexually promiscuous. At the time her son came out to her, she was concerned that he was sexually active with too many men and was perhaps even prostituting himself. When her son began a serious relationship with one man, it helped to quell her fears:

> When he told me he was gay, there were no disappointments, just worries. I was, very worried that he would be raped or would get a disease or he was selling his body, for all I knew. I was worried, because he was getting presents and money and that was the only thing that had me worried. . . . Now, he has one boyfriend instead of ten. And I am happy he is going back to school to get his GED.

Her son knew that his mother had concerns for his lifestyle and also recognized that having one stable boyfriend helped his mother feel better:

> Well, yeah, I used to leave the house with different dudes and stuff. I guess it would get her to think being gay was a bad idea. That made her approve even less. I guess she is dealing with it. I don't know for sure, but I am guessing she is dealing with it for the simple fact that now she approves of my boyfriend. I can see that she likes him.

Children's Impressions of What Helped and What Didn't

In over half of the families in this study, children and parents agreed on the factors that contributed to parental adjustment. The beneficial effects of

PFLAG meetings were apparent not only to parents but also their children, many of whom recommended PFLAG to their parents when they came out. Children also noted that their relationships had improved with their parents and tended to be in agreement with them that this was helpful to parental adjustment. They also knew that parents feared for their well-being and safety and were particularly concerned being gay meant they were destined to face discrimination and, particularly if they were males, HIV.

However, in twenty-seven (about 42 percent) of the families, the children and their parents did not agree at all as to what contributed to parental adjustment. In most of these families the children believed that their happiness and confidence facilitated their parents' adjustment while their parents did not believe there was *anything* their children were doing that was helpful. Instead, these parents were more likely to attribute their own adjustment to PFLAG participation, talking to supportive confidants, reading books, the passage of time, or some combination of these factors. As stated by this next young man, who was nineteen at the time of the interview:

> I was just very confident about it. . . . And she was really worried about me in school getting picked on by the other kids, and I was like, "No, I'm not. I'm fine." And then it just all opened up. . . . I started the Gay/Straight Alliance in my school, and that just really took over, and she was learning more about how liberal my high school was and how supportive the teachers were. And then, you know, she felt confident.

This respondent's mother stated that going to PFLAG and talking to an understanding friend is what helped her the most. She claimed that nothing her son did helped her adjustment. As a matter of fact, her son's lying and becoming romantically involved with an adult while still in high school actually made it harder to get used to the idea her son was gay.

Several young lesbians and gays believed that the pressure they applied pushed their parents to face and adjust to their sexual orientation, especially if it seemed as if parents were having a particularly hard time. Remember the Latino graduate student whose parents suggested he have brain surgery to "remove" his homosexuality? When asked if anything he did helped or hindered his parents' adjustment, he reported:

> Yes, baptism by fire. I brought my boyfriend home. I argued with them about where he would sleep. I forced them into every situation. I said, "You

know my boyfriend is sitting at the Christmas table." So basically I brought it down to that. They had no options, I forced them into everything. I said, "This is me. You might as well start dealing with it now, because it's not changing."

His mother initially felt shocked, anxious, sad, and briefly suicidal as she struggled to reconcile her strong Catholic beliefs with her son's sexual orientation. She recalled her son's efforts to educate her, which she agreed were somewhat helpful:

Over a period of time now, maybe the first year or whatever, and still to this day he is still trying to educate me. He knows now I am much better, but even if I make a comment that I don't even realize is wrong, he will correct me. He is a very cocky person anyway, nothing to do with his sexual orientation, so sometimes I just chalk it off and say, "OK, that's Raul." But then I do pay attention to what he says. I won't admit it to him, but he is right on a lot of things when he corrects me. But I can't give him that, because he is too cocky and his head will be really swollen, as we say.

However, like the parents quoted earlier, the main thing that helped her adjust was when she came to the conclusion that her son's sexual orientation was innate and unchangeable.

This next young man pressured his parents by ceasing contact with them until they agreed to be more accepting:

What happened was . . . after I came out and had this awful relationship with them I proceeded to shut them out of my life. . . . I traveled all over the country when I was in college, singing in this Jewish a cappella group, and we recorded albums and . . . I remember my parents crying when they received this album with me on it, and they didn't even know that I could sing. I had all these friends, and they didn't know them at all. And I think it became so apparent to them that it was either shit or get off the pot—that if they really didn't start to process this they were going to lose me. And the reason I can say that with some degree of certainty is because when my boyfriend was going through these issues with his parents they [my parents] said, "Ronnie just needs to start to ignore what his parents think and exclude them." My mom said, "You know, that's what happened to us. When we realized that your life was going on and we weren't a part of it—that was when things started to change."

His father did not find his son's pushing the least bit beneficial: "James could have been much more patient and understanding, but that is not James's nature. What it would have done is it would have brought harmony to the family instead of the anxiousness that everybody was going through."

What is interesting is that parents whose children reported pressuring them either did not recall being pressured or did not report that being pushed assisted their adjustment. The mother of the previously quoted respondent described: "He was allowing me to control the way it happened. And the fact that we didn't throw words at each other I think was a good thing. I think that helped the process." This next nineteen year old recalled:

> Well, I am really up-front, so I would constantly ask my mother why she didn't want to know about what was going on in my life. I would ask her why she doesn't want to know who I'm dating or where I am going or things like that. And I think that helped her become more comfortable, like, "Wow, this isn't going to change, and I need to get it together."

His mother struggled with anxiety and depression because she initially felt to blame for her son's sexual orientation. She was previously quoted as becoming concerned over her son's cigarette smoking and extreme dieting. When asked what, if anything about her son or his behavior helped her adjustment, she credited PFLAG as well as seeing her son become happier after he came out—not his pressure. His mother did not believe her son did anything to help her adjust.

One possible explanation of these discrepancies is that children might be overestimating the influence of their own behavior on their parents' feelings. The reasons for this might be twofold. First, when we are anxious about something, we search for ways we can be in control of it, even if just a little bit. We all know about athletes or people in the entertainment industry who carry a charm or don lucky underwear before an important match or performance because they believe it helps, especially since there are so many factors out of their hands. If we feel a sense of control, it can help us calm down. For these kids it is probably too scary to look back on their coming out and think that they ran the risk of being rejected with nothing they could have done about it.

Another factor might have to do with the developmental stage of these families. Remember when you became old enough that, for the first time, you could do something to help your parents? For many of us, this moment was the first flush of feeling grown-up. As children grow into adults, they perhaps realize more and more that their relationships with their parents are more mutual than unidirectional, that interactions can be reciprocal, and therefore can be influenced by the youth themselves. Filled with the sense of power brought to the fore by this realization, the adolescents and young adults may be prone to overexaggerate.

Conversely, parents may be reluctant to recognize their children's growing influence on them because to do so would acknowledge a shift in the power dynamics of the family—not so easy for parents who are accustomed to being the ones in charge, sources of help and support. It is easier and perhaps less anxiety provoking, particularly when children are at the threshold of adulthood, to think that the parent-child relationships are still all about what Mom or Dad does TO the child rather than a function of reciprocal interactions *between* parent and child. It might have been embarrassing for parents to acknowledge either to the interviewer or to themselves that they needed to be pushed by their children to accept their gay sexual orientation. Even if they did feel pushed, as did the previously quoted father, they did not necessarily see this pressure as catalyzing adjustment or acceptance. Understandably, parents want to preserve their self-image as good parents, an image that probably does not include being forced by their children to accept them. Though it is difficult to know for sure the reason for these discrepancies, the important takeaway message is that in some families there can be vastly different perceptions as to what helps and what hinders parental adjustment, and therapists need to keep this in mind when they assist such families.

Summary of the Family Recovery Phase

Having nonjudgmental, optimistic people to talk to can help parents cope with and eventually resolve feelings of mourning and self-blame for their children's homosexuality. In this study some parents found support through PFLAG meetings where it was soothing and reassuring to hear from parents like themselves who were experiencing (or had experienced) similar feelings. Parents who did not join PFLAG found it useful to talk to someone who was empathic, tolerant, and hopeful. Both situations demonstrate how nonjudgmental others can reassure parents they are not to blame, that their children can live happy and healthy lives as gay adults.

It is important to recognize that children can also play a significant role in family recovery. These parents reported that their adjustment was enhanced if their child was mature, confident, and did not show cross-gendered behavior. However, parental adjustment can be impeded if children appear "obviously" gay, are involved in risky behaviors, or are experiencing developmental problems. Perhaps, due to the nature of parent-child boundaries during family recovery, children might be unaware of how their behaviors can impede parental adjustment to acceptance. Nevertheless, child factors that enhance or impede family recovery should not be overlooked because they suggest significant implications for clinical work with these families.

Parent-Child Interaction During Family Recovery: Relief and Closeness

The good news from these findings is that it is possible for parent-child relationships to improve once the child comes out, and this may be a primary contributor to parental adjustment. In this study, children experiencing relief that their parents did not reject them began to interact with their parents more positively once they came out. Parents were relieved to see their children's moods improve and began to respond in ways that reassured children and strengthened parent-child relationships. These reciprocal, mutually reinforcing patterns of behavior can be further enhanced when children perceive that their parents are trying to educate themselves about lesbian and gay people. Ways for therapists to promote this positive interaction pattern are described later in this chapter.

Treatment During the Family Recovery Phase

More on Separate Sessions with Parents

These findings make an even more compelling case for the recommendation in the last chapter, namely, that therapists encourage parents to find supports outside the family to assist them in coping with their feelings. In addition, individual sessions can be a safe place for parents to express their array of feelings.

In this research, parents felt somehow reassured when they reached the conclusion that their child's sexual orientation was indelible and immutable. However, on the road to this conclusion, parents might ask mental health professionals if it is possible for their children to change and become heterosexual, and they might want to find a therapist to help "convert" their gay child. As stated previously, the practitioner should be aware that some therapists believe it is possible to change one's sexual orientation through individual psychotherapy, group psychotherapy, prayer, or a combination of all three. Internet-savvy parents might discover this information either before beginning treatment or sometime during the therapeutic process.

However, the therapist should inform parents that there is no consistent evidence that these methods are effective in permanently eradicating homosexual attractions. Further, since homosexuality is not a disease, many professional organizations to which mental health professionals belong, such as the National Association of Social Workers (2008), the American Psychological Association (2002) and the American Psychiatric Association (Commission on Psychotherapy by Psychiatrists 2006) consider such treatment unethical, and its practitioners risk censure as well as suspension or revocation of their licenses. I myself tell parents that I agree with conclusions of my own professional organization, the National Association of Social Workers. I also tell parents that there is good reason to believe that reparative and conversion therapies, besides being ineffective, are psychologically harmful to gays and lesbians, which is another reason I do not recommend them and will not assist families in procuring such treatment.

Parents might want to know from a practitioner what causes a child to be gay or lesbian. As stated earlier, there is still a great deal that needs to be learned about sexuality. Therapists need to feel comfortable sharing the incomplete available information with inquiring parents and, if relevant, should acknowledge that this ambiguity can be confusing and unsettling for parents trying to deal with the fact that their daughter or son is gay. The therapist and the parents should resist the temptation to get into a drawn out analysis of the causes of homosexuality, as this might derail the treatment and distract the parents from a discussion of their own feelings and, in turn, their adjustment. After a brief discussion of the issue, it is sufficient to conclude "We just don't know" and then shift the focus to parental reactions and the maintenance and growth of family relationships through the adjustment process.

More on Individual Sessions with Youth

Parents need a lot of support during the entire family trajectory, especially during the family recovery period. However, youth will also need a place to continue to express their fears and frustrations with their parents. It is difficult to wait for parents to come around, and young lesbians and gays might need a place to talk about this. As described in the last chapter, the youth need help dealing with their frustrations and fears that their parents will not adjust, and they will also need reminders that their parents need time.

However, based on these findings, young gays and lesbians may also need assistance recognizing what they can do to facilitate parental adjustment. Are there ways the young people can demonstrate to their parents that they are competent and able to handle their lives? Can they find ways to communicate to their parents that they are contented? Nevertheless, children may not be able to accept their ability to influence their parents' adjustment until they feel their anger and fear is understood. Thus the guidelines mentioned at the end of the last chapter also apply here.

As the findings of this study suggest, sometimes youth felt it was helpful to apply some kind of pressure to their parents, like distancing or pushing them to include their partners in family gatherings. However, in most of these families, pressuring parents did not occur, nor did it seem necessary. Young gays and lesbians who are angry and anxious might need some help deciding what, if any, kinds of pressure might be effective and when to apply it. Based on these findings and my clinical experience, gently forcing the issue may be useful for parents who are distressed but who do not seem like they are doing anything to help themselves adjust. As stated in the previous chapter, if parents are taking steps such as going to PFLAG, talking to supportive friends, or getting information, then "the rock is rolling down the mountain" and therapists are advised to encourage their young clients to hang in there, be patient, and avoid applying any additional pressure.

Family Therapy

One of the most compelling factors that aided parental adjustment, in this study, was the improvement in the parent-child relationship following the child's coming out. Parents described increased closeness between themselves and their offspring after the child's coming out, and this closeness helped them feel better about their children's sexual orientation. Enjoying this renewed intimacy, particularly when their children were on the threshold of adulthood, was perhaps a balm that soothed parents' feelings of distress and even suggests that having a gay child can have beneficial aspects, which are described further in chapter 5. Thus family therapy might be a natural choice for parents and children in the family recovery phase. However, the caution described in the last chapter bears repeating; before bringing family members together, therapists should be reasonably certain that sessions can be productive.

Parental guilt, anger, and fear could inspire parents to say things to their children that are provocative and hurtful, leading to wounded feelings and destructive arguments. Communication is, of course, a good thing, but sometimes the "communication" sought by members of distressed families consists of dumping their hurt and anger onto other family members. That is why a clinician should always be prepared to interrupt fruitless, destructive squabbling to redirect the conversation.

Many parents and children in the family discovery phase had the wisdom to avoid discussing certain aspects of parental feelings in an effort to keep the peace, even if this created a temporary distance. Pushing them together to talk about their feelings before they are ready can be fruitless and potentially destructive. As recommended in the last chapter, before meeting with the family, individual assessment of parents and children might be a useful step to ascertain whether they are too hurt or angry to talk calmly in family therapy.

Sometimes it is not possible to know for sure if parents and children will be able to productively express their feelings until they are brought together for a session. As stated in chapter 3, if family members seem too angry or too reactive to carry on a (mostly) civil discussion, then family sessions might need to be postponed and replaced with additional individual sessions until family members are sufficiently calmed down. As far as I know, Kenny Rogers never did a lick of family therapy, but when it came to poker—and to life—he understood the importance of knowing "when to fold 'em and when to hold 'em." In keeping with this wise insight, when it comes to family sessions, it is advised that the therapist be prepared and willing to advance—and know when it is necessary to back off.

CONFLICT AND HOPE. Families usually don't seek family therapy if they are planning to reject their kids—they just go ahead and do it. As underscored throughout this book, families who seek treatment, like families who are willing to be interviewed, consist of parents who want to find ways to maintain and even improve their relationships with their gay children. Practitioners working with families of young lesbians and gays should keep this in mind and find ways to reinforce this momentum by shining a light on the positive motivations of family members. This can be done through complimentary strength-building statements such as "I really appreciate and respect that you want to find ways to deal with this difficult issue" or "By seeking help, I know, despite these tough times, that you are committed to staying connected to each other—which I respect and admire." I recommend therapists include a generous helping of such statements as they assist family members to express and listen to each other's fears and concerns.

When a caring, open-minded therapist encounters an angry parent spewing hateful, homophobic venom such as "How did you become a pervert?" "No son of mine is a faggot!" it is perfectly understandable for the clinician to want to rescue the child. However, as discussed in chapter 3, taking sides and defending children from "bigoted" parents is an example of "help" that's just not helpful.

When working with family members in conflict, it is important to validate feelings as well as get people to talk to each other about the deeper, more vulnerable feelings that lurk behind their anger—it is a therapist's job to create a safe place for this to happen. Once people feel understood, they may become ready to open up to new ideas and other points of view (Kegan 1982; Rogers 1951; Stone Fish and Harvey 2005). There are several useful techniques that can assist with this. Stone Fish and Harvey describe the importance of encouraging family members to engage in "difficult dialogues" whereby therapists create a "crucible of refuge" or a safe space in their sessions so that family members can discuss their most painful and frightening feelings. De Jong and Berg (2002) have modified an intervention from Carl Rogers in which they get each member of a conflicted dyad to take turns discussing his or her feelings on a topic on which they disagree, while the other, without attacking or defending, simply listens and summarizes. An essential component of each of these techniques is that people avoid the unhelpful patterns of attack-defend, attack-counterattack, or attack-withdrawal and replace them with the sharing of real feelings that lie below the surface of anger and defensiveness.

The harsh parents' statements quoted earlier mask feelings of self-blame and worry for their children, and it is the therapist's job to bring these feelings out into the open. Children, who can harbor different ideas from parents as to what helps or hinders parental adjustment, should be helped to hear their parents' underlying concerns and understand that parents need information and time, just as they did when they themselves realized they were gay. Like some of the children in this study, sons and daughters who push their parents too hard toward acceptance (or who distance to protect themselves from rejection) can be encouraged to directly express to their mothers and fathers their fears of disapproval and rejection along with their sense of being over-exposed—and parents can be coached to listen and hear them.

A combination of love, fear, guilt, and shame are at the heart of most of the conflicts at the family discovery and family recovery phases, and the clinician can help expose these issues through the use of careful reframing and the encouragement of dialogue that gets to the heart of people's fears and wishes. Once people are heard, they might be ready for the education and type of renewed closeness that can be a benefit of the coming out process.

Considering the mutually reinforcing patterns of interaction found among many of these families, it is important to ask family members what, if anything, is better since the child has come out. Are there any improvements in the parent-child interactions, such as more honesty or increased closeness, that can be used as a foundation upon which the family members can build acceptance and stronger connections? If so, the therapist should frame these improvements as signs of caring and hope and use them as jumping off points for strengthening or, if necessary, rebuilding family relationships. If you have ever been in a dark room that opens to the outdoors, you know that it is sometimes possible to see sunlight through the small gap between the door and its frame, and it is the therapist's job to point out this bit of light leaking into the darkness.

A statement such as "Junior, you tell me that even though you and your folks are arguing a lot, you are still glad to see they are reading information on the PFLAG Web site, and you, Mom and Dad, are hopeful that your son is finally speaking openly and honestly with you. What needs to happen to keep these positive changes going—while you guys are trying to sort out your feelings about (your parents' disapproval, your son's many boyfriends, your daughter's butch hairstyle)?" Even in the most strained families, the therapist is advised to be on the lookout for positive signs, no matter how small, and build on them to help these families get through their rough times.

ASSISTING TROUBLED GAY YOUTH IN THE FAMILY CONTEXT. As can be seen in this study, lesbian and gay children can experience emotional problems or difficulties with school or work that can get in the way of parental adjustment. The therapist can encourage families to talk about these problems and organize or reorganize themselves to assist their children. In some ways therapists can reprise the same skills they use whenever they are helping a family that has a young adult child who is floundering. For example, they may need to assess the family relationships for complementary behavioral patterns and interactions that impede a child's autonomy.

However, the issue of sexual orientation adds a unique twist to traditional, structural, and systemic family therapy. Young respondents in this study who struggled to establish physical and emotional autonomy in relation to their parents seemed to be traumatized by a history of verbal and physical abuse at the hands of their peers. Even accepting, nurturing parents could not erase the wounds of this past cruelty. Family therapy can help these families discuss these issues and get them to brainstorm ways to help their son or daughter cope. It should be kept in mind that family dynamics might not have caused this problem, so reshaping them might not be the solution. The young people may need assistance in pursuing sources outside the family to raise their self-esteem. Support groups for lesbian and gay youth—even a good group of gay friends—can go a long way in helping a young person feel better about being gay. Of course, drug and alcohol treatment as well as antidepressant medication should be considered as needed.

As the findings of this study suggest, parents may worry that their children are making themselves targets of stigma by appearing too effeminate or butch. Does this mean that therapists helping families in which the parents are disturbed by their children's appearance should advise young people not to "look gay?" Should therapists coach children to act and dress in ways that are traditionally gender-congruent?

The answer is a resounding no. Therapists and other helping professionals must resist any urge to join either the conformity police or the gender patrol. I have known clinicians and educators who have said to scapegoated gay kids something along the lines of "Do you understand that when you dress like that, it calls negative attention to yourself and invites ridicule?" Even though it makes many people uncomfortable to see boys who act like girls and vice versa, it is not our job to reinforce what are arguably restrictive and nonsensical norms regarding gendered behavior.

However, it would be equally wrong to overlook the possibility that violating these norms could make one a target of discrimination—even violence. A way to deal with this dilemma is to simply share the information offered by this study: that parents might be uncomfortable if their children appear obviously gay, pointing out that choices about behavior and dress have implications in a world that (albeit wrongly) stigmatizes gay and lesbian people. Throughout their lives, gays and lesbians must continually decide how open to be about their sexuality and whether they are willing to face whatever consequences result from admitting they are members of a stigmatized group. In that vein, LGBT youth can be encouraged to evaluate the risks and benefits thoughtfully and make *their own* informed decisions about disclosure, dress, and behavior, knowing the potential effects of such decisions on people in their lives, including their parents.

Arguments between parents and adolescents about clothing are so common and predictable, we should probably consider them a part of normal family development. However, for families with a lesbian or gay child, the issue becomes more personal, as it could communicate intolerance or even rejection. Under these circumstances, the issue can be discussed, but the therapist should assist the parents in communicating their concerns at a deeper level. Indeed, an ongoing concern for parents throughout the family adjustment trajectory was fear for their children's happiness and safety. Perhaps therapists could coach parents not to focus their discussion so much on their children's appearances but rather on their fears for their well-being, encouraging dialogue between parents and children about safety, discrimination, and the ways in which the children will handle these issues. For example, here is how an interchange might go between a seventeen-year-old lesbian, her mother, and the family therapist:

MOTHER: Why do you have to dress like a man—with the short hair and men's shirts and everything? That makes you look like a bull dyke!

DAUGHTER: Fuck you! I will dress anyway I want. You just can't accept that I am a lesbian. You always wanted me to wear those stupid dresses, which I hated, and, now that I'm old enough, I don't have to, so just deal with it!

THERAPIST: Whoa! Hold on, hold on! Let's slow this down a bit. I can see there are a lot of strong feelings here that we need to look at. First, I will start with Mom. Tell me; what are your fears and concerns about the way your daughter dresses? Your daughter thinks you are rejecting her.

MOM: Well, of course I love my daughter and I am trying to learn to accept this part of her and it hasn't been easy. But, with her clothes and hair, I worry that she is letting everyone know she is gay, and once people know that they will judge her and maybe try to hurt her.

THERAPIST: So your concerns for the way she dresses are about your fears for her.

DAUGHTER: Why can't she let me make my own decisions?

THERAPIST: Hold on. I agree that you are almost an adult and you have a right to make your own choices, but did you hear what your mother just said? Can you tell me what she just said?

DAUGHTER: Yes, she is afraid people will pick on me and judge me because they will know I am a lesbian. But she doesn't have to worry. I can take care of myself!

THERAPIST: Of course—also, I am guessing, you are learning how to how to deal with discrimination and other people's reactions. Perhaps you can share some of what you have learned right now, right here, with your worried mother. She needs some help not to worry so much.

Rather than react to their parents in an emotional or rebellious manner, young gays and lesbians can be encouraged to discuss their thoughts on discrimination and visibility with their parents. How do they make decisions about how to appear and to whom to disclose their sexual orientation in light of these risks? Furthermore, can they talk to their parents about their plans to protect themselves (as much as it is possible) from discrimination, harassment, and violence? Parents can be coached to listen and understand their children's sensitivity to rejection and parental control and, in a nonattacking way, provide feedback and, if appropriate, support for such plans. By enacting such conversations, therapists can create an atmosphere in which productive discussions replace painful, destructive arguments.

As stated repeatedly in this chapter, renewed or newfound closeness in family relationships helped parents adjust to the news that their child was gay. Meeting with family members conjointly to help them discuss what both parents and children can do to assist parental adjustment might not only clear the air and solve problems but could also have the *metapurpose* of fostering the type of closeness the parents in this study found so helpful. Hopefully, therapists can assist such families to go beyond simply getting used to the idea that their daughter is a lesbian or their son is gay and get to where they understand that accepting their children and loving them the way they are, not the way their parents want them to be, can be an enriching experience for the family. Not all families can get to this place, but there are great rewards waiting for those who do, as we shall see in the next chapter.

CHAPTER 5

Family Renewal

The Gift of the Gay/Lesbian Child

Crises refine life. In them you discover what you are.
—ALLAN K. CHALMERS

A WISE COLLEAGUE OF MINE, WHOSE JOB IT WAS TO COUNSEL people in crisis, would tell her clients the following story. When Mount St. Helens erupted in 1980 it left a path of destruction. Rivers of molten rock incinerated the once lush forests that grew on the mountain, leaving it covered in ashes and barren of any life. However, after a few weeks, something surprising began to happen on the bleak mountainside. Small green plants began to sprout, nourished by the fertile new soil. Within a few months the mountain was covered with lush new plant life that would eventually become trees and forests. After telling this brief story, my colleague would then ask her clients how it might relate to them—in the midst of their panic and despair could they see anything positive, any sign of growth that might result from their crisis situation?

There is evidence that some people who experience trauma or hardship, such as child abuse, addiction, or serious illness are able to identify some way they benefited from these most difficult times (McMillen 1999; McMillen et al. 2001). In their samples, McMillen and his colleagues found that a frequently mentioned benefit was that people developed more closeness in their personal relationships. Close to half of the parents and children in this study were able to recognize new personal growth and family closeness in the year or so that passed from the time the child came out, and most of the remaining respondents reported that their relationships recovered to the positive state they were in before the child came out. While the coming out period could be seen as a volcanic eruption, obliterating old expectations and shaking family relationships to their core, for some fortunate families the period that followed was a reforestation—a time of new openness as family members renewed and revised their relationships.

Hansen and Johnson (1979), scholars in the field of education, have described how in some families a crisis can stimulate a *regenesis*, whereby "members accept disruptions of habit and tradition not so much as unwelcome problems, but more as opportunities to renegotiate their relationships" (584). In their thoughtful and sensitive account of parents struggling to adjust to their children's homosexuality, Herdt and Koff (2000) discuss how family relationships can be renewed and strengthened as parents integrate new understandings of their children and themselves into their lives and move forward. In the study described in this book, it was also found that some families were able to get to a place where parents and children saw the youth's coming out as something positive. Borrowing from Herdt and Koff and also Hanson and Johnson, I call the final stage of adjustment *family renewal*, and it marks the period when families can identify the benefits of having and adjusting to an out gay child.

Of course, not all families make it to this point, and the fact that many of the parent respondents could identify the benefits of having a lesbian or gay child could have been an artifact of the sample. Remember, families who have ongoing difficulty coping with the fact that their child is lesbian or gay are unlikely to participate in a study such as this. Shame, stigma, and religious conflicts probably obstruct their adjustment and, in turn, make them unlikely to want to talk to a stranger, particularly a gay or a gay-positive interviewer, about their feelings. Therefore, voices of the most troubled families are notably absent from this research.

Nevertheless, the reports of these successful families can help therapists understand the rich rewards of new or renewing family closeness that potentially await those who seek their help. It was possible for some parents to adjust to their gay children's sexual orientation to the extent that they went beyond tolerance and were actually grateful for having a gay child.

As you will recall, some family members described a new or renewed closeness during the family discovery period, and more families experienced this closeness during the recovery phase. In these families there may have been a reciprocal effect whereby children felt relieved and acted warmly toward their parents and parents, noticing that their children felt better and were less distant, responded to them positively. As described in chapter 4, these improved family relationships played a significant role in parents' adjustment to their children's sexual orientation. However, this renewed closeness was viewed by parents to be a significant "gift" of having and adjusting to a gay child and seen by the children as the most beneficial aspect of coming out.

Proud Parents + Happy Children = Happy Families

Throughout the research process, Bethann Albert, who was one of my research assistants and the mother of a lesbian, often reminded me that parents want two things for their children: to be healthy and happy. Based on my experience as a family therapist, family researcher, and family member, I would add that parents also want their children's ongoing affection and love, and they want to be proud of them. Moreover, children of all ages want to bask in the warm glow of their parents' pride.

When asked what, if anything, was positive about having a gay son or a lesbian daughter, many of these parents talked about how pleased they were to know their children were happy and relieved, and it made them proud to see how their kids were integrating their sexual orientation into their lives. In chapter 4 I noted the ways in which parents seeing their children happy and flourishing contributed to their adjustment to the news that their child was gay. However, in the family renewal phase some parents recognized and took pride in how their children were successfully integrating their homosexuality into their young adult lives.

Remember Joelle, the young African American lesbian who, among other things, provided the first quote in chapter 1 of this book? Her mother Nancy, who initially struggled with a strong, painful sense of self-blame, eventually reached the point where she became proud of her daughter: "I guess, in some small way, I contributed to her being spiritual enough to accept people at the soul level, regardless of the physical form, and that I raised a child who is confident enough to be comfortable with who she is in her own skin. I think that is good."

Some parents saw that their children's homosexuality played a role in their social, academic, and professional achievements. As this father stated:

RESPONDENT: Well, I think it's helped his career as an artist. It has given him something unique to write about that I think people are interested in reading. That's one thing. It makes him special in a certain way, not like everybody else.

INTERVIEWER: It makes you feel proud?

RESPONDENT: To the extent that Larry can be successful and self-supporting, it's positive for me. It's good to be successful. I feel proud about his commercial success. That's not directly because he is gay, although his homosexuality enabled him to be that way.

A year prior to her interview, when this next mother found out her daughter was a lesbian, she grew so depressed that she began a course of antidepressant medication. However, as time passed, this mother began to take pride in the leadership skills her daughter had acquired through her involvement in a gay organization in her high school: "Lately she has been getting a whole lot of recognition. Lots of really good things have been happening for her. God, even my father can't even help but be proud of the things she has done and accomplished."

Like almost all the youth in families that reached the renewal phase, her daughter felt closer to her mother since she came out because she felt that she could be more open with her. As a matter of fact, forty-one of the young lesbian and gay respondents discussed how their relationships with their mothers improved from the time they came out. When asked how, if at all, her relationship with her mother changed from the time she came out, the daughter of the last respondent explained how being able to be herself around her mother contributed to the improvement in their relationship: "Yeah, It took away my burden of hiding and trying to be someone I am not so . . . umm . . . yeah, I am a lot more confident now. And it is helpful that I can be interested in something or I can check out a girl with my mom. She doesn't care anymore. Yeah, we are a lot closer, and she really knows me now."

This African American mother of a lesbian reported that when she first learned her seventeen-year-old daughter was gay four years ago, she cried uncontrollably and, in the weeks following her daughter's disclosure, she became deeply depressed. Now she carries a sense of pride as she watches her daughter negotiate life as a young lesbian woman:

She is always happy and joking—I think that is her way of dealing with it. Everything rolls off of her shoulder, nothing bothers her. And she is very outspoken and very proud of her gayness. I appreciate that. I think I had something to do with that. I raised this kid to be strong. Any adversity, she is willing to take on.

Her daughter described her mother's gradual process of acceptance. Along the way there was a period of distance, which began to dissipate when she showed her mother she understood her feelings of loss. This young woman, demonstrating a maturity beyond her years, was able to really understand the grief with which her mother was coping. She said:

> It was a building process. Like first we went through this thing where we didn't speak at all. Just, "Hi, how you doing, bye." Then, each night, "Goodnight, bye." It was cut and dry. I think as I got older, I saw her point of view, which was she is a mom . . . and all parents have little fantasies when their kids are born: they are going to walk down the aisle, if it is a girl, with a guy and if a guy with a girl. And I saw her point of view, and she took time to see mine. She started to realize, "This is her life—and that she is going to do what she wants." And eventually my mother was like, "Hey, if you want to date a dog, I don't give a darn, as long as you walk across that stage at high school graduation and go to college." Now that I am about to graduate high school and have gotten into college, we can talk about anything.

This young woman's sensitivity to her mother's feelings and awareness of her mother's pride may have fueled the positive interactions between this mother and daughter, leading to their current closeness.

Imagine the feelings of relief, liberation, and gratitude felt by daughters and sons who initially distanced from their parents in anticipation of their disapproval and rejection but now found themselves bathed in the warm sunshine of their parents' growing pride. Parental pride can inspire young gays and lesbians to want to be closer to their parents, as evidenced by the more honest and intimate relationships in families that reached the renewal stage. Seeing that their children wanted a closer relationship with them after a period of distance led some of these parents to, in turn, respond warmly. For lucky families, such positive reciprocity can push parents, beyond tolerance, to the point where they realize the special advantages of accepting a gay child.

Gays and Lesbian Children and Their Lucky Parents

Currently, gay rights activists seek tolerance and social justice for gay and lesbian people. Lesbians and gay men are fighting for legislation that, among other things, gives them legal protection from discrimination, grants them the right to legally marry and adopt children, and enables them to pursue hate crime prosecution against those who commit crimes against them because of their sexual orientation. These important objectives must be vigorously pursued until lesbians and gays have the same rights as all citizens in this country. But what would it be like if, as a society, we went beyond tolerance and fairness and actually recognized and prized the presence and contributions of gays and lesbians?

At a recent talk I gave for staff at a youth residential treatment facility, an audience member asked me what the likelihood would be that if one twin were gay the other one would be as well. I summarized the available knowledge in this area (Bailey, Dunne, and Martin 2000; Kendler et al. 2000; Hyde 2005) by saying: "If the twins are monozygotic or identical, and one is gay, the other is more likely to be gay than a sibling who isn't a twin or is a fraternal twin. However, one gay twin does not guarantee that the other will be gay also. Only the luckiest families get TWO gay or lesbian kids." The nervous surprised laughter that followed indicated how foreign-sounding it was to suggest that gay and lesbian children might actually be desirable.

Greenberg and Bailey (2001) wrote a controversial article arguing, if the technology were available to determine that a child was gay before she was born, that it would be morally defensible for parents to abort the fetus. If we really appreciated lesbian and gay people and their contributions, I would argue, such a notion would be irrelevant, preposterous, and such an article unpublishable. If such technology had been historically available, and parents were able and willing to use it, the world would never have benefited from the contributions of famous gay men and lesbians, including (but certainly not limited to) Leonardo Da Vinci, Michelangelo, Virginia Woolf, Oscar Wilde, Willa Cather, Gertrude Stein, Alan Turing, Jane Adams, and Truman Capote. Moreover we would have lost out on the more current contributions of Congressman Barney Frank's political leadership, Martina Navratilova's superb athletic ability, along with the contributions of Ellen DeGeneres and k. d. Lang to entertainment (again, this incomplete list just scratches the surface). We also would have missed out on the smaller but nonetheless important contributions of less famous lesbians and gays. If, like several tribes of Native Americans, we truly revered the presence and perspectives of lesbians and gays (Gilley 2006, Lang 1997; Williams 1986), the idea that parents might wish for two or more gay children might not seem so surprising.

Some of the parents in this study grew to believe that there were special qualities they attributed to their sons and daughters being gay or lesbian that enriched their lives and relationships. Often these reports reflected common, albeit positive stereotypes such as mechanically inclined lesbians and sensitive, creative gay men. Positive stereotypes can be harmful and limiting when we believe people can do no more than what we expect them to be good at. For example, if we assume all gay men are artistic and all lesbians are athletic, we might have trouble understanding that a gay man can be professional basketball player (John Amaechi) and that a lesbian can be a talented, highly successful photographer (Annie Leibovitz). Nevertheless, there sometimes seems to be a grain of truth in these stereotypes. For example, gay men are certainly well represented in the field of fashion. Thus, perhaps parents invoking such stereotypes might be forgivable, particularly if they contribute to positive parent-child interactions.

When asked what, if anything, was positive about having a gay son, this mother spoke of how she enjoyed her son's attention to her appearance, which she perceived as a sign of caring:

> We can talk about product for our faces. He's more into my face and my wrinkles than I certainly could ever have time for. He's very, very caring. He's planning a little vacation for me now and he's just genuine. He tells me, "You know, you've got to lose some weight, Mom. This is what you've got to do." But I have good conversations with him, you know, so that's a real plus.

Fathers could also recognize a positive aspect to their children's sexual orientation. This father of a gay man who initially had a painful reaction to his son's sexuality, worrying about HIV and his son having a rough life, stated: "What's positive? Gay people . . . they're art! I think they have certain skills that the regular population doesn't have, I know that. And it's not limited just to cutting hair. Architects, engineers, designers. There are football players, basketball players, so it's everything and maybe more."

This next mother attributed her daughter's "boyish" protectiveness to her lesbianism:

RESPONDENT: She's very protective of me.

INTERVIEWER: Is she? And you think that's due to her being a lesbian?

RESPONDENT: I guess, yeah, because, whether you believe it or not, boys have a tendency to protect their mothers.

INTERVIEWER: And the fact that she's boyish makes her protective of you?

RESPONDENT: Yeah. With girls and their mothers, you always have that rebellion against each other, you know? And with my lesbian daughter I don't have that.

When children were asked what, if anything, was better since they came out, they almost always described increased honesty and closeness in their relationships with their parents. The twenty-three-year-old lesbian daughter of the last mother quoted, who recently moved into her own apartment, also perceived the enhanced closeness between her and her mother as a decided benefit:

Our relationship is very, very open. We talk about things. It's like, at this point, we're friends. So, it's weird when I see other people because it just seems like it's just business with other people and their families. I say to some of my friends, "Well, don't you talk to your mother about this?" "No, I could never talk to my mother about that." And it just seems awkward, it seems wrong. I know it just wouldn't feel natural if it [the relationship between my mother and I] were any other way. How do I know that we're closer? 'Cause for a while there we didn't talk about personal things like my relationships and, now that I'm out and older, we do. Even though she hasn't been in a lesbian relationship, there are universal themes. So she can understand, and I ask her advice. Whether or not I take it, it's always good to have it there. We've become much closer.

Susan, the previously quoted mother of a gay son, Mitch, initially felt terribly guilty when she first found out her son was gay. Mitch had been out to his mother for about twelve months, and, at the time of her interview, Susan still felt a bit guilty and worried for his well-being. Nevertheless, she enjoyed aspects of her son that seem to fit the prevailing stereotypes of gay males.

He has great taste (*laughing*). And always did! You know what? Looking back, I should have known that. He has always been a clotheshorse. That is kind of cool. And he is sensitive. He has always been a sensitive man. He likes the kind of music I like. Some of those things we share. He likes the kind of movies I like . . . he likes a good love story . . . we can sit and cry together. That is good stuff.

In chapter 4 Mitch was quoted as describing how the relationship with his mother was good before he came out, was distant during the beginning of the family discovery stage, then improved significantly as his mother learned more about gay people.

Cynthia, who initially felt terribly guilty and mournful when she first learned her son Kenneth was gay, six years ago, mused:

You know what? Gay people are nice people! They are very caring about everybody, the human race. I really like that. I like the fact that he is very understanding in most situations, and I think it has to do with that [being gay]. He is nondiscriminatory—he just isn't at all. And I think it has to do with that also, and that is very pleasing to me.

Kenneth believed that coming out improved his relationship with his mother. When asked how his relationship changed, if at all, since he came out, he stated:

RESPONDENT: It is really good. We talk a couple times a week. I see her once or twice a year. And we talk about everything.
INTERVIEWER: Has the relationship changed at all since you came out to her?
RESPONDENT: Yes, it has improved. We talk more. I got over my teenage angst.

Joe, one of the fathers who grew closer to his gay son, was a recovering alcoholic and began to attend both PFLAG and Alcoholics Anonymous (AA) meetings at the local gay community center after his child came out. He observed:

Well, I think he [Tony] is special because he is gay. One of the things I have really come to understand about the gay people I've met at the center in the last ten years is really how creative and special many of them are. In many ways I went to those twelve-step meetings because I felt like I was dealing with people who were much more in touch with their feelings than many of the people at straight meetings I would go to. Gay people could talk about their feelings more easily than straight people could at twelve-step meetings. That is an issue I've always had trouble with. I think my son is very good about that. He has much less difficulty than I had at his age, being in touch with his feelings.

Tony described how coming out to his accepting father helped him feel better about his own decision to come out. "My Dad's acceptance reinforced my feeling that coming out was a really good thing. That figuring this out about yourself and starting early was a good thing. One of my father's friends in his AA meeting is a gay man in his fifties who didn't come out until he was fifty-one or fifty-two. That makes me sad—very sad." Gloria, an actress and previously quoted mother who initially struggled with self-blame when she learned her son was gay, noted:

> Because gay people are gay! That is why gay people are called "Gay!" There is a wonderful spirit . . . And this is not a broad generalization . . . a lot of them are theater kids too. They are sharp and sometimes because of the hard times they have had they are very kind and understanding. Noah is very kind and very understanding and so is his partner Rick.

For some young people, like Tony and Noah, their parents knowing and being so accepting helped respondents feel more certain of their sexual orientation. Noah described: "I guess fundamentally, like at a really base level, it just, like, cemented myself—not just the image, but like who I am. Like it cemented the sureness of who I am."

Once again, it is possible that parents' recognition of the special qualities of gay people played a role in how they interacted with their children, and children, relieved over not being rejected, and also feeling more confident, sought more interaction with their parents leading to reciprocal patterns of positive communication and improved relationships. One mother, a teacher who was very involved with the Catholic Church, cried hysterically when she first found out her daughter Crystal, aged eighteen, was a lesbian. Now, two years later, when asked what, if anything, was positive about having a gay child, she answered:

> What's positive about it? Oh, my God. She doesn't worry about guys. She's very self-confident. I see that difference between her and her sisters. . . . She

just doesn't care what people think about her because I think at sixteen she had to stand up for herself, "This is what I am," and she accepts herself for what she is. She's very confident. That's the positive part. And the other thing is—this is a stupid little anecdote. One day her girlfriend Jackie was over, and this was when they were in high school still. Jackie was waiting for Crystal to finish her homework, and I had a pile of towels downstairs. Jackie comes upstairs and says, "I was waiting, so I folded them for you. I said, "A boy would never have done that, Jackie."

Her daughter sees a clear improvement in the relationship since coming out. "Yes. My relationship with my mother is so wonderful. I can talk to her about anything and she'll be understanding about it. And my mom is really a strong woman, and she was determined to have a good relationship with me, no matter what it took."

Here we see an indication of reciprocity whereby the mother recognized the special qualities in lesbians and Crystal saw her mother as extremely committed to their relationship. Perhaps as a result, Crystal felt willing and able to share more of her life with her mother. As mentioned before, it is tempting to ask what came first, the mother recognizing and appreciating her daughter's special "lesbianlike" qualities or the daughter being more open—and, once again, it is impossible to know for sure. What is important is to recognize that both factors work together in tandem to stimulate ongoing positive parent-child interaction.

A New World

If a person chooses too . . . having a gay child and really working with it can be the biggest growth experience of your own life because it forces you to stretch yourself . . . to stretch your understanding of people . . . of what love is . . . it is an opportunity to do some political activist work, whether it is marching in a parade or whatever you do. I just think if you really go with the flow it is a lesson in compassion and courage. And you watch a child come out and blossom into a wonderful person with a relationship, and all that stuff, that is normal, and this is a privilege.

This is from Rachel, a previously quoted museum curator who was devastated when she found out her twenty-year-old daughter Beth was gay. Rachel's statement represents the best possible outcome to be expected after a child comes out—an outcome we would wish for all parents of lesbians and gays.

According to McMillen (1999), some people search for meaning in misfortune, which, when found, can profoundly alter their view on life. As stated in the beginning of chapter 3, the definition the family makes of the event plays a role in how they will cope with it (Hill 1971), so if parents come to believe that learning and adjusting to their children's coming out has enriched their lives, they are obviously going to have an easier time than parents who see this event as a painful disappointment.

Parents in nine of the families discussed how having a gay child eventually opened up a new world to them, both socially and politically. Not only did these parents broaden their social circles by meeting other gay people and parents, as some did in PFLAG, but they also developed increased sensitivity to the burdens of others. Such newly found empathy can be a positive outcome for people who have been through a traumatic event (McMillan 1999), and some of the parents in this study were fortunate enough to find this silver lining.

Remember Ann, the mother of Mike, the young man who tried to commit suicide in the presence of the family priest right before he came out to his parents? When asked what, if anything, was positive about having a gay son, she explained:

> It has opened up the world to me. I have met some of the nicest people [parents] I've ever known, in PFLAG. And I have also met some very interesting gay people . . . It has just really expanded my universe, and I think it has made me a better person. And I mean I always considered myself an extremely tolerant person . . . my parents set that example, but . . . because Mike was gay and I got involved in PFLAG and I started to speak at high schools and stuff . . . this brought it out.

Children of parents who mentioned these broadened worldviews saw their relationships with their parents grow closer during the family adjustment trajectory—for them this was a great benefit of coming out. When asked to describe changes in his relationship with his parents since coming out, Ann's son Mike described an enhanced openness: "Awesome. We are buddies. We talk. . . . It was always pretty good, but now there is no wall, no area we couldn't get into. You know, we just chat, talk, even about guys." Mike's parents, Ann and Fred, were members of the PFLAG speaker's bureau. Fred

was visibly moved when he described the profound emotional impact of the
warmth and gratitude from gays and lesbians he met during his first speech
as well as when he marched as a member of PFLAG in the annual gay pride
parade. He also reflected on the eye-opening experience of encountering
aspects of what can best be described as gay and lesbian culture:

FRED: I am not much of a speaker and I was nervous during our first talk.
Then it was surprising to have somebody gay come up to us from the audience afterwards and thank us for being there. It was like, wow, we are just
parents! And then that first gay pride parade . . . Wow! We are assembling
on 56th Street and we got the woman in the clown outfit on a tricycle in
front of us—Dyke on Bikes—and the guys in the leather were across the
way in chains and stuff. We were like, are we in the right place? Are we
sure we want to be here?

INTERVIEWER: What was that like for you to see?

FRED: Strange. We were walking down Fifth Avenue, and there was a float,
and there were all these guys—they were in very skimpy bathing suits and
they had their music playing and they were hosing one another down.
And they were dancing and they had this disco-type music going and
they had feathers. And I was like, "Wow! Over the top! Talk about rainbow . . . " It was like, "Am I in the right place? Do I belong here? Am I
out of place? I don't seem to fit into this."

And then you get to the next block . . . to the first viewing stand, and
they say, "And here comes the North Jersey PFLAG." And then people in
the crowd start making eye contact and saying, "I love you, Dad." And
then you start saying it back and by the time you get to the Village you've
got people coming out of the crowd, crying and hugging. And then you
are talking to people. It is overwhelming. It is like, "Wow, I am glad I
did this."

If you have never been to a gay pride parade, I would urge you to find
one and watch what happens between the lesbians and gays on the sidelines
and the PFLAG parents as they march by. Don't be surprised to see lots of
enthusiastic and tearfully appreciative LGBT people shouting, "I love you,
Mom! I love you, Dad!" and PFLAG parents smiling back, some warmly and
some in stunned surprise. Many gays and lesbians have either been rejected
by their parents, worry about future rejection (if they are not out), or, if they
came out and were not rejected, recall dreading this possibility. Those of us

who are gay react viscerally when we watch PFLAG march by because almost all of us have feared rejection, yet, at the same time, yearned for parents like these PFLAG marchers who not only accept us but are willing to proudly and publicly proclaim their love and acceptance. When lesbians and gays whose parents are unaware or who have been less than positive encounter PFLAG parents, they project onto them their wishes to be fully loved by their own mothers and fathers for who they really are. In return, PFLAG parents, like Fred, are humbled by the magnitude and power of the reactions of lesbians and gays who are strangers and also surprised by their newfound heroic roles in the community.

Some parents gained a new sensitivity not only to the trials and tribulations of gay people but also to other oppressed minorities. As Janet, the previously quoted mother of Robert, an eighteen-year-old gay man, described:

JANET: You meet a whole new group of people that you might not have met otherwise. I can appreciate that. I mean even getting involved with PFLAG has been an interesting experience. And I have become more sympathetic to outsiders in general. It is very easy to be smug in life. You do develop a little more generosity.

INTERVIEWER: What kind of outsiders?

JANET: Oh, any kind of racial or oppressed group. There are so many in our society . . . I mean we got involved through the parent and faculty gay/straight alliance. Then we got involved in the diversity group at our kid's school and stuff . . . and got involved with all sorts of issues which have to do with race and class. It was kind of very interesting stuff that probably would not have been so interesting to me had I not had a gay son. So I sort of recognize that is the positive thing that has come out of it.

It is no accident that all of the respondents quoted in this section are white. As a matter of fact, all but one of the parents who described how having a gay or lesbian child changed their worldview and made them more tolerant of other oppressed groups were white. A possible reason for this could be that white parents, once their children identified as gay, realized that not only their children but they themselves were now part of a stigmatized group—for the first time in their lives.

Unlike African Americans or Latinos, many white people, particularly if they are from the middle or upper socioeconomic classes, may not fully understand oppression and marginalization in our society, because, for the most part, they have never been its targets. McIntosh (1998) goes a step further and suggests that white people are taught not to recognize the unfair benefits they receive as a result of being a member of their race, such as having the opportunity to receive a better education, live in better neighborhoods, and work in higher paying jobs than their nonwhite counterparts.

Once the white parents in this study learned their children were gay, they began to understand oppression on a very personal level and what it was like to live as a stigmatized person. Perhaps the African American and Latino respondents did not mention increased understanding of intolerance as a result of their children coming out because, presumably, they had a better understanding of what it was like to be among its sufferers and having a lesbian or gay child might simply have added to what they already understood and experienced. More information on how race and ethnicity might affect families of lesbian and gay youth coming out will be presented in chapter 6.

Ongoing Family Difficulties

It would be great to be able to say that all the parents in this study reached a point where they had not only adjusted to but also realized the benefits of having a gay son or lesbian daughter. However, in this research, as in real life, this was not the case. In particular, father-child relationships that were distant or otherwise troubled before the child came out stayed the same or worsened afterward, according to the young respondents' reports. Second, parents of gay children had ongoing worries and fears that may have abated somewhat but never completely dissipated.

Unchanged Father-Child Relationships

American family life is suffering from a famine of fatherhood. When it comes to paternal attention, love, and affection, many, or perhaps most of us, straight or gay, are badly malnourished. Though it may be satisfying to bash individual fathers, they are not completely to blame. What my experience as a family therapist and researcher has taught me is that despite some shifting in sex roles in the past fifty years or so, fathers are still judged by how they materially provide for their families—not how they emotionally nurture their children. Furthermore, as the findings herein suggest, the way families structure themselves may leave little opportunity for fathers to provide this type of nourishing sustenance.

In many of the families of this study, fathers existed on the emotional periphery of their children's lives, and, in most cases, the child's coming out did nothing to change this. Sometimes it even made things worse. As stated previously, close to two-thirds of the youth described how coming out to their mothers improved their relationships with them. An additional ten said their relationships were always good and, with the exception of a few rough patches during the precoming-out and discovery phases, these relationships remained strong. In comparison, when asked how, if at all, coming out changed their relationship with their fathers, only eleven young people reported that their relationships with their dads improved. The other young respondents said their paternal relationships stayed the same, meaning they remained distant or grew more so in the months and years following the child's coming out.

Remember M. C., the previously quoted young man who enjoyed a continuously close relationship with his mother, with whom he frequently played Scrabble and watched political shows? He had been out to his parents for five years and told of how his postdiscovery relationship with his father was just as distant as his relationship with him prior to coming out:

> Basically, it is the same as it was before, in the sense that we are not really ones to speak that much or that often. We are sort of distant. That remains the same. He probably wants a closer relationship with me, but I don't know why. I think part of it is that I don't have any interests in common with him. He likes golf, watching TV, but we watch different things. He likes seeing cars go running around and around and around, five hundred times. I don't . . . I find football quite annoying.

The coming-out process could aggravate already tense or distant father-child relationships, and eight of the youth talked about how their relationships with their fathers got worse during the coming out trajectory. As described in chapter 4, fathers of sons faced special obstacles in their adjustment. Mitch's father did not agree to participate in this study, but according to Mitch's report, his father expressed a combination of homophobic disgust and dread that is particularly common among anxious heterosexual men. As mentioned previously, when his father found out he was gay, he kept asking him in horror if he knew what two men did in bed. When asked how his current relationship with his father was and how it compared before and after he came out to him, Mitch summarized things succinctly: "It was OK before I came out. When I came out absolutely horrid. And as of now borderline horrid."

Fathers of lesbians could also have a very difficult time adjusting. Jennifer was the previously quoted twenty-year-old girl who was embarrassed and ashamed when her mother, Martha, read her diary six years ago and found out she was gay. When asked whether coming out changed her relationship with her father, from whom her mother had been divorced for most of her life, she replied:

> No, it stayed distant. And I didn't tell him until I was a senior in high school so that was three years after I had been out to almost everyone. He definitely was not OK with it. He didn't express it with me. He didn't tell me that it's not OK, but he is like, "I need time with this." I don't even know how he is now with it. He won't let me come over with a girlfriend for dinner or anything. He said he is not comfortable with it. After I told him I was gay, he didn't get back to me for a long time. He wouldn't respond to my phone calls or e-mails, and he likes to e-mail a lot. He wouldn't respond, and finally I was like, "Dad, why aren't you responding?" And he is like, "Well, I don't know how comfortable I am with your friend."

In contrast to the positive reciprocity that led to parental adjustment in some families, there might have been a negative interaction effect between distant, disapproving fathers and their children. As stated previously, detachment in father-child relationships might be a function of men's socially scripted tendency to be less engaged in the emotional lives of their children. Due to an already distant relationship, some children might not speak directly to their fathers about their sexual orientations, leaving it up to their mothers. When a father, who already shares a distant relationship with his child, learns the child is gay, his guilt, grief, or discomfort might lead him to further disengage. In a reciprocal fashion, the child, feeling uncomfortable and anxious about the father's increased disengagement, might also increase the distance. Thus coming out and its ensuing dynamics could perpetuate and aggravate the detachment already present in these relationships.

However, in other instances, we saw, in chapters 3 and 4, how fathers became closer to their children in circumstances when struggling mothers pulled away. This suggests that father-child distancing might be, at least partially, systemically related to mother-child closeness whereby maternal relationships may in some ways inhibit the connection between fathers and their children; or alternatively, mothers and children become close to compensate for paternal distancing—perhaps both dynamics occur simultaneously. So, while distant relationships between fathers and children might be in part a function of sex-role expectations, it is important not to overlook systemic factors such as how mother-child interactions either foster or make up for unsatisfying father-child relationships.

As described elsewhere in this book, father and child perceptions of the paternal relationship before coming out can differ, and in some families there were also discrepancies between the fathers' and children's perceptions of the relationship several months after the child came out. Three fathers whose children said the relationship remained distant or became more so once they came out perceived the relationship as having improved. Wanda, a previously quoted college student, described her current relationship with her father Frank, a butcher, who participated in this research and was previously quoted:

> We don't really have a relationship. It's horrible to say. We don't talk about anything. The only way I can bond with my father is at the bar or if we're drinking together, and even then nothing serious is discussed. It's just shooting the shit, as they say. Sorry. That's it. That's all I've ever known from him, unless I'm going to go fishing with him or I go drinking with him.

However, Frank believed the relationship got better. He reported: "I'd have to say we're closer . . . we joke around more now than we ever did." This next father did not say whether or not his relationship with his son improved, but at the time of his interview he saw it as pretty normal and positive: "I'd say we have a good relationship—as close as you can be to a college age kid. He doesn't tell us everything." His son described: "Oddly enough, it has kind of come full circle. We don't talk that much. When I was a kid or in high school, driving to school we would talk about superficial stuff like school, the weather, politics, sports, whatever . . . and it is just kind of the same way now." As stated earlier, fathers tend to have relationships with their children in which they provide them with material and physical assistance rather than emotional support, and it seems in at least a few of these families this did not change once the child came out. In chapter 4 Lily's father Rocky described how, after she came out, he believed that he and Lily got closer, with Lily more available for Rocky's hugs. When Lily was asked how coming out changed her relationship with her father, she replied, "We don't discuss much and we've kind of gone into our own corners . . . I trust him. I care about him. We may not talk about things, but when I got in a car accident the first person I called was him. He is always there and he always will be."

Possible explanations for these discrepancies are similar to what has been described before. Fathers might not want to admit to an outsider how their relationships were less than ideal, particularly to an interviewer who is gay or a parent of a lesbian. A second factor might also be at play, whereby children and fathers have different standards as to what constitutes a good father-child relationship. Whatever the reason, it is hard to read these interviews and not feel sad over the inability of these fathers and their children to fully, emotionally connect.

It is worth noting that in each of the families previously quoted the child's relationship with the mother improved after coming out. Only three children reported that relationships with their mothers suffered since they came out. This next African American girl, aged sixteen, lived with her mother in a blighted urban neighborhood: "We are not as close as we used to be. She works a lot and we don't spend much time together. And, when we do spend time together, all we do is complain." Her mother, a security guard at an office complex, recognized the current problems and attributed them to her own stresses:

It could be better. I am very tense because I don't like living here. I am not happy with my job. So I am very tense. That affects us because, well, Linda tends to repeat the same things. It might seem like little mistakes, but they are consistent. Like putting empty containers back in the refrigerator, not putting tops back on anything, leaving lights on. I have an eating disorder, and she knows I have issues with food. So don't eat certain things when you know that is going to create a problem. And she will anyway.

Another respondent felt mostly satisfied with her relationship with her mother but was disturbed by her mother's new tendency to talk about her own sex life. It was almost as if the daughter telling her mother she was a lesbian left her mother feeling she now had the freedom to talk in detail about her own sexual interests. The third respondent felt frustrated because he wished he could spend more quality time with his mother but was unsure whether her unavailability had to do with her feelings about his sexual orientation.

Fear for Children's Well-Being

Let's face it, most parents worry about their children, whether they are gay, lesbian, or straight, and will continue to do so as long as they live. To nurture and protect a child from infancy and then to watch her go out into the world beyond their protective reach is a difficult transition for many parents, who, understandably, never loose the desire to keep their children safe. This tendency is particularly strong for parents of gay and lesbian children. If it is true that parents' primary wish for their children is that they be happy and healthy, then it follows that they would be deeply troubled by the thought that their gay and lesbian children would encounter threats to their well-being—particularly those related to being gay such as such as harassment, discrimination, and HIV infection.

Most of the parents in this study, even those who recognized and could articulate the benefits of adjusting to and accepting a gay child, continued to worry about the well-being of their children, and this anxiety persisted no matter how long it had been since their children had come out to their them. The African American woman who lives in the inner city and whose daughter came out four years ago was quoted earlier in this chapter on how her pride in her daughter's academic accomplishments helped her adjust to her sexual orientation. However, the recent murder of an openly lesbian young woman in her neighborhood filled her with worry. She remembered: "She said they are going to this new gay club, tomorrow or Friday, in Newark. I think it's called the Globe or something—she'll tell you about it. It scares me to death, so I keep telling her to be careful." Her daughter, who knew the murdered young woman, was well aware of her mother's concerns for her safety.

Mac, a retired gay firefighter, was previously quoted as fearing for the safety of his fourteen-year-old, newly out lesbian daughter, Jillian, who understood his worries: "Yeah, he said to be careful in school and stuff—that not a lot of people are OK with it, and I realized that too. I told him that I have seen what goes on in school. I realized that it was not really the safest thing to go and parade around in school, with teenagers who aren't exactly mature."

A child's appearance could play a role in parents' ongoing fears. This next mother, whose daughter Emma had been out three years, described:

> I think it is, for me, a worry because of her presentation. Because a lot of her friends—you don't know that they are gay unless they want you to know that they are gay. But Emma is not like that: she is out . . . Yes, that

is the thing I worry about, that it will put her in danger. I know there are people in this world who are crazy. And who, for whatever reason, don't like gays and want to hurt them. So I do worry about that.

Her daughter described:

When I cut my hair, she was really worried that something might happen. She still doesn't want me to put a rainbow flag on my car, just because she doesn't know what would be done to my car. She worries that, because I am very open and out, that I'll get hurt or that somebody will do something to harm me. She told me that, probably right after I cut my hair. And then in January of freshman year in college is when I got my car, and I wanted to put a rainbow sticker on it. She was like, "I don't really want you to."

Parents could be worried about discrimination in their children's future careers, particularly if the family was middle class. When asked what, if anything, was difficult about having a lesbian child, this father, an architect whose daughter had been out for three years, offered: "The only difficulty I can see, it would be, again, how other people, other than family, would construe her, especially people in the business world."

Sons and HIV

In the U.S. and other Western countries, adolescents and young adults, particularly males, are notorious risk takers (Johnson and Malow-Iroff 2008). Considering this youthful propensity, along with parents' natural lifelong tendency to worry for their children, it must be very frightening for parents to launch a gay young son into the world knowing he is exploring sexual relationships among a population of people in which a sizable proportion are believed to carry a dangerous, sexually transmitted virus.

In chapter 4 we saw how parents' angst about their sons contracting HIV could get in the way of their adjustment. Even among parents who adjusted to the news their son was gay, the fear of HIV remained an ongoing concern. Parents worried about their sons' well-being, particularly if they in any way seemed to be jeopardizing their health through their sexual activities.

This Latina mother described her current feelings about her son's homosexuality, one year after finding out: "Honestly, it is not about the sexuality itself. It is about being promiscuous with strangers, dating people he didn't know, doing drugs, drinking—drinking a lot. And it is just a main concern about him being at the wrong place at the wrong time." Her worries were at least partially allayed by her son's current involvement with a steady boy-friend. Nevertheless, her son knew his mother feared he would contract HIV. For parents of gay sons, HIV-risk was a large, looming fear that did not dissipate as time passed from the initial discovery.

This next mother described: "He has told me that he has no problem jumping into bed with whomever because he thinks is cute (*laughing*). That is when the condom conversation starts." Her son, when asked if he thought his mother worried about him getting HIV, responded, "I'm sure she does . . . She has tried to give me the talk, and I always shut her up. Because I'm like, 'You are my mother! We are just not going to have this conversation!' . . . I don't want to hear about them, so why do [they] want to hear about me?" This next mother described: "Like any kid, he doesn't want to talk to me about sex, so since my current thing is fear about his sexual activity . . . I wouldn't be sort of in [his] face about it. But I am with him about this. So he gets mad at me. You know, 'Leave me alone. I know all that.'"

Ann, mother of Mike, who tried to commit suicide right before he told his mother he was gay, spoke of how she tried to talk to her son about his sex life:

> Well, I realize it is totally up to him but I have been very blunt with him and said; "I hope that you are practicing safe sex." And he said, "Oh, Ma!" And I said, "I have to say it." We always joked when they were kids, if they didn't like something I did, I would say, "I am required by law; it is on my mother's license. I have to do this. And if I don't they will revoke my license."

Imagine being a frightened parent who sees a child facing a risk to his health and life but who feels helpless to do anything about it. As these quotes indicate, the parents in this study tried to discuss HIV risk with their children, but their kids, clearly embarrassed by their parents' wish to talk specifically about sex—especially sex that is considered taboo—resisted their efforts. Thus the parents' fears must have been compounded by their feelings of helplessness. Clearly, as indicated by the reactions of these young men, it is quite difficult to deal with this issue by talking about it directly.

Nevertheless, there is some good news—family relationships *can* have an impact on a son's sexual behaviors. As I explain elsewhere in more detail

(LaSala 2007), a little over half the gay male youth in this study revealed that their parents had in fact influenced them to engage only in safer sex. However, the influence they cited was not their parents' efforts at educating or monitoring them, which felt like intrusive nagging. (Does that ever really work?) Instead, it was the young men's feelings of obligation to their parents to stay healthy that inspired them to either avoid anal sex altogether or consistently use condoms when they engaged in it. The young gay respondents knew that if they contracted HIV their families would be devastated.

After reading my article on this topic, a respected colleague of mine who does research on HIV prevention asked, with stunned incredulity, "Are you saying that a child's guilt is a good thing?" After a pause—during which I briefly felt . . . well . . . guilty for thinking guilt can be a good thing—I responded, "Yes, if it keeps the child safe." Guilt can be beneficial if it reminds children that their behavior has implications for those who love them, but can be a problem if parents use it excessively to control their behavior.

Courtesy Stigma

As stated previously, when parents learned they had a gay child, they very quickly realized they were now living in a world that stigmatized not only their children but also themselves. Suddenly, these parents were involuntarily drafted into a club whose members were disparaged by others. For some parents, particularly those who were white, this was their first bitter taste of the injustice of stigma, and it was eye-opening in ways that were painful and frightening.

As described throughout earlier chapters, there are two types of courtesy stigma: *vicarious stigma,* or the suffering parents feel empathically because their loved one is suffering, and *public stigma,* which is the stigma family members experience because they are thought to be to blame for their loved one's stigmatizing condition (Corrigan and Miller 2004). These two types of stigma were clearly issues for parents in this study. When asked, "What was the most difficult thing about having a gay or lesbian child?" most parents (close to two-thirds of the parent sample) gave replies that described coping with stigma. In response to this question, this mother of a twenty-three-year-old gay son described:

What other people say. Like I can't stand, I mean I don't care about gay jokes, I am Italian—I can rattle off one thousand Italian jokes, whatever, but outright nastiness. If I am somewhere and someone says something derogatory about gay or lesbian people—that bothers me. My friends know, so they would never ever say anything that would hurt me or my son in front of me ever, and I would assume they wouldn't do it behind me either. I am talking about being at a restaurant or something and strangers saying something, particularly about gay marriage. That is hard, because I just want to turn around to them and say, "Is it hurting you? My son is gay, and you don't know him. How is that bothering you?" I don't, but I would like to.

Fred, the father of Mike, observed:

> It's hard with people you meet socially. Professionally, most educators are very positive . . . We've talked at two different high school health classes. For the most part, teachers have been supportive. However, this last time around, after we had done our presentation, a mother talked about her son, and I talked about my son. And then we turned it over to the class for questions, and there weren't many questions, so the teacher got involved and asked questions, and he was pretty ignorant. I was kind of surprised.

Sometimes parents were sensitive to the possibility of being judged negatively for having a gay or lesbian child, like Rocky, a previously quoted father of a lesbian: "Yes, there is a social stigma. Yes, I am hiding it. I only tell people I want to tell [who] I know are gay or people that are important in her life that she wants me to tell. Will I tell my boss or the people I work with? No. I never will . . . yes, there is still a stigma about being gay, and I can't tell general society." Sometimes people worried that others would judge or blame *them* for their child's homosexuality. In these circumstances, parents feared being the direct target of stigma. This Latina mother of a gay male described:

RESPONDENT: I think the hardest part is people finding out . . . because you have to deal with people who want to find fault with you. They pretend to be your friend, and I don't feel that they are friends enough for me to tell them my son is gay. I don't think they care enough for me to say this is what is going on with my son. So I think the hard part is if people found out, how they would react. To me it wouldn't make a difference, because I wouldn't speak to them anymore anyway, but with members of the church, I don't know how they would react to that.

INTERVIEWER: You don't tell them so they don't think badly about your son or so they don't feel bad about you?

RESPONDENT: Yes, so that they don't feel bad about me. I still realize there is a stigma to having a gay child. Somehow I might have done something wrong. I am not saying I don't feel good about Carlos being gay, I feel good about telling the people he wants me to tell and the people I am comfortable talking to—my good friends. But have I told anybody I work with, any of my employees or my clients? No, other than the gay ones, no. It is my choice, but I am not ready to go there. I still think it is a problem; I am not ready to shout it to the world. I am not going on any PFLAG march, because I still have those feelings that somebody important to me might be turned off. I still feel that way, I have to admit it.

Other parents reported experiencing the stigma vicariously. Like all good parents, they wanted to protect their children. When they heard antigay hostility from others, they were reminded of the stigma their children would encounter. As remarked by Rachel, who was quoted earlier in this chapter:

I learned who to talk to. I would become more aware of people's comments about gay people and then decide who I might not want to reveal her identity to. Or I . . . would just be quiet in a situation. It is hard. And you worry about them. You know, when they are young . . . you worry about them anyway, and when you have got a gay teenager you worry about them.

Also, as stated by Susan, the mother of Mitch:

I have a new friend at work, and I just want to tell her. I just kind of want to try it out on her. But I haven't yet. I don't think the moment has been there yet. I was at lunch with a girlfriend last week, and it is a girl I have known for a number of years, and she said something about a mutual acquaintance of ours, a single woman, and she says, "You know, did you ever think she was gay?" And I said, "Yeah, I did." And she said, "I don't care." And I said, "Well I certainly don't care." And I thought that was the opportunity to say, "I certainly don't care because my son is gay." And I thought I missed that opportunity. I could have tried that out on her and saw what happened.

I still feel like I might lose some friends over this. I would be a little more upset if I would lose some family. But I also think that I underestimate people. People that love me should love me and love my son. But I am still afraid. I am not ready to take that risk yet. And I don't know. I hope I wake up and someday think I am ready. It would be hard for me to be ready before my husband because if I told close friends he would be uncomfortable. I don't want to do that to him.

This next mother of a lesbian claimed never to have had a problem with her daughter's sexuality. When asked what, if anything, was currently difficult about having a lesbian child, she replied:

I think the difficult thing is the reactions of others. I know I shouldn't let that bother me, but I worry are they going to change the way they treat her or not talk to her because they don't know what to say or are uncomfortable? That is the thing I find difficult, worrying about how certain people are going to be towards her.

If you are a gay, lesbian, transgender, or a bisexual person, or someone with a concealable disability, the thoughts and feelings of these parents must seem familiar; LGBT people, along with others whose stigmatizing conditions are hidden from public view, have to make decisions on an almost daily basis as to whom to disclose their distinguishing characteristic—having to scan their environments and find ways to determine who will be accepting and who won't are frequent exercises for LGBT people as well as many others. Once parents of lesbian and gay people are aware of their children's sexual orientations, they learn that they too must find ways to manage stigma.

The children of parents who worried what other people would think were not aware of their parents' struggles to manage stigma. They knew that their parents worried they could be hurt by others but were ignorant as to the specific ways parents wrestled with their reactions to other people's real or anticipated feelings and opinions. This is a shame, considering that the young gay and lesbian people themselves are going to have to, or already have, found ways to cope with ongoing discrimination, oppression, and persecution in their lives. Based on these findings, ways of dealing with stigma would be a good topic for family discussion, and this will be further explicated in the clinical implications section of this chapter.

Summary and Clinical Implications

Parent-Child Interactions During Family Renewal: Gifts and Growth

There's good news for families of lesbian and gay children and that is that parents can reach the point where they are proud of their children and value them for their uniqueness. They can use the experience of adjusting to a lesbian or gay child to broaden their perspectives on life. They can also develop sensitivity to other marginalized groups—no doubt because parents of coming-out children abruptly find themselves potentially stigmatized. As a result, or perhaps as a function of these benefits, parent-child relationships can improve, and families can become stronger than ever following a son or daughter's coming out. Now the million dollar question is, what is the alchemy that transforms troubled parents and children into families that can reap such rewards?

Reaching for Positives

Seasoned therapists are familiar with the difficulty, even impossibility, of getting families to see the gold nuggets between the silt and stones of trouble and misfortune. We are rightly suspicious and cynical when experts offer easy-sounding solutions to this challenge—because we know none exist.

Nevertheless, the stories of the respondents in this book offer important clues that may suggest some relevant guidelines. As indicated in the last chapter, parents can be guided to get emotional relief and reassurance from nonjudgmental confidants outside their immediate families. Clinicians can point out to children the role played by their own interactions and behavior in their relationships with their parents. Furthermore, reports of parents who believed their lives improved suggest that practitioners need to be actively vigilant for this possibility among client-families of coming-out children. We will never know whether there is gold in the hills unless we look for it.

However, in our search for positives, we must be careful not to impart the message to our clients that we are uninterested or incapable of listening to their suffering—or that there is something wrong with them if they don't find something good in their pain. In previous chapters I talk about how clients must feel that their suffering is heard before they are ready to accept referrals, education, or, if in conflict, their opposing family member's point of view. I would add that clients must feel their guilt, shame, loss, and fear are understood before they can even think about how having and adjusting to a gay or lesbian child can be in any way positive.

McMillen (1999) suggests some gentle, sensitive questions clinicians can ask their clients about possible benefits and wisely cautions that this should be done in a way that does not invalidate people's grief, anger, and anxiety. In keeping with his advice, well-timed questions are proposed, such as "I see how painful and difficult this is for you right now, but I am wondering what, if anything, you are learning from the experience of having a gay child? What is it teaching you about yourself, your child, your family, life in general?" or "I can really hear the (pain, grief, disgust, shame, anxiety, fear) that this is causing you. What, if anything, might be positive about having a gay or lesbian child?"

In addition, it would be advisable for the therapist to have the previously described catcher's mitt ready so that she can hear and, perhaps, gently reinforce anything the client recognizes as positive. In so doing, therapists can give families who are struggling some hope that there is not only a possible end in sight to their suffering but also that something constructive might eventually come out of the coming out crisis.

Engaging Fathers

The finding that many strained or disengaged father-child relationships did not change or improve in the months or years after the child came out further suggests that therapists must work to engage detached fathers. It bears repeating that family therapists must be careful not to collude with a societal tendency to exclude fathers from the emotional lives of their children. Instead, they need to find ways to engage them and draw them out. Like swimming upstream, this is not easy, but, in my experience, I have seen too many family therapists demonize fathers for acting in the ways in which they have been socialized—if we really want to help families, we need to stop doing this.

Many men tend to clam up when asked directly about emotionally charged issues, especially if they don't really know the person doing the asking. They are not trained to recognize their emotional needs, never mind discuss them. Thus, when the conversation turns to feelings, particularly painful feelings, they might feel as if the therapist and the female family members are speaking a foreign language. That is why, early in therapy, direct questions such as "how does that make you feel?" are often ineffective. Both my personal and my professional experiences have taught me that, sometimes, the task of getting a man to talk about his sadness, fear, and anger is like coaxing a squirrel into a cage—sudden, dramatic movements are best avoided.

Instead, to engage reluctant fathers, it is better to start slowly by discussing issues with a low emotional charge, such as their work or hobbies, until they seem to feel at ease. Then, as they get more comfortable and the relationship with the therapist becomes established, the therapist can ask family-oriented questions that do not necessarily leave the client emotionally vulnerable, such as what makes them most proud of their sons and daughters. Once fathers seem more relaxed, as evidenced by the free flow of conversation, therapists can gently probe such topics as how they feel about their daughter's or son's sexual orientation.

De Jong and Berg (2008) point out that, quite often, in marriage or family therapy, men are involuntary clients—even though there might be no legal mandate, they are in therapy because someone else, namely, their wives, thinks they should be. Thus, as is advisable with most involuntary clients, it is a good idea for therapists to initially take their time to get to know them, making them as comfortable as possible before slowly drawing them out. It is important, specifically in families with lesbian and gay children and distant, distressed fathers, that we are sure to engage and then gently pressure them to add their voices to family issues.

We must also be mindful that family dynamics might function in a way that both keeps fathers peripheral and mothers overburdened with the emotional needs of their children. So, as clinicians invite fathers to be more engaged, they might at the same time need to get the family to make room for his participation. Coaching certain enactments like "Mom, do you have any idea how Dad feels about this? He seems like the strong silent type—but can you get him to talk to you about this right now?" or asking Father directly, "Dad, you are an important part of this family and a big part of Jason's life. Let's give Mom a little rest and hear what you thought about when your son told you he was gay." Then clinicians may need to patiently wait for Dad's response, and help other family members do the same, while at the same time standing ready to interrupt any interruptions. Such interventions can push fathers to talk and also give therapists an opportunity to show other family members how they might be letting Dad off the hook by not asking him such questions or blocking his participation by interrupting him when he attempts to speak. Whatever clinicians do, they must be sure they don't leave fathers out and avoid getting induced by the family into doing so.

Once Dad is talking, there are new challenges, particularly if his views are angry or harshly critical. Remember, fathers are raised in a world where homosexuality is too often about dominance and humiliation. As stated earlier, go anywhere heterosexual males are together in a group and accusations of homosexuality can be heard as a taunt or a put down. Thus some of fathers' reactions may have to do with their own special shame and anguish, which must be recognized. As stated throughout this book, gays, lesbians, and parents need to become social critics, and fathers need to recognize the myths they have been taught about homosexuality so they can begin to unlearn them.

HIV and Helping the Family Launch a Gay Son

When we are confronted with danger and feel we cannot protect ourselves or those we love, of course we are going to feel anxious. Parents who are launching their children must learn to give up trying to feel in control (Garcia-Preto 1999). They must find a way to reconcile themselves to the helplessness they feel when they realize they cannot fully prevent their children from engaging in risky behaviors, nor shield them from the consequences of such behaviors. However, customary parental fear is perhaps much worse for parents who must launch a gay son into a world in which a moment of simple carelessness could leave him with a potentially fatal illness. The natural tendency when we become anxious is to try, as much as possible, to be in control. Nevertheless, nervous parents who seek control of their children risk choosing methods that not only don't work but instead push their children away. In this study, parents urging their sons to talk about their sexual experiences or hounding them to use condoms was ineffective. Sons found this behavior intrusive, embarrassing, and irritating—not exactly the result parents were trying for.

What seemed to have some sway in the young gay males' behavior, however, was not necessarily what parents *did* but the *relationship* parents maintained with their children. The young men knew that if they were sexually careless and got sick they would not only hurt themselves but also those who loved them. In keeping with this, therapists helping families cope with the fear of HIV might find that parents and children are engaging in ineffective interchanges like this:

MOM: You'd better be using a condom, young man. There are a lot of diseases out there!

DAD: Yes, would you like me to buy you some condoms? I can if you are embarrassed.

SON: Eeewwww! Gross! Get off my back! I am not talking to you about my sex life—do I ask you about yours? Why the hell are you asking me about mine then?!

In families in which this type of interchange is occurring, it is the therapist's job to try to coach family members to replace such conversations with dialogues that include personal reflections of feelings, including, love, caring, and fear.

THERAPIST: I see this is a difficult topic to discuss. Mom and Dad, as good, concerned parents, you are worried for your child's well-being, and you, Junior, are understandably embarrassed to discuss your sex life with them. I am wondering if it would be helpful to dig a bit deeper. Mom, Dad, can you tell your son about your fears and what you would like from him? And, for now, Junior—as yucky as this seems—would you just sit back, not say anything, and just listen?

MOM: I know you are a young man and you make your own choices, but I love you and I would be devastated if anything bad happened to you.

DAD: It's a dangerous world out there. I remember Rock Hudson dying of AIDS and I don't want the same thing to happen to you. I just want to make sure you are safe, son.

Clinicians can also coach gay sons to reassure their parents.

THERAPIST: Of course you don't want to talk about your sex life with your parents. That's normal. But is there something—anything—you can tell them that can calm their worries, without getting into the details of your sex life?

SON: "Mom, Dad, I know I understand how to keep myself safe—they have been teaching us in school since eighth-grade health class. I'm not stupid—I don't want to die! I don't do anything that will make me sick. I promise."

This hypothetical excerpt is not meant to insinuate that this conversation will go as smoothly in real life, but instead is offered to demonstrate one way to coach family members to have more authentic, and therefore more productive, discussions about this especially anxiety-arousing subject. In reality, family members will probably need repeated prompts from the therapist before they are able to talk meaningfully and effectively about this stressful issue.

Managing Stigma Is a Family Affair

Like a slap in the face, when parents discovered their newly stigmatized status, it was sudden and jarring, particularly for white parents who were unaccustomed to dealing with stigma. Based on the findings of this study, it is likely that therapists working with families of lesbian and gay youth are going to confront parents who have ongoing concerns about how to handle their somewhat newly stigmatized status as parents of gay children.

For members of minority groups to be mentally healthy and strong, they must develop the ability to be critical of the society in which they live. They must be able to question the prevailing views on sexuality and gender and eventually understand that they are excessively narrow. Parents of gays and lesbians, like their children, must be able to withstand the slings and arrows that come with living in a world that persecutes those who challenge its restrictive norms governing sexuality and gender. In order to develop and maintain good self-esteem, gays, lesbians, and those who love them must grow to learn that some of the established ideas are just plain wrong.

In my own practice, my most troubled gay clients are the ones who cling to the notion that being gay is shameful, perverted, and indicative of weakness. In their minds, the treatment lesbians and gays receive is justified and proof of how wrong they are for having same-sex attractions. Until lesbians and gays and their parents develop the ability to be critical of society, I find they are unable to attain or preserve their self-esteem.

Since stigma is something the entire family must face, it is good grist for the family therapy mill. Although siblings were not interviewed for this study, during this research and in my clinical practice I have been made aware of incidents when brothers and sisters faced jeering taunts from peers who accused them of being gay or lesbian because they had a gay sibling. Lesbians and gays and their parents must find ways to handle the effects of discrimination and prejudice, so a discussion of these topics that includes the entire family could prove useful. The therapist can stimulate dialogues or enactments whereby family members conjointly discuss and strategize ways to handle stigma. For example, the clinician can introduce topics for family discussion and problem solving such as, who gets told about the child's sexual orientation? How do children make the decision as to whom to disclose? How do parents? How will family members handle the challenges of discrimination? Or, more specifically, what does one do when overhearing or being told an antigay joke?

It must be remembered that our young clients knew they were gay or lesbian a lot longer than their mothers and fathers knew they were parents of gay children. Based on the experiences of families discussed in chapter 1, many youth have had to find ways to survive the verbal and physical harassment of peers. Therefore, it is likely that they will have developed some coping tools forged in the fire of these painful challenges. Thus, by the time they come out, they can potentially share their expertise with their parents. In my own practice I have coached children to talk to their parents about their experiences with discrimination, whether from employers, teachers, school administrators, or peers. I have found that it can be quite effective when children share with their parents the strategies they have found useful.

Furthermore, it is important to consider that most of the families who are struggling with these issues do so at a time when the child must become more autonomous and adultlike. I have written of how satisfying it can be for children to know they have reached the level where they can be helpful to their parents. Thus it is no doubt gratifying for youth to be able to help their parents cope with something with which they have developed some proficiency. A simple directive that the young people talk about their experiences and make suggestions to other family members could be enough to spur a fruitful discussion in this area. Such an intervention can have the beneficial side effect of helping young clients and their families recognize and appreciate the child's competence—a good thing, considering the developmental stages of these families.

As mentioned earlier, it might be especially difficult for white parents to understand and cope with being newly stigmatized. That is not to say that things were easy for African American, Latino, or other minority families. Though many of the issues faced by families of color were the same as those encountered by whites, some unique cultural factors emerged that impacted the family trajectory and will be discussed in the next chapter.

CHAPTER 6

Race and Ethnicity

A T AN AMERICAN ASSOCIATION OF MARRIAGE AND FAMILY Therapy (AAMFT) conference several years ago, Nancy Boyd-Franklin, a leading expert on therapy with black families, told a personal story that brought to life one of the many complex challenges faced by these families. One afternoon she came upon her teenaged sons and their friends playfully tossing a realistic-looking toy gun around her living room. She became terrified as she imagined what would happen if these black teenagers were seen engaging in the same behavior in certain neighborhoods near their home, and so she gave them a very stern, if somewhat anxious, warning.

Professor Boyd-Franklin's anecdote powerfully illustrates how frightening it can be for parents to launch ethnic and racial minority youth into a world where they are potential targets of discrimination, violence, and police harassment and how such families must actively prepare their children to deal with the inevitable racism they will encounter. Despite improvements in race relations in this county in the past fifty years, including the election of a black president, race still matters, and, as the findings of this study suggest, it can play a role in how families respond to the news that a son or daughter is gay or lesbian.

Compared to whites, African Americans and Latinos suffer disproportionately higher rates of poverty, unemployment, incarceration, and stress-related illnesses (Boyd-Franklin 2006; Garcia-Preto 2005). Young black men aged eighteen to twenty-five are five times more likely to be victims of homicide than their white counterparts and stand a one in five chance of entering prison. Latinos have a one in ten likelihood of being incarcerated compared to white males, whose chances are less than one in twenty (U.S. Department of Justice 2008). In addition, blacks and Latinos are about three times more likely to be poor than whites (U.S. Census Bureau 2009). Furthermore, young gay men of color are more likely to contract HIV. In 2004, among a large, multicultural sample of young men who have sex with men (MSM), the HIV diagnosis rate for MSM aged thirteen through nineteen years was approximately nineteen times higher for black MSM (23.5 percent) than for white MSM (1.2 percent) and about five times higher for Hispanic MSM (6.1 percent) than for white MSM. (Hall et al. 2007). Although there is much debate about the causes of these disparities, many experts believe that the wounds of racism play a significant role.

Considering these troublesome statistics, it must be especially difficult for African American and Latino parents to watch their children grow into adulthood knowing the risks and challenges that lie ahead. Imagine, then, what it must be like for them to know their children will have yet another burden—a stigma that will not only make them more of a target but also threatens to alienate them from the very community providing the support that helps them survive in a racist society. A documented strength of African American, Latino, and Asian families is their close kinship ties, which provide safe harbor from the racist seas of the dominant culture (Garcia-Preto 2005; Greene and Boyd-Franklin 1996; Lee and Mock 2005). Loving, strong families can buffer the impacts of oppression on its members. In addition, families are also the first places where children learn ways to cope and thrive in spite of prejudice and discrimination. So for gay and lesbian youth who are black, Latino, or Asian, the thought of loosing this important resource must be particularly devastating.

In this study there were many ways in which the experiences of white, black, and Latino families were similar. (Because only a small number of Latino and Asian families participated in this study for reasons that will be described, the following discussion will focus primarily on the black [n = 17] family subsample.) African American youth, like their white counterparts, distanced themselves from their parents during family sensitization for self-protection and to avoid conflict. Like white parents, African American parents could still feel guilty when they first learned their children were gay. In addition, during the family recovery phase, many black families experienced improvements in their family relationships, fueled by mutually reinforcing parent-child interactions.

However, black parents were less likely than their white counterparts to report that they mourned the loss of a normal life for their children when they initially learned they were gay. Considering the elevated risk for poverty, illness, and incarceration faced by blacks and Latinos, such a "normal" life was perhaps less a sure thing all along. White parents might be more likely to take for granted that their daughters and sons would live a middle-class life-style as adults, while blacks or Latinos may not perceive that their children are promised the same opportunities for success. In light of the previously cited risks, black parents might be more concerned with issues of survival—such as avoiding jail, poverty, and violence. This may explain why, when they first learned their children were gay and throughout the family adjustment trajec-tory, black parents' most pressing concern was for the physical and psycho-logical well-being of their children. Parents of black lesbian and gay youth knew their children would be facing a double stigma—one related to race and the other to sexual orientation and, understandably, this worried them.

Stigma + Stigma

When asked what role being black played in how the family coped with the news of the child's sexual orientation, the most common response reflected the potential for double stigma. As reported by this mother, a security officer, who herself identified as bisexual: "It is harder for us to come out to our families. It is hard enough being a black woman, never mind a black gay or bisexual woman, because with black families there is just that stigma. The whole gay thing is like this whole shame thing."

When asked how being African American impacted the family's adjust-ment to Joelle's lesbianism, Nancy, her mother, replied:

I think that minorities in general talk less about issues like that [being lesbian or gay] because you already feel oppressed for being who you are naturally so you are less likely to admit to other things . . . it is like no one can look at you and say, "You are a lesbian." But they can look at you and say, "Hey, you are a minority." So why would you add that on to the load you already carry in life? So I think that in general it is not discussed . . . Also if you look around publicly you don't see too many minorities [who] are gay and lesbian stand up and talk about it. Everyone is Caucasian who is coming to the forefront of the issue so you feel like you don't have the social support from your own culture.

Nancy also mentioned issues of class:

I also think it sometimes also depends on location, where you live . . . the general acceptance in that area. I think if you live in the ghetto and you're fighting for survival, then your black family is going to take it a little harder and not be happy about the issue than, say, if you live in a more comfortable setting where your family is already comfortable, they are already close, and they don't feel in danger . . . then they feel less threatened when the issue comes up.

Joelle and Nancy were a middle-class family. Despite Nancy's perception, in this study there did not seem to be a perceived difference in tolerance based on socioeconomic class. Upper-middle-class, middle-class, lower-middle-class, and poor families struggled with the same issues, although wealthier families were more likely to worry about the impact of their children's sexual orientation on their careers. Tolerance in schools also did not seem to be related to the socioeconomic class of the students they served. There were several examples of kids in white, upper-middle-class schools who were beaten and harassed by their peers—when a few miles away, in the impoverished inner city, the students' families were financially worse off, but schools had support groups and included LGBT issues in their antibullying curricula. As a matter of fact, students in schools in wealthier districts that ran these programs also experienced less harassment than those attending schools that did not. Thus resources and support for LGBT students, rather than the socioeconomic class of the families in the school district, was what made a difference for the gay and lesbian kids in this study.

Joelle knew that worries about racism and heterosexism weighed heavily on her mother's mind. She identified the triple threat of racism, homophobia, and sexism—walls she knew her mother was forced to scale, while her white colleagues climbed the corporate ladder encountering far fewer obstacles:

Yeah, I definitely think if you are already an ethnic minority, your life is already difficult and then you add one more thing onto it plus being female . . . you are just the ultimate scapegoat for society . . . I know my mother had a childhood where her ethnicity was a major factor in how she was treated and also her gender in terms of trying to reach career goals. So she didn't want me to have any kind of obstacle to what I could achieve in my life just because of something so personal.

Norman, the father of Franklin, who was from Guyana, anticipated what it would be like for his son to live in the U.S. as a gay black man.

I know that if you are not conscious of your blackness in America, then you are living a fool's life. If you are gay and black you doubly have to have the inner strength and readiness to do battle out there. If not, then you are just going to live a minimal life and you will never live up to your full potential. So, from that perspective, I express that to him. As a matter of fact, I tell him so much, he is tired of hearing me say it. Now, when we have conversations, he is like, "Oh God, here he goes again."

His son Franklin believed that his Guyanese ethnicity made it more difficult to be gay, which will be discussed later in this chapter.

This African American young man living in an urban environment stated:

I think it is harder as an African American. I think for any minority it is harder. Number one, you are already a minority. That is one strike. Number two, there are already a lot of people who don't like you just because you are a minority. That is strike two, and then you being gay on top of that—that is like, fuck! You are just not liked, and everything is against you. Nobody should feel like that.

The issue of race came up in a startling way at a meeting of a support group I attended for gay and lesbian youth in the inner city of Philadelphia. As the group discussion began, several of the African American boys spoke of the concerns they had with their families. When they told their parents they were gay, their parents initially responded with something along the lines of "Oh, my God! As a black man you have everything going against you—and now this! This will just make your life so much harder!" Upon hearing this, I told them about how some of the parents of white sons in my study said something like, "You have everything going for you—and now this!" The young black youth were incredulous; over and over they asked, "Really?! Really?! No . . . No way!"

What this interchange suggests are the distinctly different pressures on children, particularly sons, in black families. In many white families success is expected, and it's green lights all the way—until they learn that their children are gay. For black families it is hoped that their children can surmount the obstacles society lays before them, and being gay is one more, making the climb that much harder.

Issues of Gender

Sex role expectations loom large for African American men. They are expected to be "masculine," which means they must hide their emotions, avoid appearing vulnerable, and be continually ready to have sex with women whenever the opportunity arises (Boyd-Franklin 2006). The African American male respondents in this study described how this pressure made it harder to be openly gay. This young man, who was nineteen and worked in the human services, described the expectations of his neighbors:

> Everyone feels that because you're African American in this community that you're branded to be a manly man, so you have to be really masculine. And in this community being masculine, you have to, obviously, wear the right clothes and listen to the kind of music that they like and etc. So that stigma just really alienates me and it also makes me afraid. I've been traumatized living here.

Chauncey, the previously quoted Haitian man, had a white boyfriend who lived in a predominantly white neighborhood in New York City. He spoke of how difficult it was to feel that he did not belong in either his home community or the place where his boyfriend lived:

> I have a problem being African American in a Caucasian area, but when I am in a black neighborhood . . . I look at everybody here and I see most of them are black and I see how they're dressed and how they're acting. I look at myself and think, "I'm not like that." And I'm not the one who really makes that distinction—it's really the other black people who make that distinction because of the way they act toward me or the way they see me and they think, "Oh, my God, he's not like us, he's so different."

This biracial young man explained: "The African American community is very strict when it comes to homosexuality. It's the masculinity thing." His father, a white school teacher, worried about his son being harassed and beaten up in the mostly black neighborhood where they lived. He said, "It's a cultural thing that dates back hundreds and hundreds, maybe thousands, of years. It's that the man is macho and the king of the castle and then the black woman is the queen."

This next black mother, when asked if she thought it was more difficult to be gay in the African American community, described the hard and fast rules about gender: "Yes, I do, because you are told be a man—you have to be a man. And being a man does not mean you sleep with other men. Being a man is you have a woman and you procreate and continue the family name." Like the other black parents, she worried about gender expectations in the African American community and what might happen to her son for violating them.

The young black gay males in the previously mentioned support group shed further light on the pressure gay African American youth felt from their families and communities. Several talked about telling their brothers, fathers, and male cousins they were gay and these relatives reacted with shock, dismay, and disappointment. They responded with comments along the lines of "You are making things worse for the plight of the black man . . . homosexuality is one more thing they will hold against us."

These young men also spoke of how they would encounter their heterosexual brothers, cousins, and fathers hanging out on the street with their friends. Their friends might make a homophobic comment, and in response their male relatives would tell their friends to back off. These relatives would later complain that having a gay family member was making life difficult for them on the streets. These complaints left the young gay black men in the group feeling a painful mix of anger, shame, and sadness.

The comments of these young men underscore how important it is to recognize that for black families, and particularly families of black gay men, the burdens are additive. The stigma related to racism, internal community pressures to comply with traditional notions of masculinity, and the pressure to not further damage the image of the black man in our society all intersect to make the experiences of African American families with gay children uniquely difficult.

Latino Families

Unfortunately, only five Latino families were recruited for this study, and their reports did not yield any meaningful findings regarding the uniqueness of the coming-out experience for these families. A multipronged approach was used to recruit Latino families. Advertisements were placed in local Spanish-language newsletters that targeted the Latino community. The interviewers attended support groups for young Latina lesbians and Latino gays where they attempted to recruit respondents. Further, a bicultural, bilingual Puerto Rican lesbian graduate student was hired to assist with the recruitment and the interviewing. However, none of these methods proved sufficient.

Nevertheless, this lack of findings might in fact be a finding of sorts. When I went to meetings of community agencies to recruit families, I found that young Latino gays were eager to participate. They took my flyers and were immediately willing to sign up for interviews. But, once they were told that their parents would also need to be interviewed, they responded with an oft-repeated refrain, "Me? Sure, no problem, but my parents? No way!"

When I approached my Latino gay friends and colleagues for guidance, I was told that in many families there is a "Don't ask, don't tell" policy whereby parents know, and children know parents know, but it is never discussed. Furthermore, in the LGBT youth groups for kids of color, the impression among black and Latino participants was that Latino people have a harder time with homosexuality and that Latino parents were more likely to reject and eject their children from their homes.

The reader is strongly advised against drawing any definitive conclusions from these experiences. It must be recognized that these were the responses of only a select few and are in no way presented as representative of the broad range of Latino families of lesbian and gay children living in this country. However, the Latino family code of silence cloaking this issue has been documented. Rafael Diaz, a social work scholar who has done a considerable amount of HIV prevention research with Latino gay men, found that the men in his samples believed their parents knew of their homosexuality, but the topic was rarely, if ever, openly discussed (Diaz 1998).

The existing research on Latino lesbians and gays and their families is insufficient. However, an additional study sheds some further light on this population. Merighi and Grimes (2000) interviewed a multicultural sample of gay men and described how, before they came out, their Mexican American gay male respondents feared that the culturally based expectations of their families that they be masculine, get married, have children, and not shame their families made it likely that their parents would not accept them. However, after they came out and found they were not rejected, these men came to the conclusion that the emphasis on family unity, which is a strong value among Latino cultures, trumped parental feelings of disapproval or discomfort. Improved sampling methods need to be developed (or existing methods overlooked in the study herein need to be deployed) for recruiting Latino parents of gays and lesbians so we can learn as much as we can about the strengths as well as the needs of these vulnerable families.

Asian Families

Asian families were also underrepresented in this sample. Toshi's family was from Japan, and his mother explained that, in her home country, homosexuality was openly accepted and thus it did not bother her that Toshi was gay. However, his parents were aware of homophobia and heterosexism in this country, and were therefore worried for their son's safety and well-being.

Once again, though the available literature on gay and lesbian Asian families is small and inadequate, it does begin to describe the double stigma faced by gay Asians (Poon and Ho 2008). Additionally, since homosexuality is a taboo in many Asian cultures (Chan 1989; Hom 1994), Asian parents might be less likely to talk about their children's homosexuality to a researcher. In a recent study of a large multicultural, diverse sample of gay, lesbian, and bisexual people, it was found that Asian and Asian Americans were the least likely to be out to their parents, followed by Latinos (Grove et al. 2006). It is interesting to note that in many Asian countries homosexuality wasn't always condemned. In China, for example, homosexuality was legal and not stigmatized until Western colonialism took hold (Kapac 1998). Nevertheless, additional current research is needed to capture the voices of the families of Asian lesbian and gay youth so we can know best how to assist this vulnerable population.

West Indian Families

An unexpected finding that emerged in this study was that respondents of West Indian or certain types of Caribbean heritage believed that their cultures were particularly hostile toward gay people. There were four families in which the parents were born in either Haiti, Jamaica, Barbados, or Guyana. Even though this is a small number, in each family, members spoke of how especially difficult it was to live openly gay lives in their home countries because doing so would be too dangerous. Norman, who was from Guyana and has been previously quoted throughout this book, described how his culture was murderously intolerant of gay people:

NORMAN: I think for one, being from the Caribbean, it is automatically a taboo. In Guyana you could be killed for that, by anybody. I think Jamaica is the most extreme, where people will kill you. They will cut you and, yes, kill you. People in your neighborhood, if they know . . .

INTERVIEWER: And get away with it?

NORMAN: Yes, I remember—you can look it up on the Internet—there was supposed to be the first gay and lesbian parade, and they said machetes sold out on the island and they had to cancel the parade, because people were going to kill them. Guyana has a very high rate of HIV, and people are not addressing it as they should. And because people don't really like to talk about sex too much—that is part of it.

Marie and her son Chauncey talked about how difficult things were for gays and lesbians in Haiti.

MARIE: Here [in the U.S.] they give them [gay people] a place in society, but back home . . . they have to hide their identity.

INTERVIEWER: Or else what?

MARIE: Or in some places they can't get in. Like in school—they have a lot of schools they cannot attend. But here they give you more priority, and I overheard they're going to make a law to let them get married.

Her son Chauncey felt forced out of the predominantly West Indian neighborhood in which he lived with his mother because he had been beaten, punched, and threatened on a daily basis.

One twenty-four-year-old girl whose father's family hailed from Barbados believed that the prevailing attitudes of her culture prevented her from coming out to other relatives: "I wouldn't tell my father's mother. I think that she would totally just have a heart attack. In the Barbados it's just like no

226 Race and Ethnicity

gays allowed." Her parents, who had ongoing worries for their daughter's well-being as a lesbian, also spoke of harassment experienced by lesbians and gays, particularly gay men in Barbados.

Unfortunately, the scholarly social science literature is largely silent on the issue of homosexuality among Caribbean and West Indian cultures. However, I followed Norman's advice and found numerous stories on the Internet about discrimination and antigay violence in Jamaica (Padgett 2006), Haiti (Ammon 2006), and Guyana (*Gay Guyana News and Reports* 2008). In Jamaica homosexuality is still criminalized, and it is indeed telling that some of the reggae music, popular in Jamaica and other Caribbean countries, advocates violence toward gays and lesbians—even murder (Padget 2006).

The family members described in this section coped with stigma by either avoiding members of their own ethnicity or remaining "in the closet" as much as they could in their neighborhoods and with their extended families. Though these respondents shed some light on the special challenges potentially faced by families of these ethnic groups, it must be kept in mind that this information was gleaned from a very small subsample and therefore does not reflect the full spectrum of experiences of gays and lesbians of Caribbean heritage. Like Asian and Latino families, more information is needed about the unique challenges gays, lesbians, and their families of West Indian and other Caribbean cultures face.

Race Doesn't Matter?

In six of the twenty-four families who were African American or Latino, either the parent or the child or both believed that race or ethnicity did not matter. When asked if being black, Latino, or Asian in any way made it harder or somehow different to adjust to the news that a family member was gay, some respondents said no. This seems to fly in the face of what is expected. Aren't we taught in graduate school, and even our postgraduate training, that it is important to understand how people's ethnicity shapes their experiences and how essential culture is to our clients' lives? If so, then what do we do when respondents and clients hold ideas different from those we are taught?

One African American mother who was a school maintenance worker believed socioeconomic class, not race, was a factor, but she saw the issue differently than Nancy, who was quoted earlier in this chapter. "I am not a racist, for one, but from pictures that I've seen and tapes I've watched, I think, being African American or Latino, we accept things better than white people. Because a lot of them think they are too upper class for this to be happening. It is not right—it isn't supposed to happen."

However, in the other families in which members said race or ethnicity didn't matter, family members were coping with significant problems besides the child's homosexuality. One family had a daughter who was in residential care due to behavioral problems. Another young man struggled with a tenacious addiction to methamphetamine that persisted in spite of two courses of inpatient rehabilitation. In another family, the mother was in treatment for pancreatic cancer.

My clinical experience suggests that very troubled minority clients are so preoccupied with day-to-day survival they are unable to pull themselves back sufficiently to gain a broader perspective to analyze the role race or ethnicity plays in their current difficulties. Perhaps for the families in this study, like my client families, it was too difficult and frightening to consider their problems were caused or aggravated by social factors beyond their immediate control. However, this is only a tentative conclusion based on a small subsample. Much more information is needed about the role race and ethnicity plays, or does not play, in a family's adjustment to the news that a child is gay.

Summary and Clinical Implications

Human service professionals study different cultures in their professional training and throughout their continuing education. Our professional organizations mandate that we seek information about various ethnic groups, and increasingly, continued diversity education is necessary in order to meet licensing requirements.

In this study some of the African American respondents worried that racism threatened to make the lives of their lesbian and gay children especially difficult. They believed the effects of racism and homophobia were additive and therefore they were particularly anxious about the future well-being of their children. Furthermore, young African American men had to cope with the additional pressures generated from within the black community to conform to a very traditional and narrow definition of masculinity. If they did not, they risked condemnation from their male relatives, friends, and neighbors.

Male discomfort with homosexuality may be accentuated in certain communities and may make these families at higher risk for the mutual, reciprocal distancing patterns between fathers and sons mentioned in previous chapters. In order avoid facing their fathers' disapproval and also family conflict, African American or Latino fathers and their sons might distance from each other. Unfortunately, as described earlier, when this occurs, the homophobic and heterosexist ideas fueling this disengagement are never exposed and addressed, and children's and fathers' needs for loving relationships go unmet.

Clinicians need to show that they understand the unique pressures on families from various ethnic groups and, particularly, the additional burdens they face consequential to the intersection of racism and heterosexism. Once clients feel that these stresses are understood, clinicians can eventually help them develop broader and more critical perspectives on how members of not only the greater society but also their own ethnic groups view homosexuality.

The respondents in this study did not discuss culturally related issues or experiences with oppression until they were specifically asked about them, and this has been my experience with clients as well. Clients might withhold information about their oppression because they believe their therapists are uninterested in such experiences (Teyber and McClure 2000). However, this tendency can be counteracted if practitioners specifically ask about how issues of culture and discrimination play a role in the difficulties for which they are seeking help. If clinicians introduce these topics, particularly if they are from a different race or ethnicity than their clients, they are demonstrating their willingness to learn about and address these issues. Questions such as "Do you think being (black, Latino, Chinese American) plays a role in your reaction to your gay child?" "Do you think racism somehow factors into your feelings about being lesbian?" invite clients to reflect and discuss the roles culture and oppression play in their lives. Based on my practice experience, it is also a good idea to raise this issue several times during therapy and especially when the family is discussing a topic that might be culturally based, such as sex role expectations.

However, it is important to remember that, no matter how well-meaning we try to be, our clients' perspectives might not match our own. Some clients may believe that their ethnicity plays a significant role in their problems, while others do not. Are those clients wrong? Are they simply blinding themselves, living in a world of denial, awaiting enlightenment from culturally competent therapists?

Each question has three answers: yes, no, and maybe. As I have described in earlier chapters, it is the therapist's job to shine a light on relevant issues that fall outside our clients' awareness, including the role of stigma, oppression, and prejudice in their lives. Many clients might not ever have seriously considered the role of stigma in their difficulties or they might have chosen to ignore it to the extent that they do not think it exists. Without considering these factors, clients might excessively blame themselves for problems that are, at least in part, related to environmental factors. For example, a young African American gay man who feels ashamed when his brother chides him for hurting the image of the black man might become overly self-punitive. If he could understand the role racism plays in the obstacles and pressures African American men face, and how his brother's statements might reflect his attempts to respond to these pressures, he might be better able to adopt a broader, less self-punishing view of his brother's reactions.

Though it is always good practice to ask clients about their experiences and to invite them to think about whether social and institutional racism, heterosexism, homophobia, and sexism play a role in their lives, we must always be careful not to push our views onto our clients. The relationship between culture, oppression, and family problems has not been unequivocally proven and remains largely theoretical. It is reasonable to assume that there are links between these factors, but it is wrong to think that we know how the dots are connected or that they are connected in the same way for all families of a certain ethnic group. Thus, while it is a good idea to hold on to ideas about culture and its impact on families, we must do so with a loose rather than tight grip. Practitioners must be receptive to the idea that race and ethnicity may not play a large role in the lives of some of our black, Latino, and Asian clients—if they push the idea that it does, they run the risk of imposing a kind of cultural awareness imperialism on their clients, imparting the message "I know better than you"—which can seem insensitive, invalidating, and is potentially disempowering.

Corrigan and Watson (2002) remark that one way to cope with stigma is to avoid the situations where it manifests. For example, some African Americans can choose to live in communities that are mostly populated by black people where they do not face discrimination, at least on a regular basis, so it is not something they frequently think about. As stated repeatedly in this book, good clinical work demands that therapists know when to advance and retreat, and if, after our questioning, clients do not believe culture or societal oppression affects them, our job is to believe them and let them take the lead in exploring and explaining the causes of their difficulties.

Nevertheless, by communicating curiosity about the role of race, ethnicity, and oppression in our clients' lives, we invite them to think about these issues. We also show that we have our catchers' mitts on, ready to listen and understand all their feelings. Joan Laird (1996) has advised clinicians to be knowledgeable about a client's culture "not so as to lead from our own knowledge or theory in a way that makes prior assumptions but so as to be able to fully listen—to ask questions and listen to answers in a way that lack of knowledge or fixed ideas can prevent from doing so" (1996:118). No matter what types of families they work with, family therapists and other human service workers should tape this excellent advice onto the corners of their bathroom mirrors so they can be reminded of its importance on a daily basis.

CHAPTER 7

Areas for Future Research

and Concluding Thoughts

O NE BOOK OR PIECE OF RESEARCH NEVER ANSWERS ALL
the questions about a particular topic. As a matter of fact, findings
from the best studies often leave additional, more sophisticated
questions in their wake. As illustrated in the last chapter, there is much more
we need to know about the families of lesbian and gay youth of various
ethnic groups. Furthermore, clinicians need more information on families
of bisexual and transgender people. The focus of this study was not on families of daughters and sons who identified as bisexual or transgender. However, when the net was cast for gay and lesbian participants, a small group of
bisexual and transgender respondents were found as well. The very tentative
findings from these young people and their families suggest clinical strategies
and areas for future research.

Bisexuality as a Gateway Sexual Orientation

As we have seen in the family sensitization and family discovery stages, the
prospect of telling their parents they were gay or lesbian filled the young
respondents with anxiety. So can they really be blamed for trying to find

a way to make things easier on themselves and their parents? In systemic desensitization a clinician gets the phobic client to face her fear of spiders by gradually exposing her to the object of her terror in small steps. If treatment goes well, she will eventually be able to face a live spider. Based on this logic, it is perhaps understandable why some youth thought it might be helpful to gradually expose their parents to their homosexuality by first claiming that they were bisexual. Once parents got used to the idea, the young respondents then told their mothers and fathers that they were gay. In this study, six of the young respondents tried this strategy.

Unfortunately, this strategy didn't work. One consequence of the break-them-in-gently approach was that parents came to believe that their children were confused. This mother talked about how her son, who was white, had first told her in high school he would only date black women. Then he told her he was bisexual. As a result, she began to doubt the seriousness of her son's declarations:

> Another time we were doing something, he said, "Mom, I think I am bi." I guess I was not up on things, and I said, "Bi what? What are you talking about?" He said, "Well, I like guys and I like girls." I am thinking, "OK, this is like a little joke. Now we are bi, next week maybe we are going to go out with a giraffe, I don't know."

Six months after he told his mother he was bisexual, he brought a boyfriend home to meet his parents, also proclaiming he was actually gay. Both mother and son reported that the mother was highly distressed when he told her he was bisexual and was just as upset a few months down the road when she found out he was gay. Thus thinking he was bisexual first did nothing to soften the blow that was to come.

Lydia, a college student, described coming out as bisexual when confronted by her mother: "I remember we were working together at her office, and she was like, 'Are you a lesbian?' And I'm like, 'No, I'm bisexual.' And then she became a big mess and started yelling at me. And she's like, 'Well, how do you know?'" Her mom said:

> I don't remember how I addressed my initial disappointment, but I would say to her, "Do you want to go back and see your therapist, you know, maybe you're confused." And she said, "No, I've really thought about this, I'm pretty sure." And I think actually, for a little while, she was like, "Oh,

maybe not, but maybe I'm not sure," just for a little while, but I think she told me this later to kind of appease me, make it sound like she was bisexual or she wasn't sure of her sexual orientation . . . I guess to ease me into the idea.

Franklin described a somewhat similar situation with his mother:

I ended up coming out to her as bi several times. The first time was in junior high school, the summer after seventh grade . . . A friend kind of outed me—actually an ex-girlfriend. We [the friend and I] were having some conversation about Madonna, and I was like, "I am just like Madonna." She was like, "What do you mean?" and I was like, "Because Madonna had said that she would sleep with another woman." I said, "That is how I am." "She was like, "What? Are you serious?" The way our relationship was, we were close, but we would have our arguments at points. And that same day, after that conversation, for some reason—maybe she was upset or something—but we had an argument, and I turned the ringer off and refused to take her calls. So we had voice mail on the phone, and all that time when I had the ringer off she was leaving all these messages. One of the messages was, "Mrs. Isaac, you don't know this about your son, but he is bisexual and he wants to sleep with other boys." So, when my mom got home, she checked the messages and heard the one from my friend. She was like, "Franklin, come here. Listen to this." So I actually got to hear her [my friend] state those things. I froze. I didn't know what to say. And she was like, "Is this true?" I said, "No!" She kept grilling me. She was like, "Why would she say it?" And after a while I said, "OK, yes, it's true, I'm bisexual."

Franklin's mother had passed away two years before the study. Nevertheless, according to Franklin, first disclosing he was bisexual did not make things easier once he told her he was gay. His mother was just as angry, shocked, and hurt when she learned he was gay as she was when he told her he was bisexual.

Another reason children telling parents they were bisexual did not work is because bisexuality holds the possibility that the child will choose an opposite-sex partner with whom to enter a heterosexual relationship. In light of the self-blame, grief, and worry parents face when they find out their child is gay, could they be blamed for wishing their supposedly bisexual children would choose a long-term partner of the opposite sex so they could settle into a "normal" heterosexual life?

Lydia recalled how she realized telling her mother she was bisexual was a mistake. Her mother always seemed to be hoping Lydia would find a nice man to go out with—until she finally came clean and told her mother she was a lesbian. "Yes. I guess because—even up until a year after I told her I was a lesbian, she would still be like, "Are you sure there's no guys?" Even like the beginning of this year she's like, 'So did you meet any guys?' I think she was like half kidding but half hoping. And I was like, 'No, Mom.'"

Joelle first told her mother Nancy she was bisexual then a year later told her she was a lesbian. Her mother talked about how she schemed (and still schemes) to find ways to encourage her daughter to consider dating boys:

I think that I became more manipulative. When she told me she was lesbian, I was still at the point where I thought that this was something where maybe I could alter these events because initially she had said to me that she was bi. Now my daughter, at least up until the start of this semester, was still a virgin, because she told me . . . I mean she may not come and tell me now but up until the start of this semester she was a virgin. So in my mind I kept thinking, "Well you haven't done anything with anybody so how do you know?" And she had defined herself as bi, and I kept thinking, "All right, is this going to swing either way depending on the quality of her first experience?" Because I think Joelle has been looking for some kind of acceptance and place to belong. So I think when I say manipulative it was just like can I like push her to go out with this guy or . . . ? It was just like subtly like, "Oh you want to go out with Robert? Fine. You want to stay out late with him? Fine." But it was just kind of like I felt the ball had been tossed up in the air and maybe it could still go either way. And I don't know if she really did think that she was bi, because I sometimes wonder did she say bi to me because she thought I would handle it better than if she just said "I am a lesbian?" I don't know.

In contrast to the previous examples, there was one respondent who first identified as lesbian and *then* as bisexual. Since coming out as bisexual, she knew her mother held out hope that she would eventually settle down with a man: "Well, I came out first as a lesbian, then as bisexual years later. So at first I think she was hoping that I was bisexual, so at least there was the hope of me marrying a man or ending up with a man." Like gateway bisexuality, true bisexuality could be just as confusing to deal with, particularly if the child first comes out as gay. This last respondent's mother seemed confused and weary of trying to keep up with her daughter's shifting labels, boyfriends, and girlfriends. First her daughter told her she was lesbian . . .

> Then it turned out that she had a boyfriend, and I thought about saying, "So, you're not gay?" So I just left things for a while. And then another time she said she had a girlfriend, and I said to her, "So I guess you are bisexual." She said, "I don't like to label myself." So we left it at that. Then, when I finally got comfortable with the fact that she was bisexual and seemed to be with men a little more, she would say, "No, I am gay." So I don't know what to think. The truth is it doesn't really matter.

In the end, coming out as bisexual when one is really gay or lesbian seems to only complicate matters. Bisexuality can be difficult for parents to understand, and, as the last example demonstrates, even true bisexuality could be difficult for parents to deal with. Although more research is needed, these findings suggest that coming out to one's parents as bisexual as a way to soften the blow is a strategy that, at best, doesn't work and, at worst, gives parents false hopes, which might make their adjustment to the news that their daughter or son is gay that much more difficult.

Sexual Fluidity and Bisexuality

Two young women in this study identified as bisexual when asked what their sexual orientation was during the interview, even though they first stated they were lesbian when they signed up for the study. Two additional female respondents identified as lesbian at the time of the study, but, when questioned about their sexual orientation, said they truly viewed themselves as bisexual at some point before they identified as lesbian. In addition, there were a small number of young women who tried to avoid attaching firm labels on themselves. In response to the question of what her sexual orientation was, this eighteen-year-old African American young woman gave an intriguing response:

RESPONDENT: Controversial. I am a lesbian for the time being.
INTERVIEWER: What do you mean by that?

RESPONDENT: You never really know what can happen. I am about to go to college. There are going to be some nights I am not going to recall participating in.

When asked about her sexual orientation, this next young woman, who was in law school, responded:

> This is always a fun one. I would personally describe it as not straight. I am very strongly not straight, but I don't really feel that I fit very well into the other categories. I let people believe that I am gay, because that is easier and less complicated. I first identified as gay when I came out, because back at the time I thought that anything else would be too wishy-washy. And, because I was a teenager, people would think "You are going through a phase" if I said I was bisexual or anything else. So I said I am gay as a way to say I am very, very not straight, I am not going back on this. It was just very important to me to come out strong, and to me that was coming out strong. I identified as gay throughout high school and then I came to college. And basically, since being at college, it ceased to matter so much. I am at a women's college, we have a very large GLBT population. It is a very positive atmosphere . . . But I feel closer to the bisexual and transgender community than the gay and lesbian community. I have my own sense of what those communities are, but I identify more with the queer people than the gay and lesbian people.

Remember Bob's daughter Ellie? When asked about her sexual orientation, she replied: "Bisexual. I am lesbian, but I don't believe in the complete removal of other genders." Even Joelle, when she spoke of her sexual orientation, seemed to want to avoid being definitive. At first she told her mother she was bisexual as a way to soften the blow. Then later she told her mother she was indeed a lesbian. When I asked her about her current sexual orientation, she identified as lesbian but seemed to leave the bisexual door open:

INTERVIEWER: How would you describe your sexual orientation?
JOELLE: Don't have a definitive line. I used to associate myself as bisexual, but now I kind of associate more as a lesbian.
INTERVIEWER: What made that transition?

JOELLE: Relationships and just, like, experience and discovering what I prefer, I guess.
INTERVIEWER: So would you say you are attracted sexually to women . . .
and men?
JOELLE: I would say more so to women than men, but both.

The replies from this small number of women suggest that the relationship between sexual identity and sexual attractions can be complicated. These
responses lend some evidence to the idea, introduced in chapter 4, that sexual
feelings, along with related self-identified sexual orientations, are not always
firmly set but instead might be changeable, depending on an individual's
culture, environment, and available partners.

There is good reason to believe that women's feelings of sexual attraction
are less fixed and more flexible than those of men. Sex researchers have examined the factors related to women's and men's sexual arousal and have found
that, no matter what their stated sexual orientation, women were more likely
than heterosexual and gay men to become sexually stimulated in response to
erotic images of *both* women and men (Chivers, Seto, and Blanchard 2007).

Another researcher followed a sample of one hundred lesbians over a
period of ten years to determine whether there were any changes in their
sexual feelings over time (Diamond 2008). She found that women who identified as lesbians could find themselves periodically attracted to and sexually
active with men then women then men again. Some women could be having
relationships with members of both sexes at the same time. In fact, only one-
third of the women who identified as lesbians reported exclusive sexual attractions and behavior toward women over the course of the study. The greater
likelihood of women, no matter what their self-described sexual orientation,
experiencing attractions to both women and men could explain the greater
propensity for some girls and young women in this study to be a bit more
flexible in how they described their sexual orientations.

Although this previously cited research focused on female sexuality, there
is evidence that male sexual attractions and behaviors can also shift. First
of all, men in other cultures, including non-Western societies and those
of ancient Greece, have been known to participate in a transitory period
of homosexuality at some point during their lives (Halperin 1990; Herdt
2006; 1984; Hubbard 2003). Second, it is possible for a self-identified
gay man to have experienced sexual attractions to women before he identifies

as gay. Even though Franklin described himself as gay, he recalled his previous attraction to a woman: "I don't know how I phrased it at that point where she would still agree to go out with me but I let her know that I was attracted to men. But, for some reason, I don't know, she was very attractive, so I guess some part of me was still attracted to women at that point."

The reports of Franklin and the other respondents quoted in this section, along with the research cited, raise interesting questions as to what leads people to identify as gay or lesbian. Is it the relationship they are in? Is it the pressure not to appear undecided or on the fence, like the previously quoted law student who did not want to appear "wishy-washy"? Or is it in response to the common belief that bisexuality does not really exist? Does society push people, including those who are not inclined to limit their sexual identities and activities, to pick a definitive sexual orientation (straight, gay, or lesbian)? It should be noted that when I was gathering a sample for this study I specifically called for gay and lesbian youth and their families in my recruitment materials. That may be why most of my respondents identified as gay and lesbian and reported that their attractions corresponded with their identities. Perhaps respondents who were attracted to both men and women did not see themselves as clearly different from their gay and lesbian counterparts—at least not different enough to refrain from volunteering to be interviewed.

In my clinical practice I have found that a large part of my initial work with bisexual clients is demonstrating that I truly believe they are bisexual. In light of the skepticism bisexual people face, it makes sense that these clients need to be reassured that their therapists do not think they are either confused or trying to shield themselves from the discrimination and prejudice gays and lesbians experience. One of my recent bisexual clients referred to gay men, lesbians, and heterosexuals as "monosexuals who just don't understand."

Of course, no matter what our sexual orientation, it is our job to understand how our clients see themselves. Those among us who are "monosexual" therapists who have trouble understanding that bisexuality exists need to get themselves educated. A good way to start would be to become familiar with the Kinsey reports, which found that bisexual behavior was much more prevalent than originally thought (1948, 1953). This discovery still has relevance in today's world. Diamond's (2008) study is also recommended reading, and good overviews by Weber and Heffern (2008) and also McClellan (2006) can be found in social work texts describing work with LGBT populations. Therapists should also consult the *Journal of Bisexuality* as well as a volume of research examining this much misunderstood topic (Fox 2004). It might also be beneficial for therapists who are new to these ideas, or are uncomfortable with them, to find bisexual individuals to interact with and learn from.

If a therapist is confronted by a young gay man or lesbian woman who is thinking of coming out to his or her parents as bisexual to soften the blow, this should be discouraged. Of course, the children's anxiety is understandable, and a sensitive clinician will empathize with their young clients' motives to try to make a very difficult task a bit easier on both themselves and their parents. However, based on these findings, gradually coming out in this way is not a good idea. Perhaps young gays and lesbians who are considering such a plan are not quite ready to come out and need to wait until they are more emotionally prepared to face their parents' possible reactions to the truth.

However, therapists might be confronted with the potentially difficult task of helping families in which a truly bisexual child has come out. Some of the previously mentioned clinical suggestions for working with parents who are just finding out their children are lesbian or gay could prove helpful. Parents might need to vent their grief, self-blame, and worry as well as their confusion and hopes that the child will eventually "pick the right team" and develop a relationship with an opposite-sex partner. It is reasonable for parents to want their children to avoid the consequences of societal stigma by choosing a heterosexual relationship, and therapists need to empathize with these parents' wishes. However, ever since the times of Romeo and Juliet (and no doubt before then), parents' plans to influence their children's love lives have been known to fail miserably.

Thus, parents need to be coached to back off and try to eventually support their children's choices. As recommended in earlier chapters of this book, when the family is ready for conjoint sessions it is a good idea for therapists to encourage productive, open conversation between family members about coping with stigma—particularly as it relates to the child's choice of partner.

It seems that, as a society, we are slowly realizing how complicated the relationship is between social pressure, stigma, sexual attractions, sexual orientation, and identity. People, within and outside the lesbian and gay community are beginning to become more knowledgeable about bisexuality. It would be interesting and useful for future studies to further explore issues of sexual attraction, sexual identity, and social pressures and how they get processed in families, particularly those with bisexual members.

Transgender Youth

If you thought it might be hard for a parent to hear that a child is gay or lesbian, imagine what it must be like to hear that your son feels he was born into the wrong body and is really a woman or that your daughter is certain she was meant to be a man. As described previously, parents, like most people in our society, are uncomfortable with cross-gendered behavior, especially in their children. So it must be especially difficult for a parent to adjust to the news that their children feel as if their psychological gender is at odds with the bodies they were born into. Mallon (1999) and Lev (2006) describe how deeply distressing such a disclosure can be for parents and how children coming out as transgender are at great risk for being thrown out of their homes.

In this study two youth reported they were lesbian when they signed up, but identified themselves as transgender during their interviews, and one additional young woman who originally identified as lesbian came out later as trans once the study was over. Of course, no real conclusions can be drawn from the families of two or three respondents. However, when Eula found out her son was impersonating a woman (first described in chapter 2), her strong reactions suggest the magnitude of panic and resistance a parent might feel at the thought that a son or daughter might be transgender.

> Andrew . . . he wasn't sure what he was, and he was telling people he was a girl. And I got terrified one night . . . I had this man call here, a young man, who was straight . . . and met Andrew, and Andrew told him his name was Alexis. This man called here and he was giving me all this, "I don't play that . . . " And it scared me to death and . . . I was trying to talk to [my son], "Andrew! No! You are not a girl, you are a gay man! You are not a girl!" And I said, "Andrew, you've watched Jerry Springer. You've seen when these men come on here and tell these men that they are really men although they have been thinking for months that they are women. They beat the hell out of them! And that is the fear I have. You are not a woman! You are a gay man!" And that was the first time that we actually had a long, quite civil discussion. I also had . . . a couple of my friends talk to him . . . gay male friends. And I don't know what they talked about. I didn't ask them how the conversation went. I wasn't there. But I know that after they talked to him we didn't have anymore of the Alexis issue. It was Andrew the gay man.

She described her attempts to get her son some help:

> He would never admit to me that he was telling people he was a girl. He was always denying it to me, and I'd start throwing out names of men who had called here and asked for Alexis—and it was just like a total denial on his part. I even at one point made an appointment . . . I can't remember the doctor's name now . . . he is a black psychologist who specializes in transgender youth. My doctor gave me his name. We made an appointment . . . and I ended up really telling him off . . . We never even got in his office . . . We were sitting there, and I had a phone interview with this man, explained the whole situation to him, which is why he (Andrew) was going to see him. He came out, and the attitude he approached us with . . . it just put Andrew on the defensive right away. His arrogance . . . first he is calling him a girl. Then his secretary or nurse, whatever you want to call her, she is just like, "Well tell her . . . " And I said, "No. He is a boy. His name is Andrew." She said, "Well he's got long hair." Andrew's hair is long under those braids. So I told her, "Help me understand . . . if he were white and had a guitar in his hands it would be OK for him to have long hair? Kenny G's got long hair. Jesus had long hair. But because he is black and has long hair and has a very attractive face . . . Why are you here if your mental attitude is that way?" It just ticked me off.

INTERVIEWER: So they just assumed and started treating him as a girl?

EULA: Oh yeah. And then when I corrected them that he was a boy the arrogance came out on me . . . the defensiveness came back towards me as though I was wrong for correcting them.

INTERVIEWER: So the psychologist and his staff were attacking you for not considering him a girl?

EULA: Yeah.

INTERVIEWER: Without any discussion, without even talking to your child?

EULA: Because I corrected them. And you are right they hadn't talked to my child. No. He hadn't opened his mouth. We had filled out the forms. Andrew. Sex: male. Damn! You can't read either? So we never went back.

Was Andrew really transgender? Maybe, but I will never know for sure. During his interview, he sported long nails, long hair, and seemed like he was wearing cosmetics, yet he denied thinking he might be a girl. Perhaps he did not—or perhaps his mother's fear led him to put the idea aside, at least for the time being.

Another mother became extremely anxious when she began to talk about her daughter's cross-gendered behaviors. She seemed to enter a dissociative state, becoming highly agitated, disoriented, and unable to speak once she started to think aloud that her daughter might be transgender. (Her daughter freely admitted she was transgender, but she reported that she did not mention this to her mother, instead telling her she was a lesbian.) Her mother's reaction, along with that of Andrew's mother, shows how very distressing it can be to think that one's child might be transgender.

Nevertheless, the experience of a third family suggests that these families may be similar to those of gay and lesbian youth, whereby parents might employ the same methods to help themselves adjust. This mother, a teacher living in the suburbs, recalled how her twenty-two-year-old daughter seemed to show signs of being transgender from an early age:

> Since she was born it seemed like she was allergic to her skin. Then when she stated she was a boy and she had a penis and everybody should come and see her penis—I mean that's pretty out there . . . She may not have known it, I may not have acknowledged it, but she was out from four years old, five years old. She was identifying herself as a boy, and at school that would cause problems for her, because she was rather vocal about it. But yet, on the other hand, she was very self-conscious. So she was kind of a, a strange mix, you know? Extreme self-consciousness and yet announcing things to the world that were causing her problems.

Like many of the parents of the gay male and lesbian respondents, this mother was initially very depressed when her daughter told her three years ago that she was transgender. What helped her adjust was the passage of time along with the information she sought out. She came to the conclusion that gender was innate, even if it didn't match up with one's biological sex, and this helped her feel better.

Her daughter came out as gay first and then later as transgender. Like some of the lesbian and gay respondents, her daughter overestimated the beneficial effects of her own self-confidence in who she was. Furthermore, her daughter thinks her mother is now comfortable with her dressing and acting very masculine, which, by the way, she isn't. However, both agree that their relationship has improved since the daughter came out.

The findings from this mother and daughter suggest that some issues for transgender families might be similar to those of lesbian and gay youth. For example, parents may have early suspicions, and parents and children might have distinctly different ideas about what helps parents adjust. Arlene Istar Lev (2004) developed a stage model of how families might adjust to the discovery that a member is transgender, and her model shares some similarity with the stages described in this book. In a study of eighteen mothers of female-to-male transgender children, respondents spoke of feelings of loss, the need for support outside the family, and how seeing their children happy helped them adjust (Pearlman 2006). Undoubtedly, however, there are unique issues faced by families of transgender children, and more research in this area is needed. In the meantime therapists needing information are advised to consult Lev's seminal text, *Transgender Emergence: Therapeutic Guidelines for Working with Gender-Variant People and Their Families*.

Siblings

What is it like to have a sibling who is gay or lesbian? Based on the little bit of information in this study as well as the small amount of scholarly literature in this area, it seems that siblings may share in the stigma of their gay brothers and lesbian sisters whereby they may have to cope with taunts from peers, which include accusations that they too are gay. Remember the young African American men in the group mentioned in chapter 6? These men talked about how their brothers and other male relatives felt they were adding to society's already negative image of black manhood. Like parents, their brothers also felt they had to find ways to handle their peers' homophobic comments and behaviors.

A sensitive, insightful anthology consisting of essays written by siblings of lesbians and gays reveals how sisters and brothers feel they too become objects of abuse and intolerance, sharing in the stigma of their gay siblings (Gottlieb 2005). However, like some fortunate parents, people who learn their siblings are lesbian or gay can find ways to grow and gain new perspectives. Several of the contributors to this volume discussed how they formed especially close bonds with their gay brothers and sisters and, like some of the parents in this study, developed new, more tolerant worldviews that enriched their lives.

The paucity of available information about siblings of gay and lesbian youth does not mean their issues are small or unimportant. Effective family therapists are accustomed to incorporating siblings in their sessions, even if they do not initially seem to be suffering or playing a significant role in the presenting problems, and it makes good sense to include siblings when working with gay and lesbian families.

In my clinical and research experience, sisters and brothers might need help coping with feelings of shame that they have someone gay in the family. They may also need help dealing with peer condemnation and harassment once it is found out that they have a gay or lesbian sibling. Furthermore, they may be anxiously questioning their own sexuality—even if they have no same-sex attractions. A lack of such feelings does not necessarily preclude a sibling from wondering "Could *this* happen to *me* too?"

In addition, I have also seen parents with good intentions isolate their gay child's younger siblings, keeping the gay child's sexual orientation a secret and therefore excluding brothers and sisters from family discussions of this topic. Sometimes parents do this because they want to protect their younger children from information they believe they cannot handle. At other times this is done inadvertently when, after the gay child comes out, parents and gay kids emotionally withdraw from the family, leaving siblings to deal with their reactions alone. If the siblings are not aware why the family is in turmoil, they can even feel more confused, isolated, and distressed. In either scenario there is no one left to help the sibling(s) deal with their feelings.

For all these reasons it is a good idea to pay close attention to siblings in families with coming-out gay and lesbian youth. Early in treatment, therapists should encourage parents to give siblings age-appropriate explanations they can understand. Parents might fear that by telling younger children they might upset them too much or reveal something sexual that the youngsters are not ready to hear. However, there are ways to explain homosexuality to a small child without getting into the nitty-gritty sexual details. For example, "Mary wants to marry a woman instead of a man when she grows up" or "Johnny told us he wants to date other boys rather than girls, and Mommy and Daddy are surprised and are trying to understand." Many therapists who have worked with young children, whose prejudices are usually not fully formed, know how surprisingly flexible they can be when it comes to understanding topics such as homosexuality if they are explained in ways that are in line with their cognitive abilities.

Once siblings are aware of what is happening, the guidelines regarding family sessions mentioned in earlier chapters still apply. If the family is too distressed and reactive, it is recommended that siblings be seen alone, at least initially, so the therapist can get a sense of their concerns and also offer support and education. Since dealing with courtesy stigma might be an issue for brothers and sisters, it would also be a good idea to include siblings in the family discussion of how to cope with issues such as societal intolerance and other people's prejudices.

Mothers and fathers might also fear that such information could influence the younger sibling to actually "turn gay." Parents need to be reassured that such concerns are unfounded. There is no evidence that having a lesbian sister or a gay brother can persuade a child to become gay. Furthermore, one gay child in a family does not necessarily mean that others will be as well. However, there is some evidence that, compared to families with no gay siblings, if one son in a family is gay, his brothers are statistically more likely to be (Dawood et al. 2000). Thus therapists need to be prepared for the possibility that there might be more than one lesbian or gay sibling in a family.

In this study there were two families that included two siblings who were gay, and in both cases it seemed that by the time the parents found out about the second child they had an easier time adjusting than they did when they found out about their first child. However, it is possible that some parents might experience exponentially more self-blame, guilt, loss, and worry if they have two or more gay or lesbian children, so the therapist may have to work twice as hard to help parents deal with their feelings. Hopefully, more research will be forthcoming to provide guidance in helping families with the special challenge of having multiple gay children.

How families of different races and ethnicities cope with a coming-out gay or lesbian child, the special concerns of families with transgender and bisexual youth, how mothers and fathers cope when they have multiple LGBT children . . . these are all areas for future research, each of which could constitute a book in and of itself. Moreover, many of the findings about gay and lesbian families in this book, particularly the divergent perceptions and recollections of parents and children about various components of the adjustment trajectory, cry out to be further investigated. Nevertheless, it is hoped that the information here further enriches the existing literature and provides yet another set of tools that will enable therapists to more effectively assist these vulnerable families.

Some Closing Thoughts

Anyone who has grown up in a northern climate knows what it feels like to trudge though cold and snow after a long day—to see home waiting in the distance. As we get closer, our dark, tired mood begins to lighten. Whether it is a house or an apartment, there is something so reassuring about the shining lamplight glowing in the windows telling us that, despite the harsh weather outdoors, inside is filled with warmth, light, and life. As we enter the house or the apartment, we almost involuntarily exhale a sigh of relief. We're home—and the people there, our family members, are happy to see us. Not all of us have experienced these feelings, but as children, each of us needed to—a warm, safe, secure, loving home is the birthright of each and every child.

For lesbian and gay children and their parents, this safety and security is perhaps even more vital, while more at risk. Families need a way to shelter themselves from the cold wet storm of societal intolerance, which can leak through the roofs of even the sturdiest houses, dampening the relationships of those inside. When this happens, some families will turn to us, family therapists, social workers, school counselors, and other human service professionals, and we need to be ready to help them patch things up.

Parents need to talk about their grief and self-blame, and they also need help broadening their views of what constitutes a happy and healthy life for their children—letting go of old images to make room for new ones. Children need a buffer from the harsh realities of societal homophobia and heterosexism, but they also need to find ways to be patient with their parents, at least temporarily doing without their parents' comforting while their mothers and fathers regain their footing. Furthermore, and perhaps most important, both parents and children need to see how growing to adjust to a gay or lesbian sexual orientation holds out the promise for new, stronger relationships and a broadened, more humane view of the world.

During one of my visits to an LGBT group, several of the members spoke of how, when they told their parents they were gay, they were asked to leave their homes. Upon hearing this, one African American girl exclaimed, "Parents throw their children out of their homes because they're gay?! You mean mothers and fathers reject their children?! That's wack!" Indeed it is—and it is my fervent hope that, in some small way, the stories of the families in this book, in which parents and children rode out the storm holding on to each other, not only will make it less likely that parents reject their children but also more likely that parents reap the rewards of learning to accept and indeed cherish their gay sons and lesbian daughters.

Appendix: Research Methodology

Design

This descriptive, exploratory study qualitatively examined parent-child relationships following the discovery that a daughter or son is gay.

The Sample

My research assistants and I qualitatively interviewed a multicultural sample of sixty-five self-identified gay youth (aged fourteen to twenty-five) and seventy-six of their parents. (It should be noted that during their interviews two of these young women identified as bisexual and two others as transgender—see chapter 7). In order to be eligible for the study, the son or daughter and at least one parent needed to agree to participate.

Recruitment

Respondents were recruited primarily from the New York City and Philadelphia metropolitan areas, including northern, central, and southern New

Jersey. Families were recruited via advertisements in local newspapers ($n =$ 21) and on Craigslist ($n = 23$), a Web site of electronic classified advertisements. Fifteen families were recruited from Parents, Families, and Friends of Lesbians and Gays (PFLAG), which is a support group for parents of gays and lesbians. The remaining six families were recruited through high school and community service organizations that ran support and social groups for gay youth. I would give talks at PFLAG meetings and community organizations about coming out to parents and, at the end of each talk, I would describe the study and distribute flyers, asking the audience members to consider volunteering.

Interested potential respondents were instructed to contact me to schedule an interview. Parents were asked to check with their children to be sure they were willing to be interviewed. If young gay men or women contacted me asking to participate, they were instructed to have their parent call or e-mail me to arrange an interview. This was to ensure that parents were indeed willing to participate. The interviews were done in person and by telephone from the fall of 2003 until the spring of 2005.

The Youth

Thirty-five of the youth were female and thirty were male. Forty-one of the youth were white, seventeen were black or biracial, six were Latino, and one was Japanese American, with parents born in Japan. Their ages ranged from fourteen through twenty-five, but only four were under eighteen. Their mean age was twenty-one. The time they were out to their parents ranged from 6 months to 9 years with a mean of 3.8 years; 61.5 percent of the youth described experiencing mental health symptoms of anxiety or depression before coming out.

The Parents

Fifty-nine mothers and seventeen fathers participated in the study. Fifty-four parents were white, sixteen were black, five were Latino, and one mother was Japanese. The parents' ages ranged from thirty-four to sixty-nine, with a mean age of fifty-one; 53 percent reported symptoms of anxiety and or depression after discovering that their son or daughter was gay or lesbian and 44 percent reported that religion was important or very important in their lives. Families came from a variety of socioeconomic backgrounds and had household incomes ranging from over $1,200 to over $200,000 per year.

For the most part, the parents were fairly adjusted to their children's sexual orientation by the time of the interviews, so it is important to recognize the external validity limitations of the sample. Because an unknown proportion of the population of lesbian and gay youth do not publicly identify themselves, investigators in this area lack sufficient information to determine and derive a truly representative sample. Nevertheless, it is important to recognize that the goal of this study was not necessarily to discover findings that could generalize to the larger population, but to develop data-based theory about family adjustment that would be useful to practitioners.

This research was approved for human subjects by the Rutgers University Office of Research and Sponsored Programs, Institutional Review Board, in March of 2003.

Data Collection

A combination of grounded theory (Glaser 1978, 1992) and narrative methods (Lincoln and Guba 1985) were used to collect the data. Interviewers were carefully trained to capture the respondents' true voices and to avoid influencing their interviewees' responses. They were also trained to be vigilant for social desirability effects. The interviewers (myself included) continually reassured respondents that we wanted participants to be truthful and that they would not be negatively judged for any of their responses, no matter how harsh. Parents and their children were interviewed separately because it was believed that individual respondents might edit their responses in front of family members. Interviews were done mostly in person, but occasionally an interview was done over the telephone if a child or parent lived out of town or was away at school.

Below are the primary research questions, followed by some of the interview questions:

1. How do parents react upon discovery that a son or daughter is gay or lesbian, and what factors are related to changes in their reactions?
Parents were asked to describe parent-child relationships historically and immediately prior to the discovery. They were asked how they learned of

their child's sexual orientation and about their behavioral and emotional reactions, including whether they experienced mental health symptoms. They were also queried regarding any changes immediately following and up to a year after the discovery. In addition, their lesbian daughters or gay sons were also asked for their perceptions of parental reactions.

2. What effects do parents' reactions have on their gay and lesbian children?

Gay and lesbian respondents were asked the specific effects of parental reactions on their self-esteem and whether they experienced mental health symptoms after their parents learned of their sexual orientation. They were asked to describe their responses to their parents' reactions so that specific interactions could be identified. They were also asked to describe changes in their parental relationships immediately after they came out and up until the time of their interviews.

3. What helps or hinders parental adjustment?

Parents were asked how their attitudes and behaviors changed since their initial discovery. They were asked about factors that enhanced or interfered with their adjustment, including child-related factors. Children were also asked for their impressions of the changes in their parents' reactions since the initial discovery and what factors influenced these reactions.

Probes were used to elicit factors that facilitated or hindered parental adjustment. Each interview lasted anywhere from ninety minutes to two hours.

Two research assistants assisted with the interviews: Bethann Albert is a white social worker who is the mother of a lesbian adult; Rita D. Velez Carreras is a bilingual, native Puerto Rican lesbian woman, who was twenty-five at the time of the interviews and had recently graduated from college with a degree in women's studies.

Respondents initially were paid twenty dollars per interview. However, halfway through the data collection this compensation was raised to forty dollars, and this increase served to attract more respondents from lower socioeconomic backgrounds including working-class and poor African American families.

Data Analysis

All interviews were audiotaped, transcribed, and analyzed using a combination of cross-case analysis and grounded theory methods (Padgett 2008; Corbin and Strauss 2008). Using cross-case analysis, transcriptions of answers to the same question were grouped together and the texts of their responses were analyzed. In keeping with grounded theory methods, these grouped responses were read, and preliminary codes were developed. Through constant comparative analysis, axial codes led to the primary themes, which included the family adjustment stages, the importance of strong parent-child boundaries, and the reciprocal interactions of parents and children.

As the principal investigator, I regularly debriefed with peers who were family therapists, social workers, parents of adult gay and lesbian children, and gay lay people. Repeated reading of transcripts, coding, and discussion of the findings with peers and research assistants led to the concepts and theory that described family adjustment. As a reliability check, one of the research assistants coded portions of the interview transcripts into the key codes that I developed, and agreement ranged from 84–100 percent, with a mean of 94.5 percent.

Additional Study Limitations

Throughout this book, and especially in chapters 6 and 7, I have diligently tried to point out the limitations of the findings of this research, and in this section I reiterate some of these and add others. It bears repeating that this sample consisted primarily of families with parents who had mostly adjusted to the news that a daughter or son was gay, so the findings must be interpreted with that in mind. It would be helpful, though rather difficult, to recruit and interview parents who had rejected their children in order to examine how child factors such as cross-gendered mannerisms, developmental problems, and parent-child interactions play a role in parents' decisions to reject their children.

Further, it would be helpful to know more about how families of Latino, Asian, and other cultural backgrounds adjust to having a gay or lesbian child, as it is likely that culture plays a strong role in parent's and children's feelings about homosexuality. Principal investigators who are bicultural and bilingual might be more likely than I, a third-generation Italian American white man, to have sufficient insider knowledge as to how to recruit such parents and encourage them to discuss these deeply personal issues.

All but five of the parents were living in the New York City and Philadelphia metropolitan areas, which are known to be fairly liberal parts of the country. It is expected the findings would be different if the study took place in a different region of the country. For example, if families from an area known as the Bible Belt were interviewed, religious conflicts might have played a more central role in family reactions. Thus a similar study that includes a sizable sample from more religious and traditionally conservative areas of the U.S. could prove illuminating.

Last, this study was cross-sectional and asked for retrospective recall, meaning that all respondents were interviewed at one point in time about incidents that occurred in the past. Such reports can be biased, whereby the way in which respondents remember events can differ from what actually occurred. Throughout this book, I discuss how such a bias could affect respondent reports. A longitudinal study of this topic, in which parents and children are interviewed close to the time the child comes out and then at various points in time afterward, could further test the family stage model identified in this study and determine necessary modifications.

Despite these limitations, the findings of this study provide additional insight into an important but understudied area of research. Hopefully, human service professionals will find these results useful in their work with this potentially vulnerable population of families.

American Psychological Association. 2002. *Ethical Principles of Psychologists and Codes of Conduct.* http://www.apa.org/ethics/code2002.html. Retrieved September 26, 2009.

Ammon, R. 2006. *Gay Haiti.* http://www.globalgayz.com/g-haiti.html. Retrieved September 26, 2009.

Appleby, G., and J. Anastas. 1998. *Not Just a Passing Phase: Social Work with Gay, Lesbian, and Bisexual People.* New York: Columbia University Press.

Avery, A., J. Chase, L. Johansson, S. Litvak, D. Montero, and M. Wydra. 2007. "America's Changing Attitudes Toward Homosexuality, Civil Unions, and Same Gender Marriage 1977–2004." *Social Work* 52:71–79.

Bailey, J. M., M. P. Dunne, and N. G. Martin. 2000. "Genetic and Environmental Influences on Sexual Orientation and Its Correlates in an Australian Twin Sample." *Journal of Personal and Social Psychology* 78:524–36.

Bergling, T. 2001. *Sissyphobia: Gay Men and Effeminate Behavior.* Binghamton, NY: Haworth.

Bernstein, R.A. 2007. *Straight Parents, Gay Children: Keeping Families Together.* Rev. ed. New York: Thunder's Mouth.

Besen, W. R. 2003. *Anything But Straight: Unmasking the Scandals and Lies Behind the Ex-Gay Myth.* New York: Harrington Park.

Bieber I. H., P. Dain, M. Dince, H. Drellich, R. Grand, M. Gundlach, A. Kremer, C. Rifkin, T. Wilbur, F. Bieber. 1962. *Homosexuality: A Psychoanalytic Study.* New York: Basic Books.

Blanchard, R. 2001. "Fraternal Birth Order and the Maternal Immune Hypothesis of Male Homosexuality." *Hormones and Behavior* 40:105–14.

Blumstein, P., and P. Schwartz. 1983. *American Couples: Money, Work, Sex.* New York: Morrow.

Borhek, M. V., 1993. *Coming Out to Parents: A Two-Way Survival Guide for Lesbians, Gay Men, and Their Parents.* 2d ed. Cleveland: Pilgrim.

Boyd-Franklin, N. 2006. *Black Families in Therapy: Understanding the African American Experience.* 2d ed. New York: Guilford.

Brown, M., and E. Henriquez. 2008. Socio-demographic Predictors of Attitudes Toward Gays and Lesbians. *Individual Differences Research* 6:193–201.

Brown, W. M., C. J. Fin, B. M. Cooke, and S. M. Breedlove. 2002. "Differences in Finger Length Ratios Between Self-identified 'Butch' and 'Femme' Lesbians." *Archives of Sexual Behavior* 31:123–27.

Carr, C. L. 2007. "Where Have All the Tomboys Gone? Women's Accounts of Gender in Adolescence." *Sex Roles,* 56:439–48.

Carrier, J. 1995. *De Los Otros: Intimacy and Homosexuality Among Mexican Men.* New York: Columbia University Press.

Carter, B., and M. McGoldrick, eds. 1999. *The Expanded Family Life Cycle: Individual, Family, and Social Perspectives.* 3d ed. Needham Heights., MA: Allyn and Bacon.

Cass, V. 1979. "Homosexual Identity Formation: A Theoretical Model." *Journal of Homosexuality* 4:219–235.

Celentano, D. D., L. A. Valleroy, F. Sifakis, D. A. MacKellar, J. Hylton, H. Thiede, W. McFarland, D. A. Shehan, S. R. Stoyanoff, M. LaLota, B. A. Koblin, M. H. Katz, and L. V. Torian. 2006. "Associations Between Substance Abuse and Sexual Risk Among Very Young Men Who Have Sex with Men." *Sexually Transmitted Diseases* 33:265–71.

Chan, C. C. 1989. "Issues of Identity Development Among Asian-American Lesbians and Gay Men." *Journal of Counseling and Development* 68:16–20.

Chauncey, G. 1994. *Gay New York: Gender, Urban Culture and the Making of a Gay Male World, 1890–1940.* New York: Harper Collins.

Chivers, M. L., M. C. Seto, and R. Blanchard. 2007. Gender and sexual orientation differences in sexual response to the sexual activities versus the gender of actors in sexual films. *Journal of Personality and Social Psychology* 93:1108–21.

Cochran, S. V., and F. E. Rabinowitz. 2003. "Gender-Sensitive Recommendations for Assessment and Treatment of Depression in Men." *Professional Psychology: Research and Practice* 34:132–40.

Coleman, E. 1982. "Developmental Stages of the Coming Out Process." *Journal of Homosexuality* 7:31–43.

Coltrane, S., and M. Adams. 2008. *Gender and Families.* 2d ed. Lanham, MD: Rowman and Littlefield.

Commission on Psychotherapy by Psychiatrists (COPP), American Psychiatric Association. 2006. "Position Statement on Therapies Focused on Attempts to Change Sexual Orientation (Reparative or Conversion Therapies)." In J. Drescher, and K. J.

Zucker, eds., *Ex-Gay Research: Analyzing the Spitzer Study and Its Relation to Science, Religion, Politics, and Culture.* pp. 29–34. New York: Haworth.

Corbin, J., and A. Strauss. 2008. *Basics of Qualitative Research: Techniques and Procedures for Developing Grounded Theory.* 3d ed. Thousand Oaks, CA: Sage.

Corrigan, P. W., and F. E. Miller. 2004. "Shame, Blame, and Contamination: A Review of the Impact of Mental Illness Stigma, on Family Members." *Journal of Mental Health* 13:537–48.

Corrigan, P. W., and A. C. Watson. 2002. "The Paradox of Self-Stigma and Mental Illness." *Clinical Psychology Science and Practice* 9:35–53.

Craig, L. 2006. "Does Father Care Mean Fathers Share? A Comparison of How Mothers and Fathers in Intact Families Spend Time with Children." *Gender and Society* 20:259–81.

D'Augelli, A. R. 2002. "Mental Health Problems Among Lesbian, Gay, and Bisexual Youths Ages 14–21." *Clinical Child Psychology and Psychiatry* 7:433–56.

D'Augelli, A. R., A. H. Grossman, N. P. Salter, J. J. Vasey, M. T. Starks, and K. O. Sinclair. 2005. "Predicting the Suicide Attempts of Lesbian, Gay, and Bisexual Youth." *Suicide and Life Threatening Behavior* 35:646–60.

D'Augelli, A. R., N. W. Pilkington, and S. L. Hershberger. 2002. "Incidence and Mental Health Impact of Sexual Orientation Victimization of Lesbian, Gay, and Bisexual Youths in High School," *School Psychology Quarterly,* 17:148–67.

Davies, D., and C. Neal, eds. 2000. *Pink Therapy 2: Therapeutic Perspectives on Working with Lesbian, Gay, and Bisexual Clients.* Briston, PA: Open University Press.

Dawood, K., R. C. Pillard, C. Horvath, W. Revelle, and J. M. Bailey. 2000. "Familial Aspects of Male Homosexuality." *Archives of Sexual Behavior* 29:155–63.

DeGeneres, B. 1999. *Love Ellen: A Mother-Daughter Journey.* New York: HarperCollins.

De Jong, P., and I. K. Berg. 2002. *Interviewing for Solutions Instructor's Resource Manual with Test Bank.* 2d ed. Pacific Grove, CA: Brooks Cole.

—— 2008. *Interviewing for Solutions.* 3d ed. Belmont, CA: Brooks Cole.

Diamond, L. M. 1998. "Development of Sexual Orientation Among Adolescent and Young Adult Women." *Developmental Psychology* 34:1085–95.

—— 2008. *Sexual Fluidity: Understanding Women's Love and Desire.* Cambridge: Harvard University Press.

Diaz, R. M. 1998. *Latino Gay Men and HIV: Culture, Sexuality, and Risk Behavior.* New York: Routledge.

Dovidio, J. G., B. Major, and J. Crocker. 2000. "Stigma: Introduction and Overview." In T. F. Heatherton, R. E. Kleck, M. R. Hebl, and J. G. Hull, eds., *The Social Psychology of Stigma,* pp. 1–28. New York: Guilford.

Drescher, J., and K. J. Zucker. 2006. *Ex-Gay Research: Analyzing the Spitzer Study and Its Relation to Science, Religion, Politics, and Culture.* New York: Harrington Park.

Ferriter, M., and N. Huband. 2003. "Experiences of Parents with a Son or Daughter Suffering from Schizophrenia." *Journal of Psychiatric and Mental Health Nursing* 10:552–60.

Festinger, L. 1962. *A Theory of Cognitive Dissonance*. Stanford: Stanford University Press.

Finley, G. E., and S. J. Schwartz. 2006. "Parsons and Bales Revisited: Young Adult Children's Characterization of the Fathering Role." *Psychology of Men and Masculinity* 7:42–55.

Floyd, F. J., and R. Bakeman. 2006. "Coming-out Across the Life Course: Implications of Age and Historical Context." *Archives of Sexual Behavior* 35:287–96.

Foner, E. 1988. *Reconstruction: America's Unfinished Revolution, 1863–1877*. New York: Harper and Row.

Fox, R. C. 2004. *Current Research on Bisexuality*. Binghamton, NY: Harrington Park Press.

Frable, D. E., C. Wortmen, and J. Joseph. 1997. "Predicting Self-Esteem, Well-Being, and Distress in a Cohort of Gay Men: The Importance of Cultural Stigma, Personal Visibility, Community Networks, and Positive Identity." *Journal of Personality* 63:599–24.

Gallo, K. M. 1994. "First Person Account: Self-Stigmatization." *Schizophrenia Bulletin* 20:407–11.

Gallup Organization. 2006. *Gallup's Pulse of Democracy: Constitutional Amendment Defining Marriage as Only Between a Man and a Woman*, http://www.gallup.com/poll/1651/Homosexual-Relations.aspx. Retrieved September 26, 2009.

Garcia-Preto, N. 1999. "Transformation of the Family System During Adolescence." In B. Carter and M. McGoldrick, eds., *The Expanded Family Life Cycle: Individual, Family, and Social Perspectives*, pp. 274–86. 3d ed. Needham Heights, MA: Allyn and Bacon.

—— 2005. "Latino Families: An Overview." In M. McGoldrick, J. Giordano, and N. Garcia-Preto, eds., *Ethnicity and Family Therapy*, pp. 153–65. 3d ed. New York: Guilford.

Gaustad, E. S., and M. A. Noll, eds. 2003. *A Documentary History of Religion in America to 1877*. 3d ed. Grand Rapids: Eerdmans.

Gay Guyana News and Reports. 2008. http://www.globalgayz.com/guyana-news.html. Retrieved September 26, 2009.

Gilley, B. J. 2006. *Becoming Two-Spirit: Gay Identity and Social Acceptance in Indian Country*. Lincoln: University of Nebraska Press.

Glaser, B. G.. 1978. *Theoretical Sensitivity: Advances in the Methodology of Grounded Theory*. Mill Valley, CA: Sociology.

—— 1992. *The Basics of Grounded Theory Analysis*. Mill Valley, CA: Sociology Press.

Goffman, E. 1963. *Stigma: Notes on the Management of Spoiled Identity*. Englewood Cliffs, NJ: Prentiss-Hall.

Gottlieb, A. R. 2005. *Side by Side: On Having a Gay or Lesbian Sibling*. New York: Harrington Park Press.

Graff, E. J. 2004. *What Is Marriage For? The Strange Social History of Our Most Intimate Institution*. Boston: Beacon.

Greene, B., and N. Boyd-Franklin. 1996. "African American Lesbians: Issues in Couples Therapy." In J. Laird, and R.-J. Green, eds., *Lesbians and Gays in Couples and Families: A Handbook for Therapists*. pp. 251–71. San Francisco: Jossey-Bass.

Greenan, D. E., and G. Tunnell. 2003. *Couple Therapy with Gay Men*. New York: Guilford.

Greenberg, A. S., and J. M. Bailey. 2001. "Parental Selection of Children's Sexual Orientation." *Archives of Sexual Behavior* 30:423–37.

Griffin, C. W., M. J. Wirth, and A. G. Wirth. 1986. *Beyond Acceptance: Parents of Lesbians and Gays Talk About Their Experiences*. Englewood Cliffs, NJ: Prentice-Hall.

Griffin, C. W., M. J. Wirth, and A. G. Wirth. 1997. *Beyond Acceptance: Parents of Lesbians and Gays Talk About Their Experiences*. Rev ed. New York: St. Martin's.

Grove, C., D. S. Bimbi, J. E. Nanín, and J. T. Parsons. 2006. "Race, Ethnicity, Gender, and Generational Factors Associated with the Coming-Out Process Among Gay, Lesbian, and Bisexual Individuals." *Journal of Sex Research* 43:115–21.

Guerin, P., and E. Pendagast. 1976. "Evaluation of Family System and Genogram," In P. Guerin, ed., *Family Therapy: Theory and Practice*, pp. 450–64. New York: Gardner.

Hall, H. I., R. H. Byers, Q. Ling, and L. Espinoza. 2007. "HIV Prevalence and Disease Progression Among Men Who Have Sex with Men in the United States. *American Journal of Public Health* 97:1060–66.

Halperin, D. 1990. *One Hundred Years of Homosexuality: And Other Essays on Greek Love*. New York: Routledge.

Hansen, D. A., and V. A. Johnson. 1979. "Rethinking Family Stress Theory: Definitional Aspects." In W. R. Burr, R. Hill, F. I. Nye, and I. L. Reiss, eds., *Contemporary Theories About the Family: Research-Based Theories*, 1:582–603. New York: Free Press.

Herdt, G. H. 1984. *Ritualized Homosexuality in Melanesia*. Berkeley: University of California Press.

—— 1999. *Sambia Sexual Culture: Essays from the Field*. Chicago: University of Chicago Press.

—— 2006. *The Sambia: Ritual, Sexuality, and Change in Papua New Guinea*. 2d ed. Belmont, CA: Wadsworth.

Herdt, G..H., and B. Koff. 2000. *Something to Tell You: The Road Families Travel When a Child Is Gay*. New York: Columbia University Press.

Herek, G. M., R. Chopp, and D. Strohl. 2007. "Sexual Stigma: Putting Sexual Minority Health Issues in Context." In I. H. Meyer and M. E. Northridge, eds., *The Health of Sexual Minorities: Public Health Perspectives on Lesbian, Gay, Bisexual, and Transgender Populations*, pp. 171–208. New York: Springer.

Hill, R. 1971. *Families Under Stress: Adjustment to the Crises of War Separation and Reunion*. Westport, CT: Greenwood.

Hill, R., and R. H. Rodgers. 1964. "The Developmental Approach." In H. T. Christenson, ed., *Handbook of Marriage and the Family*, pp. 171–211. Chicago: Rand McNally.

Hom, A. Y. 1994. "Stories from the Homefront: Perspectives of Asian American Parents with Lesbian Daughters and Gay Sons." *Amerasia Journal* 20:19–32.

Hooker, E. 1957. "The Adjustment of the Male Overt Homosexual." *Journal of Projective Techniques* 21:18–31.

Howard, D. A., and V. A. Johnson, 1979. "Rethinking Family Stress Theory: Definitional Aspects." In W. R. Burr, R. Hill, I. F. Nye, and R. L. Reiss, eds., *Contemporary Theories About the Family: Research-Based Theories,* 1:582–603. New York: Free Press.

Hubbard, T. K. 2003. *Homosexuality in Greece and Rome: A Sourcebook of Basic Documents.* Berkeley: University of California Press.

Huebner, D. M. 2002. "Mental and Physical Health Consequences of Perceived Discrimination, *Dissertation Abstracts International* 62(2):1030B (UMI No. 95016406).

Human Rights Coalition. 2008. *Statewide Employment Laws and Policies,* http://www. hrc.org/documents/Employment_Laws_and_Policies.pdf. Retrieved September 26, 2009.

Hyde, J. S. 2005. "The Genetics of Sexual Orientation." In J. S. Hyde, ed., *Biological Substrates of Human Sexuality,* pp. 9–20. Washington, DC: American Psychological Association.

Isay, R. A. 1989. *Being Homosexual: Gay Men and Their Development.* New York: Farrar, Straus, and Giroux.

Jackson, D., and J. Mannix. 2004. "Giving Voice to the Burden of Blame: A Feminist Study of Mothers' Experiences of Mother Blaming." *International Journal of Nursing Practices* 10:150–58.

Jagose, A. 1996. *Queer Theory: An Introduction.* New York: New York University Press.

Jenkins, D. A., and L. B. Johnston. 2004. "Unethical Treatment of Gay and Lesbian People with Conversion Therapy." *Families in Society* 85:557–61.

Johnson, P. B., and M. S. Malow-Iroff. 2008. *Adolescents and Risk: Making Sense of Adolescent Psychology.* Westport, CT: Praeger.

Kapac, J. S. 1998. "Culture/Community/Race: Chinese Gay Men and the Politics of Identity." *Anthropologica* 40:169–81.

Kegan, R. 1982. *The Evolving Self: Problems and Process in Human Development.* Cambridge: Harvard University Press.

Kendler, K. S., L. M. Thornton, S. E. Gilman, and R. K. Kessler. 2000. "Sexual Orientation in a U.S. National Sample of Twin and Nontwin Sibling Pairs." *American Journal of Psychiatry* 15:1843–46.

Kimmel, D. C., and B. E. Sang, 1995. "Lesbians and Gay Men in Midlife." In A. R. D'Augelli and C. J. Patterson, eds., *Lesbian, Gay, and Bisexual Identities Over the Lifespan,* pp. 190–214. New York: Oxford University Press.

Kimmel, M. 2003. "Masculinity as Homophobia: Fear, Shame, and Silence in the Construction of Gender Identity." In M. Kimmel, ed., *Privilege: A Reader,* pp. 51–74. Boulder: Westview.

—— 2004. *The Gendered Society.* 2d ed. New York: Oxford University Press.

Kinsey, A. C., W. B. Pomeroy, and C. E. Martin. 1948. *Sexual Behavior in the Human Male.* Philadelphia: Saunders.

Kinsey, A. C., W. B. Pomeroy, C. E. Martin, and P. H. Gebhard. 1953. *Sexual Behavior in the Human Female.* Philadelphia: Saunders.

Kirkman, M., D. Rosenthal, and S. S. Feldman. 2002. "Talking to a Tiger: Fathers Reveal Their Difficulties in Communicating About Sexuality with Adolescents." *New Directions for Child and Adolescent Development* 97:57–74.

Kosciw, J. G. 2001. "The School-Related Experiences of our Nation's Lesbian, Gay, Bisexual, and Transgender Youth." New York: Gay, Lesbian, Straight, Education Network (GLSEN).

Kurdek, L. A. 1988. "Perceived Social Support in Gays and Lesbians in Cohabitating Relationships." *Journal of Personality and Social Psychology* 54:504–9.

—— 2004. "Are Gay and Lesbian Cohabitating Couples *Really* Different from Heterosexual Married Couples?" *Journal of Marriage and the Family* 66:880–900.

Kurdek, L. A., and J. P. Schmitt. 1987. "Perceived Support from Family and Friends in Members of Homosexual, Married, and Heterosexual Cohabitating Couples." *Journal of Homosexuality* 14:57–68.

Laird, J. 1996. "Invisible Ties: Lesbians and Their Families of Origin." In J. Laird and R.-J. Green, eds., *Lesbians and Gays in Couples and Families: A Handbook for Therapists*, pp. 189–22. San Francisco: Jossey-Bass.

Lang, S. 1997. *Men as Women, Women as Men: Changing Gender in Native American Cultures*, Austin: University of Texas Press.

LaSala, M. C. 2000. "Lesbians, Gay Men, and Their Parents: Family Therapy for the Coming-Out Crisis." *Family Process* 39:67–81

—— 2003. "When Interviewing 'Family': Maximizing the Insider Advantage in the Qualitative Study of Lesbians and Gay Men." *Journal of Gay and Lesbian Social Services* 15:15–30.

—— 2006. "Cognitive and Environmental Interventions for Gay Males: Addressing Stigma and Its Consequences." *Families in Society: The Journal of Contemporary Human Services* 87:181–89.

—— 2007. "Parental Influence, Gay Youth, and Safer Sex." *Health and Social Work* 32:49–55.

Laslett, B., and R. Rapoport. 1975. "Collaborative Interviewing and Interactive Research." *Journal of Marriage and the Family* 37:968–77.

Lawrence v. Texas, 539 U.S. 558 (2003).

Lee, E., and M. R. Mock 2005. "Asian Families: An Overview." In M. McGoldrick, J. Giordano, and N. Garcia-Preto, eds., *Ethnicity & Family Therapy*, pp. 269–89. 2d ed. New York: Guilford.

Lev, A. I. 2004. *Transgender Emergence: Therapeutic Guidelines for Working with Gender-Variant People and Their Families*. New York: Haworth.

—— 2006. "Transgender Emergence Within Families." In D. F. Morrow, and L. Messinger, eds., *Sexual Orientation and Gender Expression in Social Work Practice: Working with Gay, Lesbian, Bisexual, and Transgender People*, pp. 263–83. New York: Columbia University Press.

LeVay, S. 1991. "A Difference in Hypothalamic Structure Between Heterosexual and Homosexual Men." *Science* 253:1034–37.

Link, B. G., and Phelan, J. C. 2001. "Conceptualizing Stigma." Annual Review of Sociology 27:363–85.

Loney, J. 1973. "Family Dynamics in Homosexual Women." *Archives of Sexual Behavior* 2:343–50.

Lopata, M. E. 2003. *Fortunate Families: Catholic Families with Lesbian Daughters and Gay Sons.* Victoria, BC: Trafford.

McClellan, D. 2006. "Bisexual Relationships and Families." In D. F. Morrow and L. Messinger, eds., *Sexual Orientation and Gender Expression in Social Work Practice: Working with Gay, Lesbian, Bisexual, and Transgender People,* pp. 243–62. New York: Columbia University Press.

McCubbin, H. I., and J. M. Patterson. 1983. "The Family Stress Process: The Double ABCX Model of Adjustment and Adaptation." In H. I. McCubbin, M. B. Sussman, and J. M. Patterson, eds., *Social Stress and the Family: Advances and Development in Family Stress Theory and Research,* pp. 7–37. New York: Haworth.

McIntosh, P. 1998. "White Privilege: Unpacking the Invisible Knapsack." In M. McGoldrick, ed., *Re-visioning Family Therapy: Race, Culture, and Gender in Clinical Practice,* pp. 147-58. New York: Guilford.

McMillen, J. C. 1999. "Better for It: How People Benefit from Adversity." *Social Work* 44:455–67.

McMillen, J. C., M. O. Howard, L. Nower, and S. Chung. 2001. "Positive By-products of the Struggle with Chemical Dependency." *Journal of Substance Abuse Treatment* 20:69–79.

Mahalik, J. R., G. E. Good, and M. Englar-Carlson. 2003. "Masculinity Scripts, Presenting Concerns, and Help Seeking: Implications for Practice and Training." *Professional Psychology* 34:123-31.

Mallon, G. P. 1999. "Practice with Trangendered Children." In G. P. Mallon, ed., *Social Services with Transgendered Youth,* pp. 49–64. New York: Harrington Park.

Mattison, A.M., and D. P. McWhirter. 1995. "Lesbians, Gay Men, and Their Families: Some Therapeutic Issues." *Psychiatric Clinics of North America* 18:123–37.

Merighi, J. R., and M. D. Grimes. 2000. "Coming Out to Families in a Multicultural Context." *Families in Society: The Journal of Contemporary Human Services* 81:32–41.

Meyer, I. H., 2003. "Prejudice, Social Stress, and Mental Health in Lesbian, Gay, and Bisexual Populations: Conceptual Issues and Research Evidence. *Psychological Bulletin* 129:674–97.

Meyer, I. H., and L. Dean, 1998. "Internalized Homophobia, Intimacy, and Sexual Behavior among Gay and Bisexual Men." In G. M. Herek, ed., *Stigma and Sexual Orientation: Understanding Prejudice Against Lesbians, Gay Men, and Bisexuals,* pp. 160–86. Thousand Oaks, CA: Sage.

Muller, A. 1987. *Parents Matter: Parents' Relationships with Lesbian Daughters and Gay Sons.* Tallahassee, FL: Naiad

National Association of Social Workers. 2008. *Code of Ethics,* http://www.socialworkers.org/pubs/code/code.asp. Retrieved September 26, 2009.

Netting, F. E., P. M. Kettner, and S. L. McMurty. 2004. *Social Work Macro Practice*. 3d ed. New York: Allyn and Bacon.

Nichols, M. P. 1995a. *The Lost Art of Listening*. New York: Guilford.

—— 1995b. *No Place to Hide: Facing Shame So We Can Find Self-Respect*. Amherst, NY: Prometheus.

—— 1998. *Inside Family Therapy: A Case Study in Family Healing*. Boston: Allyn and Bacon.

Nichols, M. P., and R. C. Schwartz. 2008. *Family Therapy: Concepts and Methods*. 8th ed. New York: Allyn and Bacon.

Padgett, D. 2008. *Qualitative Methods in Social Work Research: Challenges and Rewards*. 2d ed. Thousand Oaks, CA: Sage.

Padgett, T. 2006. "The Most Homophobic Place on Earth? *Time*, http://www.time.com/time/world/article/0,8599,1182991,00.html. Retrieved September 26, 2009.

Pearlman, S. F., 2006. "Terms of Connection: Mother-Talk About Female-to-Male Transgender Children. In J. J. Bigner and A. R. Gottlieb, eds., *Interventions with Families of Gay, Lesbian, Bisexual, and Transgender People from Inside Out*, pp. 93–122. Binghamton, NY: Harrington Park.

Ponse, B. 1976. Secrecy in the Lesbian World." *Urban Life* 5:313–338.

Poon, M. K.-L., and R. T.-T. Ho. 2008. "Negotiating Social Stigma Among Gay Asian Men." *Sexualities* 11:245–68.

Robinson, B., P. Skeen, C. Hobson, and M. Herman. 1982. "Gay Men's and Women's Perceptions of Early Family Life and Their Relationships with Parents." *Family Relations* 31:79–83.

Robinson, B., L. H. Walters, and P. Skeen. 1989. "Response of Parents to Learning That Their Child Is Homosexual and Concern Over AIDS: A National Study." *Journal of Homosexuality* 18:59–80.

Rogers, C. 1951. *Client-Centered Therapy*. Boston: Houghton-Mifflin.

Rosen, E. 1999. "Men in Transition: The 'New Man.'" In B. Carter and M. McGoldrick, eds., *The Expanded Family Life Cycle: Individual, Family, and Social Perspectives*, pp. 124–40. 3d ed. New York: Guilford.

Russell, S. T., and K. Joyner. 2001. "Adolescent Sexual Orientation and Suicide Risk: Evidence from a National Study." *American Journal of Public Health* 91:1276–81.

Sandnabba, N. K., and C. Ahlberg. 1999. "Parents' Attitudes and Expectations About Children's Cross-Gender Behavior." *Sex Roles* 40:249–61.

Savin-Williams, R. C. 2001a. *Mom, Dad, I'm Gay: How Families Negotiate Coming Out*. Washington, DC: American Psychological Association.

—— 2001b. Suicide Attempts Among Sexual Minority Youths: Population and Measurement Issues." *Journal of Consulting and Clinical Psychology* 69:983–991.

—— 2005. "*The New Gay Teenager*." Cambridge: Harvard University Press.

Schulze, B., and M. Angermeyer. 2003. "Subjective Experiences of Stigma: A Focus Group of Schizophrenic Patients, Their Relatives, and Mental Health Professionals." *Social Science and Medicine* 56:299–312.

Scambler, G. 1989. *Epilepsy*. Routledge: London.

Shavelson, E., M. K. Biaggio, H. H. Cross, and R. E. Lehman. 1980. "Lesbian Women's Perceptions of Their Parent-Child Relationships." *Journal of Homosexuality* 5:205-15.

Sheldon, J. P., C. A. Pfeffer, T. E. Jayaratne, M. Feldbaum, and E. M. Petty. 2007. "Belief About Etiology of Homosexuality and Ramifications of Discovering Its Possible Genetic Origin." *Journal of Homosexuality* 52:111-50.

Shernoff, M. 2008. "Social Work Practice with Gay Individuals." In G. P. Mallon, ed., *Social Work Practice with Lesbian, Gay, Bisexual, and Transgender People,* pp. 141-178. 2d ed. New York: Routledge.

Siegelman, M. 1974. "Parental Background of Homosexual Women and Heterosexual Women." *British Journal of Psychiatry* 124:14-21.

—— 1981a. "Parental Backgrounds of Homosexual and Heterosexual Men: A Cross National Replication." *Archives of Sexual Behavior* 10:505-13.

—— 1981b. "Parental Backgrounds of Homosexual and Heterosexual Women: A Cross National Replication." *Archives of Sexual Behavior* 10:371-78.

Spitzer, R. L. 2003. "Can Some Gay Men and Lesbians Change Their Sexual Orientation? 200 Participants Reporting a Change from Homosexual to Heterosexual Orientation." *Archives of Sexual Behavior* 32:403-17.

Stone Fish, L., and R. G. Harvey. 2005. *Nurturing Queer Youth: Family Therapy Transformed.* New York: Norton.

Teyber, E. 2000. *Interpersonal Process in Psychotherapy: A Relational Approach.* 4th ed. Belmont, CA: Wadsworth.

Teyber, E., and F. McClure. 2000. "Therapist Variables." In C. Snyder and R. Ingram, eds., *Handbook of Psychological Change: Psychotherapy Processes and Practices for the Twenty-First Century,* pp. 62–87. New York: Wiley.

The New American Bible. 1991. Washington, DC: World Catholic Press.

Tharinger, D., and G. Wells. 2000. "An Attachment Perspective on the Developmental Challenges of Gay and Lesbian Adolescents: The Need for Continuity of Caregiving from Family and Schools." *School Psychology Review* 29:158–72.

Thompson N. L., D. M. Schwartz, B. R. McCandless, and D. A. Edwards. 1973. "Parent-Child Relationships and Sexual Identity in Male and Female Homosexuals and Heterosexuals." *Journal of Consulting and Clinical Psychology* 41:120-27.

Troiden, R. R. 1989. "The Formation of Homosexual Identities." *Journal of Homosexuality* 17:43-73.

Tully, C. T. 1989. "Caregiving: What Do Midlife Lesbians View as Important?" *Journal of Gay and Lesbian Psychotherapy* 1:87–103.

U.S. Census Bureau. 2009. http://www.census.gov/Press-Release/www/releases/archives/income_wealth/014227.html. Retrieved September 26, 2009.

U.S. Department of Justice. 2008. Bureau of Justice Statistics. http://www.ojp.usdoj.gov/bjs/crimoff.htm. Retrieved September 26, 2009.

Van Wormer, K., J. Wells, and M. Boes. 2000. *Social Work with Lesbians, Gays, and Bisexuals: A Strengths Perspective.* Boston: Allyn and Bacon.

Vives, A. P. 2002. "The Psychological Sequelae of Victimization Based on Sexual Orientation: A Structural Equation Model for Predicting Suicidality Among Lesbian,

Gay, and Bisexual Young Adults, *Dissertation Abstracts International* 61(12):5983B (UMI No. 95012210).

Warner, M. 1999. *The Trouble with Normal: Sex, Politics, and the Ethics of Queer Life.* New York: Free Press.

Weber, G., and K. T. Heffern. 2008. "Social Work Practice with Bisexual Clients. In G. Mallon ed., *Social Work Practice with Lesbian, Gay, Bisexual, and Transgender People*, pp. 85–99. 2d ed. Binghamton, NY: Haworth.

Weinberg, G. 1972. *Society and the Healthy Homosexual.* New York: St. Martin's.

West, D. J. 1959. Parental Figures in the Genesis of Male Homosexuality." *International Journal of Social Psychiatry* 5:85–97.

Weston, K. 1991. *Families We Choose: Lesbians, Gays, Kinship.* New York: Columbia University Press.

Wilber, W., C. Ryan, and J. Marksamer. 2006. *Serving LGBT Youth in Out-of-Home Care: Child Welfare League of America Best Practice Guidelines (CWLA).* Washington, DC: Child Welfare League of America.

Williams, W. L. 1986. *The Spirit and the Flesh: Sexual Diversity in American Indian Culture.* New York: Beacon.

Wolf, A. E. 1991. *Get Out of My Life But First Could You Drive Me and Cheryl to the Mall?* New York: Noonday.

AA, *see* Alcoholics Anonymous

AAMFT, *see* American Association of
  Marriage and Family Therapy

Acceptance, 3; professional help and
  nonjudgmental, 59–60; *see also* Parental adjustment

Adams, Jane, 188

Addictions, 54–55, 57, 227

Adjustment; *see* Parental adjustment

Advocate, 46

African Americans, 248; bisexuality and,
  235–36; double stigma and, 218–21;
  families, 3, 10, 11, 17, 19–20, 21, 32,
  56–57, 76, 83–84, 88, 185, 216–23,
  226–27; gays and stigma, 220–22;
  HIV diagnosis rate for MSM, 217;
  HIV diagnosis rate for youth, 168;
  incarceration, stress-related illness
  and, 216–17; lesbians and stigma,
  218–20; men and gender issues,
  221–22; oppression, marginalization and, 196; parents and guilt, 217;

poverty, unemployment and, 216–17;
  views of masculinity and, 227–28;
  youth and distancing, 217, 227–28;
  youth and HIV diagnosis rate, 168;
  see also Coming out

AIDS, 25, 92, 99, 143, 167–69, 213; *see
  also* HIV

Albert, Bethann, 185, 250

Alcohol, 163, 180

Alcoholics Anonymous (AA), 191, 192

American Association of Marriage and
  Family Therapy (AAMFT), 216

American Psychiatric Association, 175

American Psychological Association,
  175

Anal intercourse, unprotected, 168

Angermeyer, M., 5

Anticipatory courtesy stigma, 82

Anticipatory disturbance, 40–41

Antigay scripture, 98

Antigay violence, 5–6, 219, 225–26

Anxiety: precoming-out subphase,

Daughters: failure to launch, mothers and, 165–66; fathers' fears about, xiii, 95; fathers' relationships with, 14–16, 108–10, 118, 140–41, 155, 199–201; gift of lesbian, 183–215; intense relationships and, 2, 17–19, 76–77; lack of personal grooming by, 18; mothers' relationships with, 9, 57, 115, 154–56, 201, 242–43; parental suspicion about, 17–22, 52; see also Coming out; Youth
Da Vinci, Leonardo, 188
DeGeneres, Betty, 129
DeGeneres, Ellen, 55, 57, 143, 146, 188
De Jong, P., 178, 211
Denial, suspicion during family sensitization, inklings and, 23–27
Depression: parents and, 82, 87, 88, 89, 95, 125, 134, 149, 154, 172, 186, 248; youth and, 41–42, 50, 51–52, 54, 57, 59, 64, 163–64, 248
Diagnostic Manual, x
Diamond, L. M., 238
Diaz, Rafael, 223
Difficulties, see Family difficulties
Discovery, see Family discovery
Discrimination, 7, 21; coping with, 181–82, 208, 214–15, 217–21; fear of, 94–96, 160; institutional policies/practices and, 5, 56
Dissonance reduction, 108
Distance/distancing, 27, 71; African American youth and, 217, 227–28; to avoid conflict, 103, 121–22, 217, 228; children and, 4, 11, 31–32, 103–6; divergent perceptions of parent/child and, 27–31, 106–10, 169–73, 200–201; family sensitization, conflict and, 31–39; fathers and paternal, 12–16, 27; initiated by youth, 103–6; mothers and, 199; parent-child boundaries and mutual, 120–23; relationship changes during family discovery and, 101–6; temporary parent-child, 82, 88

Distress: children's safety and parents, ix, xiii–xiv, 22, 81, 89, 91–94, 181–82, 202–5, 224; coming out in, 64–65; parent-child confrontations in, 77–79
"Don't ask, don't tell" policy, 223
Drugs, 163, 180, 204; addiction, 54–55, 57, 227; antidepressants, 137, 150, 180, 186; cocaine, 158; methamphetamine, 227

Elephant in the room, see Coming out; Suspicion
Ellen DeGeneres Show, 57
Environments: assessment, treatment of, and working with, 45–46; mothers in control of emotional climate and, 72; sexual orientation, distance and hostile, 39–41
Etheridge, Melissa, 146
Ethnicity: coming out influenced by, 217–22, 224, 226–27; double stigma and, 218–21; poverty, unemployment and, 216–17; race and, 216–30; stress-related illness, incarceration and, 216–17; see also specific ethnicities
Exodus International, 144

"Faggot," 69, 178
Failure to launch: Mothers, daughters and, 165–66; Mothers, sons and, 163–65, 166, 167; parents worry over children's, 163–67
Families: African American, 3, 10, 11, 17, 19–20, 21, 32, 56–57, 76, 83–84, 88, 185, 216–23, 226–27; Asian, 50, 116, 224, 251; crisis of soldiers being called to service and leaving, 40–41; HIV and gay sons launched by, 212–14; Latino, 37–38, 57–58, 90, 106, 170–71, 197, 216–17, 223–24, 226–27, 228, 229, 251; managing stigma as affair of, 214–15; myths and heterosexual, 85, 109; ongoing difficulties in, 197–208; proud parents, happy children and,

Fathers (*continued*)
140–41, 143–44; initial phase of family discovery/adjustment and, 12–16; parental adjustment and, 157–58; paternal distance and, 12–16; as scapegoat, 130; sons and disapproval of, 38–39; sons' relationships with, 13–14, 22–23, 39, 102, 116, 118–20, 171–72, 198–200; therapists engaging, 210–12; unchanged relationships with child and, 197–201; *see also* Coming out; Families; Parents

Fears: for children's well being, 202–3; coming out and, 70; of discovery, 3; discrimination, 94–96, 160; family sensitization issues, isolation and, 39–41; mental health/isolation and influence of, 6–7; of not entering heaven, 98; of other people's judgments, 96–97; parental worry and, 91–99, 163–69, 180, 181, 202–9; physical harm, 91–94; of rejection by children, 86–87; of rejection by parents, 4, 42, 49, 179, 182; of religious stigma, 97–99; of "turning gay," 245

Fortunate Families: Catholic Families with Lesbian Daughters and Gay Sons (Lopata), 129

Frank, Barney, 55, 188

Gallup poll, 5

Garcia-Preto, N., 115

Gay: appearing, 159–63; family renewal and gift of being, 183–215; parental reactions and feeling good about being, 90–91; porn, 72–75; "turning," 245

Gay, Lesbian, and Straight Education Network (GLSEN), 46, 128

Gay pride parade, 195

Gays: coming out and bisexuality as gateway sexual orientation for, 64, 146–47, 231–35; conducive school environments for lesbians and, 20,

43, 45–46; family therapy and assisting troubled lesbians and, 179–82; famous, 55, 188; identifying as gay, 238; lucky parents of lesbians and, 188–93; reparative/conversion therapies harmful to, 175; risky behavior and, 75–76; stigma and, 5; stigma and African American, 220–21; West Indian culture's intolerance of, 224–26; *see also* Boys; Coming out; Sons

Gender: race, ethnicity and issues of, 221–22; roles, 19; scholars, 159

Girls, girls' intense relationships with, 2, 17–19, 76–77; *see also* Daughters; Lesbians

GLSEN; *see* Gay, Lesbian, and Straight Education Network

Goffman, E., 4, 22

Gratitude, 157

Greece, ancient, 237

Greenberg, A. S., 188

Griffin, Carolyn, 129

Grimes, M. D., 223

Grooming, daughters and lack of personal, 18–19

Grounded theory, data and, xv, 249–51

Group affiliation, parents and healing power of, 136–38

Guilt, 134; fathers and, 84; safe sex and, 205; suspicion during family sensitization and parental, 21–23; with white and African American parents, 217; *see also* Self-blame

Hansen, D. A., 184

Harassment: peer, 5–6, 7–8, 152; at school, 5–8, 45, 92, 94, 219; stigma/isolation, parents and peer, 7–8, 64, 164; West Indians and, 224–26

Harvey, R. G., 42, 43, 178

Hate crimes, penalties for bias and, 56, 91

Heaven, fears of not entering, 98

Heche, Anne, 146

Parents (*continued*)
117, 119, 126, 128–29, 132, 146, 149, 153,
169–70, 172–73, 176, 179, 191, 194–96,
207, 248; downside to, 138–39; family
recovery, parental adjustment and,
136–39
Peer harassment, 5–7, 64, 152; stigma,
parents and, 7–8, 64, 164
PFLAG; *see* Parents, Families and
Friends of Lesbians and Gays
Physical harm, 91–94; children and, 5–6;
see also Violence
Physical health: environments conducive
to, 20; isolation and fear's influence
on, 6–7
Pogrebin, Letty Cottin, 1
Ponse, B., 8
Pornography, 3; gay, 72–75
Positive reframes, 131–33
Poverty, whites, ethnic groups and,
216–17
Prayer, 144–45
Precoming-out subphase: coming-out
and, 49–63; family therapy and,
62–63; individual counseling with
youth and, 59–62; parent-child
interaction and, 58; suicide ideation
and, 54–55; youth in need of parental
support and, 55–58
Pressures, to "act straight," 34–36, 40
Professionals: counselors, 59–62; non-
judgmental help and, 59–60; teach-
ers, 59; *see also* Therapists
Protestants, 98
Prozac, 150
Public stigma, 22, 96, 205

Questions: helps/hindrances to parental
adjustment, 250; how parents'
reaction influences child, 250; how
parents react to child coming out,
249–50; primary research, 249–50

Race: Asian families and, 224; clinical

implications and summary with,
227–30; double stigma and, 218–21;
ethnicity and, 216–30; gender issues
and, 221–22; as inconsequential,
226–27; Latino families and, 223–24;
West Indian families and, 224–26
Reactions: family discovery and parents',
81–133; parental, 82–99; *see also* Parental reactions
Reciprocity, 34, 40, 174, 187, 192–93,
199–200, 227, 251; family relationships improved with relief and, 151–57
Recovery; *see* Family recovery
Recruitment, research methodology
and, 247–49
Reframes, positive, 131–33
Regenesis, 184
Rejection, 42; within families, 39–40,
62, 158; parental reactions and fear of,
86–87; peer rejection, 4, 39, 44; from
societal groups, x
Relationships: discussing sexuality
and family, xi; family discovery and
changes in, 99–120; improved family, 113–17; intense, 2, 17–19, 76–77;
monogamy and committed, 149–50;
power of family, xiii; relief, reciprocity and improving family, 151–57;
romantic, 66–67; sons and mothers,
x–xii, xiii, 9–12; stigma as function of, 4; unchanged father-child,
197–201
Relief: family relationships improved
with reciprocity and, 151–57; feelings
of, 81, 113–14, 127; parental reactions,
youth and, 87–90; parent-child interaction, closeness and, 174
Religion: "cure" of changing sexual orientation through prayer, counseling
and, 144–45; *see also specific religions*
Religious conflicts, 97–99, 184, 252
Religious stigma, 97–98
Renewal, *see* Family renewal, gift of
gay/lesbian child and

Spitzer, R. L., 145

STDs, *see* Sexually Transmitted Diseases

Stein, Gertrude, 188

Stereotypes, positive, 48, 189

Stigma, 4, 60, 184; African American gays and, 220–22; African American lesbians and, 218–20; anticipatory courtesy, 82; Asians and, 224; of bisexuality, 146; courtesy, 22, 82, 96–97, 160, 205–8; double, 218–21, 224; family affair of managing, 214–15; family sensitization, isolation and, 4–8; homosexual, x, xiv, 5; parental fear and religious, 97–98; peer harassment, parents and, 7–8, 64, 164; public, 22, 96, 205; race, ethnicity, stigma and, 218–21; siblings of gays/lesbians and, 243, 245; structural dimension of, 5–6, 45; vicarious, 22, 205; white parents managing, 215; youth coping with, 7, 62, 79, 105, 128, 229

Stone Fish, L., 42, 43, 178

Straight Parents, Gay Children (Bernstein), 129

Strohl, D., 5

Suicide: coming out and attempts at, 3, 68–70, 85, 110, 148, 194; ideation and precoming-out subphase and, 54–55; thoughts of, 7, 50, 51, 52, 54

Support: confidants' trust and, 139–42; sharing and, 135; treatment and getting outside, 127–29; youth groups and, 56, 113, 219, 223; youth needing parents', 55–58

Suspicion: daughters and parental, 17–22, 52; initial phase of family discovery/adjustment and, 17–31; inklings, denial and, 23–27; not discussed, 20–21; parental guilt and, 21–23; parents without, 27–31; reasons for parental, 17–20; sons and parental, 19–20, 22–31, 51; *see also* Coming out

Taboos: children's sexuality and family, 105, 112, 204; homosexuality and cultural, 28–30, 224, 225

Teachers, 59

Theory, data and grounded, 249–51

Therapists, 17, 41, 58; being asked to "convert" gay child, 175; bisexuals and, 238; coaching parents away from children's appearance and on communication, 181–82; encountering homophobic parents, 178; engaging fathers, 210–12; mutual avoidance and family, 26; reaching for positives, 209–10; tolerating intolerance, 124–26; trust with, 63; working on self, 47–48; youth speaking about sexual orientation with, 41–45; *see also* Treatment

Therapy: cognitive behavioral, 60; "curative" conversion/reparative, 144–45, 147; family discovery crisis and family, 131–33; precoming-out subphase and family, 62–63; recovery and family, 176–82; *see also* Treatment

Tomboys: behavior, 19, 159; *see also* Lesbians

Transgender Emergence: Therapeutic Guidelines for Working with Gender-Variant People and Their Families (Lev), 243

Transgender youth, 159–60, 240–43, 247

Trauma, positive aspects of, 183–84

Treatment: during family discovery crisis, 122–33; family recovery and, 174–82; family sensitization and implications for, 41–47; family therapy, 46–47, 62–63, 131–33, 176–82, 209–15; getting outside support and, 127–29; individual sessions with youth, 41–45, 59–62, 126–27, 176; separate sessions with parents, 122–26, 174–75; therapists working on self, 47–48; working with children before coming out, 41–45; working with environ-